Life After Why

Life After Why

Finding My Footing and Purpose
in a Life Disrupter

Sheri Entz Blackmon

Foreword by John Ortberg

RESOURCE *Publications* · Eugene, Oregon

LIFE AFTER WHY
Finding My Footing and Purpose in a Life Disrupter

Resource Publications
An Imprint of Wipf and Stock Publishers
199 W. 8th Ave., Suite 3
Eugene, OR 97401

www.wipfandstock.com

PAPERBACK ISBN: 978-1-6667-3609-0
HARDCOVER ISBN: 978-1-6667-9394-9
EBOOK ISBN: 978-1-6667-9395-6

FEBRUARY 28, 2022 8:26 AM

This book is dedicated to my husband, Rick,
for his unflappable support and boundless encouragement.

The desperate need today is not for great numbers of intelligent people,
or gifted people, but for deep people.

RICHARD FOSTER

Contents

Foreword

Midway upon the journey of our life
I found myself within a forest dark,
For the straightforward pathway had been lost.

So Dante begins *The Divine Comedy*, a journey to beatitude that must begin in places of darkness and fear and suffering, with hope but without guarantees, with unflinching honesty but not despair, with a guide but without a map.

The thoughts and stories you are about to read are by one familiar with the forest dark. This is literally true; Sheri used to speak of vacationing in the Black Forest in Germany when for most of the rest of us in her circle of friends it was only a setting for stories by the Brothers Grimm. Deeper than that, in the chapters that follow Sheri guides us through the tangled underbrush of (several bouts of!) devastating cancer episodes and surgeries with 99% success rates that nonetheless fail her; of religious experiences that both inspire and cripple, of Holocaust survival and the crippling effects of unresolved trauma; of family secrets and infidelity and being the victim of predatory sexual damage when barely a teenager; of being an American in Germany and a German in America and at home nowhere.

This sense of being a stranger–of trying to find a pathway that is somehow lost–never really fades. (Sheri's story about telling–repeatedly–in a children's sermon how David hit Goliath "where it counts" is one of the endearing examples of this; it gives you something to look forward to.) It is one of the ways that Sheri's experience of challenge becomes one of her most effective tools in helping those of us who read. "Outsider-ness" is a universal human condition; maybe only someone who is acutely aware of it can name it with enough clarity to help everyone else.

The hope of finding the pathway does not make the forest any less dark. Among other things this is a book of lament–a book about how to lament. It is not a book for the trite or the triumphant. ("Attitude is everything!"—No it's not!) It calls us not to transcend suffering, but to learn to suffer well, and suffer together. Nietzsche famously said that the person who has a 'why' can suffer almost any how. In this book we're invited to reverse the polarity; to move from "why did this suffering happen to me?" to how it might be born with love and meaning.

What is remarkable about this book is the way that it combines a deeply personal journey through the dark forest, with an informed unpacking of clinical and social science expertise (being married to a psychologist helps), and a love of words marked by deep literacy, and razor-sharp theological reflection. What is even more remarkable is how brave, how very brave it is. There are many exhibitionist writers in our day. This is not one of them. This is a voice that is willing to disclose with great courage in the service of love.

Sheri has been a friend, and a teacher, and an encourager in times of suffering, for more than four decades in my own life, as she has been in the lives of more people than I could count. So, it is a gift to be able to write a few words here at the beginning of her story. By the time you have finished, you will be grateful to have her as your friend and teacher as well.

Some books are worth reading because of the gripping drama of the author's life. Some because of the healing wisdom they offer. Some are worth reading because they point us to God.

This is the rare book that does all three.

Bring it on.

JOHN ORTBERG
Pastor, speaker, and author of more than a dozen books among which are *The Life You've Always Wanted, The Me I Want to Be,* and *If You Want to Walk on Water You've Got to Get out of the Boat*

Preface

WHAT DOES IT TAKE to make it through a crisis with our souls intact? Just as the soul is the part of us that unites our will, mind, and body into an integrated whole, the life disrupters we experience have the potential to bring integrity and wholeness to our lives. Crises have a way of stripping away the trivial parts of our lives like dross. What remains is purer, truer, and gleaming, though it doesn't feel that way at the time. The biggest challenge we face is to allow the process of refining to take hold in our lives without resorting to crippling despair or triumphant platitudes. Both courage and honesty are needed if we want to be changed for the better by our crises.

The first time I had cancer I didn't let it change me that much. The second time the soil of my life was profoundly altered. Hard ground was plowed up, nutrients were added, and rain was absorbed like a gentle shower in a drought. I didn't do most of the work; I allowed the work to be done. How? By moving toward acceptance and eventual embrace of my life disrupter. It helps to have a picture of where you're going, and that is what I'm offering in this book.

Life disrupters are a lot like being a tourist in Venice with its *calli*, the streets that intersect the city in a confusing maze. I remember visiting there with my son, Nate, during the 2006 World Cup between Italy and France. To celebrate the victory over France, drunk fans jumped off pedestrian bridges into the murky water in their underwear. The convivial atmosphere wrapped the entire town in a confusing haze that disrupted my sense of direction. Between the rowdy crowds and meandering streets, I could not find my way around the town without a map constantly before my eyes.

There may not be a physical map for a life disrupter, but there is a mental model. It's the most effective kind of guide because a great deal of our physical battles are really battles of the mind. How do we deal with loss in an honest way? How do we keep strong without being fake? How do we keep going when we can't see the future, much less the next day? How do we allow ourselves to be redeemed and refined by our suffering? How do we find purpose and hold on to the lessons of pain? How do we refuse to let our pain go to waste?

Ultimately, pain invites us to find a renewed purpose in our lives, and that's what this book is about. It started as a compilation of blog posts that looked at the question of what to do when we don't know why something happens to us, and it developed into a memoir. Writing a memoir is scary to me because, as you will see, I'm by nature shy and reticent. It feels vulnerable and scary to put myself out there for others to see. So, what helped me overcome these innate tendencies?

My cancer journey stirred up something deep inside me. It was like I was awakening to a more intimate connection to myself, others, and God, an integration of the parts of myself I had split off. As I set aside time during the pandemic for what I call my "boredom project," I discovered a refreshing well that wanted to bubble to the surface. My writing became a gift to me that I had to share with others. I share it in hopes of bringing refreshment to you, my revered reader.

We are all connected through our experience of being human, frail, and beautiful. I hope that my story encourages you to find your footing and purpose in crisis. There is a way forward, a way that redeems your suffering and forms you into a deeper person. Deep people are what this world needs most of all, wounded healers who heal others' wounds.

SHERI BLACKMON

Part I

THE DESTRUCTIVE AND CREATIVE POTENTIAL OF DISRUPTERS

Chapter 1

Membership in a Club I Don't Want to Join

A Surreal Phone Call

I'VE WALKED THE FAMILIAR SCHOOL HALLS for nineteen years since switching careers in 2000, but this time it's different: surreal, focused, insular. It's 2:27 p.m. as I head to my last class full of spirited high school sophomores and juniors. At 2:14 p.m. I just answered a call from the gynecologist with the results of four needle biopsies to learn that three of them reveal hard-to-detect lobular carcinoma. I have breast cancer once again, but it's a different kind this time, a stealthier, more deadly kind. My first cancer was invasive ductal carcinoma with some lobular features. This time it's all lobular. The doctor tries to reassure me that its non-aggressive nature will probably only require excisions. (How wrong that would be!) The phone call ends ten minutes later, and I try to collect myself. What should I do, go to class or find a sub? Since there's no time to find a sub before my 2:30 class, I stand up, straighten my clothes and my resolve, and head out the teacher core room into the bustling hallway. I feel detached, like being in someone else's body.

Walking down the hall as I have done thousands of times, I think this is the strangest out-of-body walk I've ever had. I appear to blend into the routine, but my life is flipped over in an instant. I wonder about students who experience similar feelings of alienation in the hallway. I push down the door handle of the classroom and the news I just heard and enter the room. A memory from seventeen years ago flashes through my mind of defiantly pushing down the door handle of the Tarzana Hospital where I

3

am about to have my first breast biopsy in 2002, feeling certain that this is a waste of the doctor's time. Those were the former days of invincibility. That biopsy and subsequent surgeries and treatments initiated me into the cancer club. Today's door opening shows less of that early certainty, but it's not completely gone. Is it the myth of being special? Why do I still believe that bad things don't happen to me? Teaching that class is a robotic blur; I'm in charge, but not really; I operate by instinct, and I can't report later what we discussed.

After school, I take a moment for reality to settle in as I tell a colleague, and friend, the news. She reflects on her own dissociation after losing her college-age son a few years ago. She tells me that her grief the first year was so ever-present and palpable that she simply went through the motions of teaching. She could not report the specifics of her teaching, only that she somehow got through that year. We bond over a shared experience of loss and detachment.

There's little time to make crucial decisions. A single or double mastectomy? What kind of reconstruction and when? The plastic surgeon advises against an implant on the affected side due to previous radiation, which significantly lowers the chances of success. An alternative is to do a microscopic tissue transplant from the abdomen to the breast called a DIEP flap surgery and an implant on the right side. Cold and rushed decision-making diverts the flood of emotions into a neighboring tributary.

This diversion continues for a time as I decide how much information to share with the students, tie up loose ends, and prepare to leave two weeks before the end of the school year–and my teaching career as my retirement plans are already made before the diagnosis–amid final oral presentations and exams. I choose to be candid with my students, spurred by Joni's Eareckson Tada's comment of not wanting to waste her breast cancer recurrence. I want them to know how my faith helps me.

The support and love–hugs, prayers, meals, gifts, cards–affirm my choice. A sixteen-year-old student named Ryan even leaves a gift basket with candles, a floral English teacup, and tea on my doorstep along with a hand-written note. I'm moved because it looks like he, not his mom, authored this kind act.

Wanting to finish well, I push myself until six the evening before surgery, as students patiently stand in line for hours to complete missing assignments. Why do they always wait to the end? At this point I take up my colleagues' offers to grade extra work. With dizzying speed, my career ends at the school I helped found almost twenty years earlier. For now, the dizzying speed is a comfort, the comfort of agency and control.

Like many disrupters, cancer initiates me into a club I don't want to join. After my first initiation in 2002, I clicked the unsubscribe button as soon as possible. In the first few months after that experience, I still thought about cancer every day; then, slowly, the months and years of remission carved a wide stream out of the tributary into a normal life. Years of floating on the calmer waters carried me far away from the rocks and snarls of that small tributary. Normal was the new fantastic for me.

But here I am again, and this time it feels like I'm heading down the rapids toward a precipice. It's like a bad dream of returning to a place you think you're far removed from to find the same fears and anxieties again, only more pronounced, like being back in middle school with the bullies. In your dream, you ask yourself if it's just a dream, but it doesn't seem to be because the dream continues. "How did I get here?" I ask myself incredulously.

When I Find Myself in the One to Two Percent of Medical Statistics

I never expect to find myself in the one to two percent of medical statistics. In my first consultation with the plastic and oncological surgeons, I automatically dismiss the low percentage of failure. Under discussion is what to do after the double mastectomy (DMX). My options for reconstruction are limited. I decide on an implant on the right and a DIEP flap transplant on the left, a lengthy and specialized microsurgery transplant of abdominal tissue to the breast.

I automatically dismiss the low percentage of failure–it never enters my mind. It's a habit I have–or had–of denial. After all, my birthday is 7/11, a lucky number, right? Mixed in is the conflation of denial with strength and the feeling of being special. Deep motives are not pretty things. I'm thankful for the privilege of having excellent medical opportunities at my disposal. I calculate that prominent surgeons supported by sterling educations, a teaching position at UCLA medical school, cutting-edge experience, strong reputations, and good bedside manners thrown in as an extra, suffice to beat the odds.

A digression, why are they called "bedside manners" because one only discovers them after surgery? So, I'll call it patient rapport to be distinguished from the pedantry and intimidation of the old days where the patient obediently submits and doesn't ask too many questions. The plastic surgeon may belong to an older generation, but he is approachable, dedicated, and funny. He makes time to meet us right away for over an hour extending into the evening. The oncological surgeon is educated at Harvard with a quiet, reassuring kindness and compassion. A woman of few words, she uses touch to show she cares. My hematologist's forty-something bedside manners make me chuckle when he introduces himself: "Hi, I'm Shay" (instead of a long Persian name), listens to my story without taking notes–his NP does that–and offers a high five at the end of the appointment. Between appointments I can email him, and he gets right back to me. I like his style.

On the day of surgery, I expect to be under anesthesia between six and eight hours, but it turns out to be a celebrated five and a half hours followed by an upbeat report of how my being in shape helps the surgeons finish the radical bilateral mastectomy and DIEP flap transplant in a short amount of time. Whose pride doesn't swell at hearing the efficacy of working out and being in shape? I buy the line that I can control my health. We rest confidently on the positive report from two medical experts.

I recall blurry snippets of the night after my surgery in the ICU. Around one in the morning a machine starts beeping loudly. Why is it going off? A young nurse comes in to silence the beep, making what strikes me as an inexperienced–actually, off-the-wall–assessment of the cause, but she can't silence it. I keep trying to figure out what she means but can't make sense of it. The ICU nurse assigned to me enters with calm professionalism and kindness. She is one of those special nurses who studies her patients to figure out what they need. As it turns out, she would be assigned to me three days in a row, and I would see her at a wedding of a friend two months later. The beep still won't stop. She checks the portable Doppler ultrasound device for blood flow to the transplant site, but the signal is mixed and uncertain. As additional nurse staff flit in and out, I hear them mention the surgeons' names and "emergency surgery." There's talk of blood clots, blood thinner, scary prospects. Eight hours before, the report was crisply positive, the Doppler showing steady blood flow, but now the danger is rapidly spiraling.

A couple of hours later, the staff tries to call my husband, Rick, to inform him of an emergency surgery, but his phone is off because it's the middle of the night. They finally reach my oldest son, Andrew, who lives an hour away. The quick and efficient movements of nurses prepping a patient for surgery fill the room with hushed and rustling noises. I lie in bed, my mind dulled by anesthesia, narcotics, and confusion and my anxiety spiking.

All I know is that I am alone and afraid of facing an emergency surgery in the middle of the night. The most vivid memory of that night is the ceiling in the hallway as the nursing staff wheels me to the operating room. Time stands still as I move under its bright lights. A mental picture downloads with surprising clarity and precision. Snippets of a familiar passage appear like a screen shot to my drugged brain–lucid, unbidden, and irresistibly sweet.

The words of the psalmist which my friend Pam texted me a day before take center stage in my mind, sliding fear to the periphery:

> "Where shall I go from your Spirit?
> Or where shall I flee from your presence?
> If I ascend to heaven, you are there!
> If I make my bed in Sheol, you are there!
> If I take the wings of the morning
> and dwell in the uttermost parts of the sea,
> even there your hand shall lead me,
> and your right hand shall hold me.
> If I say, 'Surely the darkness shall cover me,
> and the light about me be night,'
> even the darkness is not dark to you;
> the night is bright as the day,
> for darkness is as light with you."[1]

In that brief moment of time the Psalm bypasses the narcotics and other drugs in my system, and I experience God's presence, like a cloud that parts for a moment, an epiphany of sorts. I know I am not alone. I'm at peace under the bright lights and cheer myself on with, "I can do this!" as I am whisked into the operating room. The particulars of the second OR blend together with the others–a total of seven surgeries in the next ten months–except for the friendly, slightly subdued banter of the staff helping me push back the fear. A stark sign saying the space is "terminally cleaned" catches my attention, though I don't know why. Next is the vivid memory of my husband's kiss in the recovery room.

---

1. Ps 139:7–12

My thoughts are muddled from the drugs, so I ask Rick to remember for me. I can't take in the surgical report and news, but the doctor hopes the transplant can be saved. It's like putting one foot on the scale; all I know is that I can't assess the actual weight of my situation. I also know that I'm slammed against the pillow with itchy hair and a body squirming in pain. Comfort evades me, and anxiety riddles my mind.

That week in the hospital is a blur of being wheeled in and out of my room for tests and surgeries. All my drug-addled attention fixates on trying to stay strong for the next challenge. It's like trying to extricate myself from a bad dream, only it keeps on going. In those dreams I'm trying to open my eyes, walk, or put the brake on a car, but I can't do it. It's a relief when I wake up from such a dream. I don't have that relief this time. The Doppler signal grows weaker and weaker. I must prepare for another emergency surgery. This time I request a big boy narcotic.

After the third emergency surgery, I awaken to the news that the transplant tissue is dead. The details of the steps the surgeon takes to keep it alive stay in my mind like a Bosch painting of grotesque figures. My battered breast has an open wound, and I'm attached to an efficient, portable "wound VAC" which *ueberheals* the skin in preparation for a skin graft to close the wound. It puts negative pressure on my breast day and night for a week. I must find a way to endure the constant pain from the droning machine and even sleep through it. My chest is tight from pulling as much skin as possible to close the incisions. The oversized abdominal wound is completely useless. Six drains, little plastic bottles that fill up with blood and need to be changed twice a day, are attached to my body. My only option for future reconstruction is a latissimus flap surgery taking muscle from the back, swinging it under the arm, and making a flap for a new breast with an implant. I can't think about that right now.

I assumed the cancer was only on my left side, but three emergency surgeries later to save the distressed transplant, I learn more hard news. The problem with the transplant is in my chest where the mammary lymph nodes are. After removing three sizable malignant tumors in the new location, four diseased mammary nodes nearby, and some bone in the chest wall, the surgeons surmise that the unexpected tumors choked the blood supply to the transplant site. One diseased node in front of the heart is left behind for the oncologists to zap. I don't find this out until months later, but I do learn that I'm the subject of the hospital's monthly cancer convocation to discuss complicated cases. The main concern is whether I can have radiation again after the thirty-five treatments in 2003. After removing all the tumors and nodes there isn't enough skin to sew me back up, so I'm left with an open wound.

My abdomen with its now taut and taunting incision tempts me to a pity party as I count a total of eleven holes and incisions. Within ten days of the first surgery, I go under for the fifth time for a skin graft to close the open wound, and I am sent home to begin healing my battered body.

What happened to all the prayers that poured in from a vast network of family, friends, and pastors? With the efficiency of a switchboard operator, Rick manages the chaos from a smartphone. He sends out prayer chains for one thing and another, but here we are with some of our worst fears realized. Doubts drive by like unwelcome intruders. I keep going back to the parting cloud on the ceiling in the hallway to the OR. It is a message that my greatest gift–and need–in this life is God's presence.

Everything boils down to this one reality. I can't control God with my faith, and God isn't bound by the confines of a contract with me. Am I owed an answer or is the divine presence the ultimate answer? When I leave this earth, nothing else is important. On this earth, presence–God's and others'–is still the most important gift.

The day of the transplant failure the oncological surgeon visits me and gently takes my hand to express sympathy over the outcome. When she jumps up to leave the room saying she doesn't want to cry, I know that the journey ahead is arduous–perhaps over several steep hills–and I must get ready. The same evening the plastic surgeon enters the room with a sympathetic, doleful look on his face, explaining what happened and why a surgery with a ninety-eight to ninety-nine percent success rate failed. He says he will leave no stone unturned to be sure of the cause. Humble and honest, the surgeon lowers himself into a chair eye to eye with us and gets personal. I have never heard a doctor openly reflect on how he wishes things were different, how he questions what happened. I have never heard a doctor open his heart to us like he does that night.

He tells us about his daughter. She was eighteen and wanted to be a medical missionary in Thailand as his parents had been, and suddenly one night, she died of the flu. They never found out why, never got answers. He struggled for a long time with profound grief, drifting into ennui, seeking support of different kinds. I don't know when the shift inside him occurred, maybe months or a year or two later, but one day something clicked. He looked at his life and who was in it–his wife, another daughter, his patients–and decided that the only way forward was to be there for these people, to serve them, to heal them. And that's what he did; and, surprisingly, that's how he healed, by embracing his family and work with renewed dedication, compassion, and humor. He tells us the story because he thinks it might help us understand that sometimes there are no answers, no reasons, that life isn't fair or easily placed into categories and boxes. Sometimes we discover the answer in giving and immersing ourselves in the life we now have. That's hard when you're in a state of limited agency and you feel like all you're doing is taking, not giving.

Every nurse I encounter speaks of his compassion, patience, and love. His personal office nurse, a petite young woman, who, I am surprised to learn, works at the County USC ER when not in the suburban doctor's office, says he is the kindest man she knows. One time the doctor tells me that as he nears sixty, he wants to travel with a purpose. He's gone on fancy trips and cruises, but they leave him with no more than the enjoyment of another trip. Weeks later, his nurse removes my drains–an incredibly painful experience at the abdominal site–because her boss is in Ethiopia on a medical mission trip for two weeks, his vacation time. A month after that I learn he's in Thailand training medical staff.

There is a special bond between doctors, nurses, and patients in crises. You feel love and an attachment to these people who are with you in the hardest moments of life. All I know at the time is that this man is giving me something important, something to help me move from invincibility to vulnerability and from fairness to fortitude, but I can't put it into words at the time. All I know is that I'm in the cancer club again, perhaps for longer this time, and he's there with me.

I Need Your Presence Not Your Problem-Solving

During the week in the hospital, the gift of presence sustains me. Two small wheels roll against the privacy curtain of my hospital room in the oncology unit. The hand that parts the curtain belongs to my middle son, Alex, and the wheels to his baby stroller. He sneaks in his three-month-old baby girl, Sage, to see grandma. A sunny person with a perpetual smile, she beams with joy. Her joy jumps into my battle-worn heart, soothing and healing it. Her brief visit on daddy's lap kindles the fire I need to fight right now.

There's also a picture on my hospital tray table of Sage and her almost three-year-old sister, Reese, that Alex and Andrea give me. It captures a moment of uncontainable joy as the girls laugh at something funny their mom does to get their attention. I hear it takes some cajoling to capture the moment. That picture is their presence whenever I wake up, before I'm wheeled out of the room, and throughout the day. This is my motivation, a symbol to direct me through acute pain and emergency surgeries. It's a handhold on a vertical climb, a place to rest for a moment from straining and reaching along a sheer wall, a chance to catch my breath up the steep climb. Their presence helps me persevere.

Another picture is in my mind's eye from a day earlier in the ICU. There's an outdoor area just outside the room where families can meet and talk. Alex and Andrea bring Reese to that area, so I can see her out of the window. In my foggy mental state, I notice her straining eyes peering in, but I don't think she sees me. I see her, my sweet young granddaughter with a heart as tender as a spring flower. The picture of her searching for me is snapped in my memory. I hope she seeks me out when she's older. I hope she tells me about her day, confides in me when she has troubles, and shares her joys with me. I didn't have a grandma watch me grow up, a grandma who participated in my daily life. I hope I get to experience that.

Later, she asks her mom how I'm doing and whether I'm feeling better. She notices the small things and remembers people well. She's not even three but already has a heart full of love and compassion. For these girls I will fight this battle. For them I will win.

It's the small things my family and friends do that keep me going during the weeks and months of recovery. It's the visits, gifts, food, and talks. It's mostly how they listen to me and want to know more. My husband, Rick, my boys, Andrew, Alex, and Nate, and their wives and girlfriend, Jenna, Andrea, and Mady, are kind, attentive, and caring. Rick's indefatigable care and love, Andrew's tears and how he holds my hand, Alex's empathy from lengthy hospital stays as a teenager, and Nate's compassion and thoughtful gifts get me through the hard days. My friend Nancy sends me a yearly subscription to beautiful bouquets of flowers, which arrive every month. My nonagenarian mother, unstable from a hip fracture, even hikes up the stairs to bring me food in bed. Alex often brings the girls over to see me during the long weeks of recovery. When you're raising three sons, you don't think of them taking time to ask you questions and listen to you. You don't think of them becoming a father of girls. You're too busy making food, doing laundry, attending games, making sure they're wearing helmets, doing their homework, learning good manners–especially true for this German mom of American boys–and so on. So, to witness Alex lovingly attend to the needs of his little girls amazes me.

Seeing the girls eases my loss, but I can't hold them because of the surgeries. I can't really touch anyone right now. This season of retirement was supposed to be different with play dates, babysitting, and outings. For now, seeing them is enough. And it is good. Until later when the realization hits that I haven't held my baby granddaughter almost half of her life.

People often underestimate the power of presence. Like trees, we are interdependent organisms. A recent trip to Costa Rica reinforces my love of trees with their iconic high canopies of graceful branches sheltering Brahmin Cows below and Howler Monkeys above. What do these trees have in common with Tolkien's Forest of Fangorn and the Ents, Shakespeare's Birnam Wood coming to Dunsinane, Dr. Seuss's dog party tree from *Go, Dog. Go!* and Colorado aspen groves? These trees teach us about what we need to survive.

Fast forward to the summer after my treatments as Rick and I enjoy a mountain bike ride through a Colorado aspen forest. I stop to take in the gray trees and the sounds of wind rushing through the grove. I'm reminded of the gray walls of the ancient Gothic cathedral in Cologne, Germany, near where I grew up. I record these lines on my phone: *An aspen forest is a Koellner Dom with spliced walls and open windows. Ruach speaks and sings in the small leaves, like choir boys sounding high and clear.* Like the trees of Fangorn, Birnam, and the dog party, aspen groves are community outreach centers extending help to neighbors in need. These trees work together to fight enemies, vanquish a malicious king, provide fun, and sustain others. They help us look beyond ourselves. They show us what kind of tree to be in our individualistic culture.

An aspen grove is an organism of interdependence. Contrast that with oak trees. I have two majestic oaks in the yard, each numbered and protected by the city. I marvel at how they sustain themselves in our dry climate with their deep roots. But oaks are solitary trees. In our area, it's common to see a lone oak in a sea of dry grasses and brittle mustard plants that look like scarecrows. Aspen, on the other hand, are connected to "hundreds or thousands more by a network of roots so deep they can survive wildfires." That's why author K. J. Ramsey describes herself as being "more aspen than oak."[2] She knows the importance of interdependence from firsthand experience.

2. Ramsey, *This Too Shall Last*, 77.

Ramsey deals with excruciating daily pain from an illness that flared up in her early twenties. She can no longer work, and on good days she is glad to make it to the couch. The first sentence of her book is, "This book is not a before and after story" but a story "from the middle where so many of us live yet so few describe."[3] She adds this weighty perspective: "The tacit message in our churches, culture, and relationships is this: Success is public; suffering is private."[4] This reality contributes to her personal isolation.

One day Sarah walks into her private pain during an early flare-up. At first, Ramsey wants to hide and not open the door because of the shame she feels over her dirty house and disheveled life, but Sarah remains unfazed and keeps coming back. Ramsey adds, "She entered the place of my confinement, the prison of my perceived uniqueness, and sat with a willingness to witness the desperation I felt."[5] Soon their roots intertwine.

Sarah bears witness to her story. More than the words they speak, Ramsey remembers "being allowed to be broken and hopeless" and over time "the darkness of shame began to recede beside the gentle light of Sarah's acceptance."[6] In what she calls the welcome of weakness, Ramsey's suffering becomes less private, opening a door out of her lonesome confinement.

Like Ramsey, I, too, don't want others' problem-solving skills, but their presence. How is presence a comfort and not a burden? It's not through pity or solutions but being a witness to my pain. This releases the pressure to get better or put the disrupter behind me with a quick and easy, "Let's move on." Rick is my best witness. When I introduce a complaint with, "I'm not looking for you to solve my problem; I just want you to hear me," he responds accordingly, and the pressure to be better or give a good solution is dissolved. Witnessing validates the reality that "This too shall last"–at least for a time–to borrow the title of Ramsey's book. It's like being an eye-witness, the most persuasive role in a court of law, a role that validates my story. Validation, in turn, contains the seeds of change whereby sufferers look outside themselves for solutions and help.

The welcome of weakness is a profound paradox. When Paul summarizes his account of sufferings with the statement, "For when I am weak, then I am strong"[7] he is touching on an important correction in our indi-

---

3. Ramsey, *This Too Shall Last*, 19.

4. Ramsey, *This Too Shall Last*, 158.

5. Ramsey, *This Too Shall Last*, 161.

6. Ramsey, *This Too Shall Last*, 162.

7. 2 Cor 12:10

vidualistic culture. Weakness reveals the vast root system of connectedness to others and helps us look up beyond the canopy to God, a help that will not put us to shame. It starts with allowing others to notice our weakness. Sometimes we may even have to tell others about it. Being vulnerable is a weakness that makes us stronger.

The Destructive and Creative Power of Disrupters

Disrupters reveal weakness as they derail our lives and cause destruction. But there's more to a disrupter. How does the word "disrupter" become so widespread that its connotations range from cringeworthy to aspirational? On the one hand, its association with unpredictable life-transitions lodges it in the mind as fated, feared, and repulsive. Author Bruce Feiler argues that *Lifequakes,* which he defines as "a forceful burst of change in one's life that leads to a period of upheaval, transition, and renewal," are increasing. The average adult experiences three dozen transitions in a lifetime, three to five of which are "massive reorientations."[8]

Feiler's claim challenges Gail Sheehy's ground-breaking 1974 book *Passages* with its predictable stages of adult development. The book's cover, spelling out passages like ascending stairs with each letter signifying a step of progress to the top, matches the idea of orderly progression within adult development. Which view best reflects actual experience? Perhaps both order and unpredictability are true. That's hard for people like me who like order, another German characteristic I inherited. Indeed, our times are marked by technological, religious, social, and political upheaval, but peace and stability punctuated by chaos and upheaval are universal human experiences from ancient times to today. Perhaps modernity lulls us into the illusion of control over chaos, and thus it needs a correction. Whatever the case, it's best to supplement the enjoyment of stability with a grittier perspective that leans into the reality of disrupters. That way we train ourselves to be fit and resilient.

On the other hand, disrupters are receiving increasingly positive press. The standard denotation from *The Oxford English Dictionary* is: "A person or thing that interrupts an event, activity, or process by causing a disturbance or problem." In biology it's a thing that interferes with or significantly alters the structure or function of a biological molecule such as a gene or hormone. Words associated with disrupter are change, alteration,

8. Feiler, *Life is in the Transitions,* 16.

revolution, upheaval, transformation, metamorphosis, and breakthrough. The traditional definition of interruption, with a largely negative connotation, is shifting with change and breakthrough on the same continuum. Disrupter is now an iconic word in business, politics, and society.

A common application is business innovation that replaces old markets and habits. Beginning with Clayton Christensen's 1997 book *The Innovator's Dilemma,* the idea of disruptive innovation becomes a way to think about successful companies not only addressing customers' current needs, but also tapping into future needs. His theory explains how minimally resourced companies displace established systems. Christensen helps shift disruption to a positive term, making it a buzzword, and like most buzzwords it now has an aspirational quality with many people claiming to be disruptive and innovative.

Entrepreneurs now dream of birthing disrupters, but one problem is that it's hard for the originator to anticipate how a disrupter will deliver the benefit, and it can take years for the true effects of disruption to present themselves in the market. For example, Thomas Edison expected that his phonograph player would be used for recording wills.

Let's not put the cart before the horse, however, by failing to acknowledge that disrupters destroy before they create something new. Personal disrupters strike like a bomb devasting a city of bricks. Structures, walls, roofs lie in rubble in the street, like Berlin in 1945. Destruction is all there is to see for a time. Impoverished Berliners scrape the last bits of food out of trashcans, children wander the littered streets, filthy and forlorn; life seems like it will never be the same again.

Then, painstakingly and with regularity, the debris is removed, plans are made, people start to rebuild, and maintenance is restored. People begin to envision a better future. There are still problems and setbacks–sometimes lasting years and decades–but eventually, the rebuilding is underway, and the city has more than just bricks, like Caesar Augustus's ancient Rome transformed from a city of brick to a city of marble. Marble is made to last. After some time, marble monuments and buildings dot the city with shiny walls and facades. Landmarks with a wretched history are reengineered and restored beyond their original drab look and dreadful use. Business returns. Politics improve. Visitors come. People stroll the *Allee* arm in arm. Something lasting takes the place of the rubble.

The process of creating something new out of a disrupter involves dealing with the rubble of loss. This book is about becoming aware of loss, assessing and feeling it, and eventually letting go of it in order to accept—even embrace in some cases—the gifts found on the other side of loss. There are no pragmatic or triumphalist claims that the gains make the loss worthwhile—even good. There is the recognition that God works for good through it all—because God *is* good. So, we can trust God. We don't grab, clutch, or control these gifts but receive them, as they are grace-deposits that come unbidden. Appreciation and gratitude shift the focus from what is lost to what remains. Our scars are a part of our story as are the new possibilities we discover after letting go. It's possible to experience a satisfying life after a life disrupter, and that is what I want to explore with you.

Don't Be a Solutions-Person

People react in different ways to disrupters: acting out, worry, fear, searching for answers, talking to everyone, talking to no one, denial, compartmentalization. Is there a right approach? A wrong one? Probably not, so we can be more tolerant of people's different reactions. My first reaction to a disrupter is to figure out a way to cope with it. "Buckle down and fight!" sweeps away the emotions that get in the way. The impact of the disrupter is thus delayed.

Others feel the pain and loss more immediately. There's no standard for how to deal with disrupters, but one thing is clear: people's pain shouldn't be minimized or dismissed with statements like "at least you don't have . . . " We shouldn't teach people a lesson in positivity or solve their problems, and yet that is often the approach people take to disrupters. The well-meaning urge to say something and be helpful overrides empathy and compassion. What's wrong with doing this? It assumes that disrupters are controllable and it's my job to provide an attitude adjustment. I saw a sign which said, "Attitude is everything!" It's not everything; it's something, but attitude is best discovered by the person who's been knocked down. Empathy creates a pathway to an attitude adjustment, and we are called to validate, not dismiss another's pain. A disrupter may not be controllable but it's manageable with the individual as the manager and the friend as the assistant manager.

In her memoir of dealing with a stage four cancer diagnosis at age thirty-four, Kate Bowler singles out the "Solutions People, who are already a little disappointed that I am not saving myself. 'Keep smiling! Your attitude determines your destiny!'" one says, "and I am immediately worn out by the tyranny of prescriptive joy."[9] That last phrase catches my attention because there's a lurking dismissal of pain in the admonition to be better. Don't put that burden on another person. Disrupters are like vertigo, the spinning and swaying imbalance that upsets a person's equilibrium and sense of control. Sometimes vertigo persists longer than anticipated.

A Tool to Survive a Life Disrupter

Let's step back for a moment to consider a framework for dealing effectively with disrupters. This framework is essentially practical, and it helps me in many types of situations that involve struggle, loss, and letting go. Rick, a Clinical Psychologist, and I stumbled upon a framework for acceptance as we discussed an upcoming marriage talk a few years ago. Exploring how to accept our partner's differences, I wondered if it was realistic to embrace everything about our mate. An acceptance scale popped into my mind, which is as applicable to marriage as to disrupters. Effective loss management–and healing from our disrupters–is a movement forward on the acceptance scale.

The Acceptance Scale

Condemn ➡ Endure ➡ Tolerate ➡ Accept ➡ Embrace

It looks like a linear model with orderly stages that reach a triumphal end, but it's not. It's not a before and after story because suffering "is not a mark on the timeline of your life. It is not a season with a clear beginning and end, or a problem you can overcome. It is a place you will visit again and again, a place whose clouds threaten and frighten but whose landscape can bring you nearer to your true home."[10]

We move forward. We get stuck. We move forward and backward again many times. After initial progress is made, it's possible to get stuck on the acceptance scale. It's an aspirational model for when we see only broken bricks to remind us of the marble. It's a framework for growth in the oscillations of life. Just like everything else we commit ourselves to, we strive to move forward on what I call The Acceptance Scale: a transitioning from Condemn to Endure, Tolerate, Accept, and eventually, though not always

9. Bowler, *Everything Happens*, 118.
10. Ramsey, *This Too Shall Last*, 108.

to Embrace. Allow me to explain the way I see the movement on the scale before I tie it into my story.

Disrupters unsettle our lives with jarring doubts like: "What if I can't handle this?" and "What if don't get back to normal?" These questions pose a significant threat that leads many people to *condemn* and reject their disrupters. Some people get stuck. Becoming helpless, they minimize their own agency and resilience, which leads to malaise and depression. For others, deep patterns of acquiring worth through achievement are interrupted, leading to questions of individual worth like, "Who am I?" or "How do I find my purpose?" Still others dive into denial by ignoring the severity of the disrupter, compartmentalizing, or shutting off their feelings.

Next comes the struggle to *endure* a new reality, a different identity. At first, we feel disoriented. After my surgical failure and complications, I feel like an amputee and battle-scared soldier. The numbness, pain, and limits of mobility make it hard to accept my body. I'm faced with the task of figuring out how to not push the loss away. Endurance is a shift from disbelief and condemnation to shorter-term persistence.

Then comes the movement forward in which we *tolerate* the loss over the longer haul. We develop coping skills. We choose perspective changes. But most of all, we take action against two primary standards we all seek to meet: certainty and comfort, as Reid Wilson argues. There are unintended consequences to banishing uncertainty and distress: "When our desire for the comfort of security and confidence turns into a requirement, it will drive a great deal of our worries, fears, self-criticisms, and disappointments."[11] It turns out that avoiding distress generates more distress in the long run. So, we have to adopt a different perspective to "Want what you don't want. Want what you've been trying to get rid of. Want difficulty, confusion, and struggle."[12] Yeah, right!

We can't do this when we're looking ahead or behind but only when we look at the present moment. Being in the moment for more than a moment is the key. Looking elsewhere engages the standard of certainty and comfort as we compare our current life unfavorably to the past and worry about the future. Disrupters pose a challenge of how to incorporate loss into a new present reality and accepting a new normal instead of comparing it to how life used to be. Questions from others like, "When is this over?" or "When are your treatments done?" along with your own plea, "When will I–or this

11. Wilson, *Stopping the Noise in Your Head*, 17.

12. Wilson, *Stopping the Noise in Your Head*, 133.

circumstance–return to normal?" drain away the ability to persevere and pull us back to condemning the disrupter when what we most need is to lower our expectations to accept the hand we've been dealt. Tolerance is chosen, clawed out, hardscrabble.

Moving forward on the acceptance scale is anything but automatic. Many months after my recurrence, with ongoing numbness and upper body and stomach pain, I naturally want to feel like before. An unforeseen intestinal condition called SIBO leaves me with constant pain and bloating. I long to get off my draconian diet to eat whatever I want again. My desire for normalcy hinders me. So, I choose to compare myself today to when the problem was more acute, not how I used to be, and that way I set a "new normal." Is the pain unbearable? No. Can I control some of it through diet? Yes. Instead of focusing on what I can't do, I focus on what I *can* do. A measure of control, even if small, lifts my spirit.

Tolerance propels me toward *acceptance*, which begins with naming, assessing, and owning my losses. That process releases the creative power of a disrupter. This does not mean we assert, "It was worth it all!" or make other pragmatic, results-oriented statements of profit and loss. Instead, we note the compassion, connection, and appreciation the experience yields. As we move from tolerate to accept, we might feel ashamed of how we used to be–task over people-oriented, a control-freak, unappreciative, dismissive of others' pain, shallow, selfish, and impatient–and a desire to become a better person. Sometimes we need to own our mistakes and failures along the way. Ownership is about allowing our wounds to be a part of our story.

The final step is to *embrace* the disrupter as it offers a new vantage point and opportunity to keep the lessons of pain alive. This step, however, is not indispensable to healing–acceptance is sufficient in some cases–because some things simply may never be embraced. I have a friend who lost her college age son through a gruesome suicide and another whose only daughter drowned at age nine. Most Holocaust survivors can't embrace the horrible losses they endured at the hands of sadists. People who endure violence or PTSD will be triggered for a long time, if not their whole lives. Just as it's not necessary to experience reconciliation for forgiveness to be real, so embracing is not necessary for healing to take place.

Disrupters are inherently destructive, but also potentially life-giving. In some circumstances it's possible to move toward embrace. When a disrupter carries the potential of finding meaning and purpose, it's good to embrace it. When it offers a restart based on innate, not acquired, value apart from what we have or do, it's good to embrace it. This requires faith, faith that there's something we gain that only comes through pain.

How I respond to discomfort and pain is a choice. It's like childbirth, especially natural childbirth, when the mother yields to the severe and exhausting contractions instead of screaming her head off. Screaming and fighting against the pain only make it more severe. Giving birth during the natural childbirth trend of the 80s and 90s–arguably a brainwashing trend I would avoid these days–I have to reach deep inside myself to yield to the pain. I become quiet, like an animal giving birth. Rick's wrist bears the brunt of the pain, though. The breathing techniques help my body work with the contractions and get my mind on top of them instead of being crushed by them. A vivid memory of all three labors is Rick's eyes fixed on the monitor telling me when the contractions spike. I cling to his two words "going down," for dear life in the agonizing seconds of pain that feels like a truck driving over my stomach. I don't care about the pain my vise grip inflicts on his wrist; in fact, I secretly like it. That is his penny payment for the pain he inflicted on me. I learn that I can endure the worst possible pain with a proper mental attitude. I am proud of my martyrdom. Pain tolerance is not always born of pure motives.

A purer motive for embracing pain and discomfort is seeing how it connects us to the suffering of others, as Bowler experiences through the people who enter her suffering: "When they sat beside me, my hand in their hands, my own suffering began to feel like it had revealed to me the suffering of others, a world of those who, like me, are stumbling in the debris of dreams they thought they were entitled to and plans they didn't realize they had made."[13] Presence propels us through pain.

It takes time, patience, and faith to embark on a journey of acceptance. The acceptance scale is a pathway for finding our footing in a life disrupter. We get stuck and claw our way out, but the commitment to keep moving is worthwhile. I want to take you through my own process on the acceptance scale starting with childhood triggers aroused by my disrupter.

13. Bowler, *Everything Happens*, 121.

Chapter 2

Trauma and Triggers

Childhood Debris

WHEN A DISRUPTER HITS, it often unearths other dormant and unresolved issues from the past. We not only deal with the circumstances of the disrupter but also with subterranean forces that create powerful emotions and a desire to condemn and push away the disrupter. Sorting through why we first condemn our disrupter is a confusing process that requires self-awareness at a time when we are just trying to survive. A survival instinct stifles awareness and insight. That's why a framework or a scaffold like the Acceptance Scale is a tool to support us in the chaos.

Experiencing a life disrupter is like a tornado. I've never been in a tornado, but I think of it as picking up everything in its path and scattering large and small debris in wild disarray. Destruction dots the landscape. Disrupters function in a similar way: They remove the things we rely on for security. Their scatter-force takes not only objects on the ground but also just below the surface, like a downed tree revealing its roots. Disrupters pick up debris from the past–unresolved problems, pain, and trauma–and leave us confused and in disbelief. We ask ourselves, "Where did that come from?"

Memories of childhood trauma subsist beyond our conscious awareness and are triggered by a sudden disrupter. In the case of trigger-ability, as Rick calls it, there are three universal reactions to trauma: numbing, hypersensitivity to danger, and re-experiencing symptoms. These secondary reactions complicate the process of dealing with a disrupter. That such memories have a physiological basis compounds the challenge of understanding them. As psychiatrist Bessel Van Der Kolk advances, symptoms of PTSD "have their origin in the entire body's response to the original trauma."[1] Research reveals that "reliving a strong negative emotion causes significant changes in the brain areas that receive nerve signals from the muscles, gut, and skin–areas that are crucial for regulating basic bodily functions."[2] Some people reexperience the physical sensations of the original event. The body remembers.

People with PTSD are often unaware of this connection–as well as the connection between now and then–but they feel like their whole life is affected. They ask themselves, "Weren't these issues distant and settled?" or "Why does it feel like my feet are tangled up in trip wire?" What is true for survivors of PTSD is also true for anyone who has experienced a life disrupter, especially in the formative years of life, though perhaps to a lesser degree. Everyone has different snares, but each person must watch out and not be surprised if old stuff comes up.

As we will see in subsequent chapters, dealing with disrupters requires understanding our losses, but a first step is to be aware of our triggers. My cancer disrupter forcibly initiates me into the cancer club, a club no one wants to join. It's a club of insecurity and loss of control. This unearths memories of other insecurity clubs I am thrust into as a child. The connections are invisible to the mind but vivid to the heart and body.

My childhood triggers are from experiences of dislocation and social pressure, which contribute to two different quests within me at odds with each other: to belong and to have my own voice. The first is an attaching or cohesive force, while the second is more of a detaching or disuniting one. The desire to belong tends to obfuscate truth, weakening my voice. The quest for a voice requires standing up for myself,–and being self-aware–qualities I lack as a child. The desire to belong pervades my childhood years, and the quest for my voice my adolescent and young adult years.

As a child I am afraid of not fitting in. This fear is one of the deepest value-distorting human drives. Teachers see students give in to the pressure not to "rat" because they don't want to be ostracized. Their focus shifts from the actual wrong to the greater violation of disturbing group cohesion. Students who rat are vilified and cast out, creating fear of reprisal.

1. Van Der Kolk, *The Body Keeps the Score*, 11.
2. Van Der Kolk, *The Body Keeps the Score*, 97.

Adults succumb to the same pressure. In the case of George Floyd, the duty to intervene might be a case of entrenched police culture running up against the fear of being ostracized and branded a 'rat.' If you're considered an individual who can't be trusted, you might not receive timely back-up from other officers. The addition of a power differential and inexperience between Derek Chauvin and at least two of the officers–rookies on the fourth day of duty–compounds the problem. Belonging compromises truth.

Flared Nostrils and a Hotline to God

I define my childhood as being an American in Germany and a German in America. My first three years are the normal life of a small child in a suburban Los Angeles ranch house. My dad is a successful Cadillac salesman in Hollywood, affording us many comforts, like fancy new cars as big as boats with expansive fins and eye-catching paint. My mom is a homemaker with three children. I'm the baby with a doting older brother, Rich, and an older sister, Joy, who is launched in the next phase of childhood. I associate images of light and color with that house. For the three of us, Malcolm Avenue is idyllic: a playhouse, flowers, neighborhood kids, birthday parties, my maternal grandparents with a house just behind us and, most of all, security. All of us carry that magic image with us throughout our lives.

At age three we move to Germany for a short-term mission trip–long enough to learn the language–and back to the U.S. for Kindergarten. It's a nomadic life for a while, a bit like the migrating Romani people whose camps dot the rural landscape of Germany. The place we plan to settle in doesn't work out, so we are looking for another place. One evening, we cross the bridge in an unknown city. Should we turn left, or right? My mom says "right," and we end up at a hotel. That hotel leads to a stay–and eventually my childhood–in Koblenz. We rent two rooms in a nearby house vacated by a family on an overseas trip where we share the house with other strangers for six months. There I learn German from another child. By the time the family returns, there is a spiking housing shortage that leads us to take what we can find.

It's one room in a crowded area below an ancient fortress. Ehrenbreitstein, a famed monument, towers above the tight dark streets made of cobblestones with ancient tenements. The room is in the lower story of a house pushed against a rock hill at the end of the crowded settlement.

Just outside the dank room sits a modest trailer my dad buys to sleep my brother and himself. Meanwhile, my mom, sister, and I occupy the room with a bed, a wash basin without running water, and an adjoining WC with spiders clinging to cobwebs near the trap window. Cold, dreary, and scary is how I remember this room. I feel the insecurity of nomadic life creep into my bones before I know it with my mind. After a few months, we escape this room for an apartment on top of the hill called Am Asterstein. It has a spacious backyard the owners allow us to use.

After a year, we kids are delighted to return to Los Angeles. Kindergarten is glorious. Nurturing teachers, comforting naps on soft rugs, and happy times with friends reset a feeling of security. My best friend, with the same name as mine, invites me to her house brimming with an overabundance of toys. I return often. For Halloween, my mom makes me a splendid satin blue princess dress. The shiny dress and crown triumph over the day even though it ends with my vomiting from too much candy. But it's my last Halloween as a child.

Church is a big part of our lives. We commute on surface streets along Santa Monica Boulevard to Hollywood before freeways are built. These are the glory years of Hollywood Presbyterian Church. Bustling and spirited, the church is a beacon in Los Angeles. On Sunday mornings, we rush to find seats, like concertgoers at a popular venue. My white taffeta dress with black velvet bodice and flowers dotting the puffy petticoat rustles, like the rushing breath of God. I find a seat next to my mother in a fancy dress with matching hat. The men wear suits and ties; boys wear white shirts, some with ties. People settle in hushed reverence awaiting the resounding organ of ornate mahogany framed by a massive choir loft above the minsters' hefty red velvet chairs and exalted lectern. The dark wood, the creaking sounds of latecomers finding seats on the balcony level above, the packed pews, and the musty smell of age give this Gothic sanctuary a sense of place. We have a sense of our place before God.

It's through this church that my mom discovers a vibrant spiritual home after her escape from war-damaged Germany a decade earlier in 1947 where she spent her entire youth as a hunted Jew. Here she is enfolded under the leadership of Henrietta Mears–a once in a century woman, as my mom calls her. She is invited to a conference led by Ms. Mears for college-age adults at Forest Home Christian Camp in the San Bernardino Mountains.

There my mom has a profound experience of forgiving the Germans whom she bitterly hates. She describes it in her book *Yola* as "a rending and painful acknowledgement of my need for God's help in dealing with . . . my hatred and desire for revenge" that enacts a miracle of forgiveness and love replacing the hate. This miracle is solely from God apart from her human will as she concludes, "No mental effort, no human resolutions, no iron will could do what he has done for me."[3] There she opens her Bible, and her eyes fall on this verse: "No one who puts his hand to the plow and looks back, is fit for the Kingdom of God."[4] "These are my marching orders" she decides as she begins to answer the question of what being a Holocaust survivor means for her future.

I think of my mom's nose at church, the earnest way her nostrils flare. As the organ ascends, the nostrils train, like an elk on a distant scent, on God. My mom's voice rises in song and floats upward, her eyes closed and small tears pushing out under the eyelids onto her cheeks. The flared nostrils signal the moment of divine inspiration. It's like the breath of God is reaching her in the pew. To my siblings and me it seems like my mom has a hotline to God.

My mom's faith is a blending of proposition and intuition. Earlier, my mom receives a verse from Isaiah which leads her to decide to marry my dad who is not a believer. The passage describes three offspring, each with different identifying characteristics. Soon my dad becomes a Christian. At that same camp where my mom forgives the Germans, she and my dad put a red pin on the world map over Germany to pray for the people there. After camp, they each receive the same verse on the same day that provides the impetus to move us back to Germany. The verse arrives after the church budget is already set. Over time a family narrative forms that God is directing each step of our journey.

My mom's belief in God's direction becomes a prominent feature of our family. Bible verses from jars, dreams, right turns, and other unexpected signals are God's provision. We children laugh at how God even gives her driving directions. I guess that's what happens when men refuse to ask for them. My mom is the Google maps voice from on high long before smart phones. On numerous occasions, she instructs my father to "Turn right!" or "Go straight ahead!" with a strong sense of certainty that makes us take notice. One time a few years later, while driving from Germany

3. Entz, *Forgive and Remember*, 145.
4. Luke 9:63

to Monte Carlo in search of her dad—we have no idea where he's staying but we know he's there on a rendezvous—another "Turn right!" leads to my grandpa's surprised face just around the corner. We embrace one another and spend a happy vacation together.

Flared nostrils and hunches have consequences, however, like the decision to trade a comfortable life for one of meaning and purpose, as she describes it. This is the family narrative, "We don't want to live an ordinary life. We want to be sold out for the Lord's work," on fire for Christ. This is the fruit of her first experience at Forest Home as she reflects on her status as survivor: "What could I do with this spared life? Making plans like normally young people make at this time of their life, seems to be out of the question. I want to keep the memories alive of those who had been so cruelly taken at the threshold of their adulthood. But I also need to turn the leadership of my life over to God who had saved me from total destruction. I have no right to plans that leave him out."[5] Since comfortable lives are lukewarm and compromised, my mom and dad have a clear mandate to eschew the comfortable life.

After Kindergarten my parents sell the house and all our belongings and move us to Germany permanently. Independent Christian workers without financial support and health insurance, they live off the earnings from the sale of the home. We can't afford luxuries, but many of our necessities are met except for health insurance. In fact, the first time I go to the dentist is at age eighteen while at college in California. I'm embarrassed by the dentist's question whether I'm a smoker derived from the accumulated gunk on my teeth. My dad makes extra money buying and selling used Mercedes. His outgoing personality and salesman skills make up for his broken German and strong American accent. He doesn't know what it means to be embarrassed. I do.

A Sensitive Girl in a Harsh Place

We return to Koblenz where we rent the same Am Asterstein apartment after a wait that sends us traveling to Spain and Portugal. Upon our return, I settle into first grade. I am an American growing up in a small bureaucratic city in Germany in the 1960s. I quickly slip into German society without an accent, and I make a few close friends. Marion is my best friend, and we are inseparable. There are carefree days of roaming the neighborhood

5. Entz, *Forgive and Remember*, 146.

without checking with parents, and going downtown by bus and the feared "Teufelstreppe" (devil's stairs) to the public pool. We jay-walk, roam city streets, climb cheery trees, do pranks.

There are no theme parks, arcades, recreational facilities, just a sparse playground with one small carousel. My mom hosts birthday parties for us in the summer. American items are hallowed, like the cans of food and candy from a local military PX my dad occasionally displays on the kitchen table. We celebrate like exiles longing for their home. I like making things, houses out of cardboard, board games, purses, knitted items, Christmas decorations, and Creepy Crawlers from a set I bring back from the U.S. and heat with a transformer. They are the rage of the neighborhood, and I sell them to the other kids. I like that part of being an American kid in Germany.

In the winter, I love the occasional day when the snow lasts for a day or two and we make human chains on our wooden sleds with feet linked to the sled behind it. Christmas has warm charms and traditions like fresh-cut candlelit trees that my parents decorate on Christmas Eve and the spicy aroma of cookies like *Zimtsterne* and *Lebkuchen*. The kids wait anxiously for hours until the tree is revealed in its splendor. Overall, Germany is a place of innocence with homespun entertainment, wholesome traditions, muted colors, nothing flashy.

A razor's edge below the surface, harshness and pedantry invade the innocence of my childhood. People everywhere cry about the woes of their early years, but nothing is quite like the German version of the 1960s: the clipped emotional landscape, spiky warnings, reprimands and dire consequences from beer-bellied fathers, middle-aged amputees, and bullying teachers aimed to produce manicured conformity and compliance in children. Even some children are harsh, like the boys on my street who throw snowballs with rocks at my friend, Marion, and me. The adults habitually instruct, correct, and scold children–perfect strangers acting like offended parents. There's always a lesson to be taught, like when the ball that goes over the fence of the neighbor's house is burned. The houses are heated by coal furnaces in the basement that are filled by the shovelful once a day. This is where our ball ends up. These experiences are not just wild outliers.

Nothing, however, matches the stupefying silence about the war. It's a funeral pall covering the remains of the deceased. No one comes near the subject of concentration camps and war atrocities. Not one syllable about the war is uttered in school. The responsibility to reckon with national sins shifts to rebuilding projects everywhere. With remarkable speed and efficiency, Germany erases even that reminder. Were it not for the middle aged men and hushed comments, it would seem like the Holocaust had never happened. Men with missing limbs in public and hushed tones of "Er ist im Krieg gefallen" (He died in the war) punctuate the silence. Signs without explanations, evidence without a claim slide the pall from the coffin. Will the remains resurrect?

Teachers are harsh to children, and children must obey. Girls stand up to curtsy adults entering the room. Boys bow. My first-grade teacher, Frau Uckermann snaps a ruler on my bitten fingernails. She looks severe and old. My brother thinks she's sixty or seventy but she's forty. I am forced to write with my right hand though I'm left-handed. When my mother objects, she faces iron-clad rules impervious to change. Left-handed writers erase cursive scribble on little black boards with tiny sponges on red strings, which first-graders use to practice their letters. The teachers claim to be helping me, but they are really helping themselves conform to the god of rules. Second grade greets me with the announcement that Frau Uckermann is my teacher again. I spend another year under her strict pedagogy.

As I advance into the Gymnasium–the university, not trade school track decided by bureaucratic edict before fifth grade–teachers become even more officious. They enter the classroom, and students rise, push in their chairs, and curtsy or bow, greeting the teacher in unison, "Guten Morgen, Herr Doktor Pausch." The feigned respect goes only in one direction. In answer to a question by Dr. Pausch, my German English teacher, I dutifully stand to answer, but he yells at me in front of the class, "Wir sind nicht in Amerika!" (We are not in America!). So, I resentfully learn British English, but I cut loose in mocking display of my British accent at home. At least my parents temporarily get their wish for me to hold onto the English language. But I'm really holding onto bitterness.

Every day, I tremulously enter the grocery store for milk with my two-liter tin can hoping the abrasive owner doesn't raise her voice at me again. She yells at me for touching her precious produce, but it feels like she's yelling at me for existing. I ask a bus driver if he's *going* to such and such a place. He yells "Nein!" (No!) and starts driving off, stops, then calls me. I happily saunter to the door when he tells me he's not *going* there; he's *driving* there, and I should get in.

Strangers tell me not to walk on the grass or sit on public steps. The train conductors with their whistles and officious voices yelling "Karte!"

(Tickets!) are the worst. That one word injects anxiety in a child's heart. In Germany compliments are in short supply, rare to the point of penury; I don't remember compliments from teachers, instructors, or adult acquaintances. I remember mostly instructions, warnings, and reprimands. Judging from the children's books, I conclude that they believe consequences motivate children to be good, and compliments give them a big head. If so, why not intensify the consequences to really make them stick?

A thousand petty lectures, dire warnings, and catastrophic consequences from people, books, and the culture–books like *Der Struwwelpeter*, *Max & Moritz*, *Gebrueder Grimm*–steadily hammer in a solid sense of shame. *Der Struwwelpeter*, replete with shocking consequences and pictures, illustrates the point in case it doesn't get through. The boy who sucks his thumb has it cut off with oversized scissors from a wizened old man leaving splats of blood bursting from his hand. The girl who plays with fire burns to death with pictures of her kittens crying over her ashes. On and on it goes. My own kids think this book is appalling and abusive, but the author–a doctor–attaches the subtitle: *Happy Stories and Cute Pictures for Children from 3 to 6 Years*. Growing up, I absorb a culture of truth-telling, criticism, and consequences. It's like living in a sparsely furnished house with hard furniture and splintering stools.

Zacharias is a soft cushion of kindness in that house. Zacharias sees me. We meet him at a conference of a German youth evangelist with ties to the Ugandan revival called "Walking in the Light." He needs housing for some of his African friends. Zacharias, a pharmacist working in a hospital in Kampala, stays with us during the conference. He's married with children. My mom never forgets a sermon he preaches at that conference. I never forget how he stoops down to look me in the eye, asking, "Sheri, how are you?" His voice is the kindest warm bass I ever heard. With his eyes at my six-year-old level, I feel the kindness of God reach my heart. He's only with us for a short time but it feels like he fills up my childhood with regular visits. He is my first love, my knight in shining armor who stoops to my level to see and hear me. The wish to marry him stays with me through childhood. I will never diminish a child's experience of love.

My dad is another cushion of comfort. My parents are involved in Christian youth work; my mom does the public speaking–and much of the upfront work. Many evenings I sit on my dad's lap listening to my mom expound a Bible passage or concept. She excels in that role and pours herself into the work of ministry. My dad excels at giving me a comfortable seat as his Sheri Becky. He's like a hearth that warms up a cold room. I feel his unconditional love.

Don't Stand Out

How do I respond to the culture around me? An insatiable desire to blend in, to refuse to stand out as a loud American, to find security and belonging overtakes me. I'm already shy with a mumbling voice, but my voice shrinks even more. I'm the baby in a family of talkers, who affix three attributes to me: spiritual antenna, sensitive, and peacemaker. The first comes from early faith experiences, like getting on my knees at a young age to accept Jesus into my heart, telling my worried family to trust the Lord on a nail-biting trip over Swiss Gotthard Pass with trailer in tow, requesting a book on Christian doctrine, and adoring God and the angels before bed. The spiritual antenna becomes a part of my identity and a dominant feature as an adult–after a rejection of that identity in adolescence.

The other attribute is that I'm sensitive and must be protected. I'm sensitive to irregularities, rejection, and discomforts, like a child bothered by an itchy wool sweater or the tag poking her neck. My family shields me from the truth out of a desire to protect me. I often hear, "Don't say that around the baby!" and "She's so sensitive" along with well-meaning cautions. These messages tell me I am weak. I feel ashamed to be sensitive and conciliatory, except for my role of family peacemaker, a useful skill in a family of five. I accept these attributes as immutable and true. They settle like cement on a sidewalk, but years later strong roots bulge through the hard ground to break the slabs.

My dad, a friendly, and assertive man is a loud American, albeit a lovable one. He doesn't know a stranger and engages people in friendly conversation wherever he goes. He is unaware of–and doesn't care about–the unwritten German rule not to talk to strangers. Sometimes his friendliness embarrasses me, so I learn to keep a strategic distance behind him in public. One time we visit a church in Spain where it starts to rain. He's wearing shorts with socks and sandals. But then he puts on a raincoat and looks like someone chased outdoors in a shower robe. Stares from strangers and a woman calling "Santa Maria!" chase us kids away embarrassed.

At times his assertiveness is easily mistaken for combativeness. From his view, the German people are inefficient and want to scam him. This is in the day when it takes months, even close to a year to get a telephone. My dad, who has sacrificed his job as a top salesman, a suburban Los Angeles bungalow-style home, and a comfortable life now has to support a family of five in a foreign country with no job and the savings from the house sale. Deep down he's probably afraid, but you wouldn't know it from the outside. He cobbles together an income by selling used Mercedes on his own. Here we are a struggling missionary family with luxury cars in the garage, a mystery conjuring up nefarious rumors in the neighborhood. He commands us to keep the garage closed at all times in order to stem the rumors. One day Rich breaks the rule and lets his friends see a sleek Mercedes 450 convertible Coupe with burnt orange and cream leather interior. That creates a ruckus in our family.

My mom is a more reserved German. As a Holocaust survivor from Berlin, she knows the consequences of standing out in Germany. Her trauma is tightly tucked away. She believes the trauma is healed at Forest Home, a one-time miracle with lasting effect. So, she plods along unaware that miracles require human effort to apply over the long haul. She embodies a practical Calvinism, an approach to living the Christian life that leans heavily on God's direction in the big and small events of life. A frequent statement is, "God carefully prepared this circumstance just for me." This applies to right turns and forgiveness. It is an idea that good things come to us as recipients. And they do, but are forgiveness and direction something only received apart from human effort? Does clawing out forgiveness day by day undermine the miracle of grace? Does following God's directives erase the possibility of making wrong choices? My mom seems convinced that the effort of decision-making is on God's end. Against this narrative, questions and doubts subtly slide to the periphery. I don't know it at the time, but I struggle to find my own voice and to figure out how God's will really works.

This leads me to a basic theological distinction of terms I learn as a young adult. Salvation, the process of being reconciled with God, is *monergistic,* meaning the effort comes from one–mono–source who is God. We simply accept the gift of grace. Sanctification, the process of living out salvation is *synergistic,* meaning God and man work together to effectuate salvation. Paul commands to "work out your salvation with fear and trembling, for God is at work in you to will and to work according to his good purpose."[6] This means that we are going to get it wrong at times, but that's okay because God works through our mistakes to redeem them.

6. Phil 2:12-13

Acknowledging our mistakes and repenting, however, remain necessary and crucial prerequisites for redemption and healing.

In my home and the surrounding German culture, admissions of wrong and regret are absent from the vocabulary except for my dad. His willingness to admit wrong endears me to him. No one else seems to be aware of the need to voice such words. Perhaps it's too threatening so close to the horror of the Holocaust. Horrible experiences can't be spoken about and are suppressed. The shame is too great; the pain is too deep, too palpable. Does all truth set us free or is some truth better kept in the dark? How long can you push down the truth? Or will it refuse to be contained, like roots breaking up the sidewalk? As a child, I don't formulate these questions, but the material for the questions gathers in the basement somewhere away from my consciousness.

My mom's reluctance to deal with her trauma is understandable, but I keep thinking about what my life would be like if she had dealt more completely with the anger and pain of her past? The truth that sets us free requires feeling and validating pain. Truth may seem like a pointed sword, but it's also a light. Anne Lamott says that "you don't always have to chop with the sword of truth. You can point with it too."[7] That pointing is an act of courage, a bravery that releases healing even to the next generation. My siblings and I all struggle in different ways with insecurity, anger, and finding our voices beyond what is normal for many people. There still is much work for us to do.

Fitting in is a Bad Fit

My insecurity as a child leads me to fit in completely, so much so that I speak exclusively German. My dad and mom speak English at home–American style–to help us kids keep up on our English, but I stubbornly respond in German, except to mock my English teacher. My mom's journal recording things I said shows the extent of it. She narrates in English, asks me questions in English, and she records my answers in German. The amount of translating we all do just to keep up a conversation is amazing. I speak without an accent, so no one can tell I'm not a German girl. I want it that way. Being different in a homogeneous culture means I don't belong. Neighbors know I'm not German, and sometimes I hear the jeer "Ami, go home!"

7. Lamott, *Bird by Bird*, 156.

Blending in continues until sixth grade when my first big disrupter knocks out my clawed-out sense of belonging. A thick blanket of fresh snow covers the area where I live on Germany's Rhine River. "Mom, I want to go sledding with my friends," I announce. We have enviable sleds, not the plastic disks in the U.S., but long, wooden ones, long enough to lie prostrate on, hitch your feet to a friend's sled and bump down the slopes in raucous unison. My mom's reply is, "No; we're moving to the States today." I am eleven, and this is my fourth trans-continental move, but this one is literally overnight.

Extenuating circumstances lead to such an abrupt move. Joy and Rich are living in California by now where Rich's life is falling apart. We have to remove him from a bad living arrangement and troubles with school and friends. My parents first consider a boarding school in Florida, but that falls through. The only option is for my mom and me to return to Los Angeles while my dad stays behind for his work with the Billy Graham Evangelistic Organization in conjunction with the U.S. military bases. At that time there are 500,000 American troops in West Germany.

Icelandic Air, a charter airline with low prices, has only that one January flight. The next flight is weeks away. I am jerked–literally overnight–out of the innocence of an all-girls school, where I walk arm in arm with my girlfriends, to a co-ed elementary school in a Los Angeles suburb for the second half of sixth grade. We leave our belongings including a stack of adventure stories I wrote between ages nine and eleven. Writing is a favorite hobby. Unfortunately, my dad gets rid of them in the hurried move as he stays behind and packs up our apartment. We say good-bye not knowing how long we will be in America and separated from my dad.

The middle of sixth grade is not the best time for a transcontinental transplant. Since my entire school life is in German, I am woefully unprepared for an American education. I only read and write German. In the new school a continent away, I reflexively stand up with a curtsy when the teacher calls on me–it's hard to undo six years of authoritarian training–until the snickers gradually extinguish the habit. I have an accent and am called the German kid. I'm put in remedial reading and picked last at sports.

The opaque veil that obscures people's opinions of me lifts as teams are picked in gym class. Team captains go around and around until, at the bottom, someone reluctantly picks me. It's never a voluntary pick with a welcoming smile; it's an obligatory pick. I don't like being an obligation. Each round nails the shingle "Unwanted" and "Bad" into my storefront where I conduct the business of pre-adolescence. My athletic inadequacy adds to the humiliation of not knowing the games, classroom rules, and social norms, which no one else, of course, needs explaining because it's common knowledge like, "Who crossed the ocean blue in 1492?"–another thing I don't know. My mom buys me a handball and I practice against the carport walls of my apartment that no one visits because I have no friends. Even if I did, I would be too embarrassed to invite them to our one-bedroom apartment where four of us reside.

California is on the cusp of the summer of love. The girls wear miniskirts with fishnet stockings. After school one day, I ask my mom what "making out" is, but she doesn't know. Joy and Rich also don't know. Belonging may be far out of reach, but it still drives me. Social failure motivates me to figure out a way to fit into this strange new world–though I'm unconscious of my motive.

In the summer after that wrenching experience in sixth grade, we move again, this time to Van Nuys, a nearby suburb. Another start from scratch. In my hurt and rejection, I resolve to never experience the humiliation of being an outcast. How? Excel at academics? Join a sports team? Run for student government? No; I decide to be popular. How is popularity achieved at Van Nuys Junior High School in the late 1960s? By joining the "bad" group, a cohort of preteen rebellion known for foolish choices.

For a time, I enjoy belonging to a group of valley girls–and boys–who roam the streets, hitchhike, and engage in risky behaviors, not that different from today's teenagers. In that phase of my life, I do things I would regret for years, even decades, but I belong, at least for a while, until another devastating event makes me an outsider once again.

Triggered Eighty Years Later

Disrupters have a way of scraping dormant wounds from childhood even though the past seems distant and sealed off. My recent disrupter raises these old feelings of insecurity once again. It's a stealthy process that catches me off guard until I ask myself why it's so hard to accept the current circumstance. Everyone has different wounds and debris, but the same principle of trigger-ability is at work. We must watch out and not be surprised if old stuff comes up.

To illustrate the fresh memory of old wounds, take my mom's recent experience of people making a wide berth around her on neighborhood walks during the COVID pandemic. As a Holocaust survivor from Berlin, my mom carries the tattered load of past trauma around with her every day. She remembers Crystal Night and the yellow Star of David with *Jude* (Jew) sewn on her lapel by her Gentile-cultural Christian-mom. Her dad is Jewish. Hitler's 1935 second degree law of *Mischlinge* (mixed race children) declares that she belongs to the Jewish race. Her parents dote on their only child, but her Jewish father flees Germany with the rest of his family on February 22, 1938, Washington's birthday. My mom is twelve, and she and her mother are left behind to care for their linen shop in East Berlin, an essential business, particularly during the war. He plans to send for them when he finds work, but the war breaks out. There is little opportunity for my grandma to nurture her daughter under Hitler's edict of destruction; she can only try to protect her.

Small events trigger my mom's memories. The well-meaning gesture of moving away from the elderly in public during the pandemic touches a raw nerve pulsing just below the surface despite eighty years of dormancy. She remembers the yellow Star of David with *Jude* sewn on her lapel. My mom is an impressionable girl–barely a teenager–in the streets of Berlin. Pedestrians do far more than provide a wide berth; they taunt, jeer, and threaten her very existence with their furtive stares of seething anger. The star gives them license to release their vitriol on an innocent child.

How does my grandma endure the cruel force compelling her to sew the star on her daughter's lapel? What goes through her mind as chooses a spool, threads the needle, knots the fiber, and stabs the coarse cloth? How does she extinguish the primal urge to protect her only child from harm? How does she persuade her daughter to wear the coat outside? She fastens the star high on the lapel to fold down in the streets, but it doesn't blunt the horror.

"It was the worst thing I ever experienced" my mom recalls with bitterness. "I cried and physically struggled with my mom as she was trying to sew on the star. I screamed at her: 'Why did you have to marry a Jew and make me suffer like that? You don't have to go out like me!' I was really beside myself. I loved my dad! But it was unbearable to me, and I just cried my heart out." She leaves the house with the lapel turned up for the Nazi spy stationed at the apartment complex entrance to see, folding it down when he's out of sight. Now, as people make a wide berth around her eighty years later, the pain reemerges. It's remarkable how grim memories are preserved like honey-colored amber; it's sad to witness their relentless force.

When it becomes too dangerous for my mom in Berlin, her mom sends her to Bavaria where she is sheltered by an anti-Nazi carpenter family called the Walters. There she survives the war even through the threats of the town's mayor and other suspecting locals. After the war, my mom finds her dad with the help of an American officer in Bavaria, whom she meets through her job as translator for a local intelligence service (CIC) to try war criminals.

Getting out of Germany is a long and difficult process. My mom and grandma travel north to the port city of Bremerhaven and must go through primitive camps for three months before they finally get on the list after giving up their last valuables. She and her mom obtain tickets to leave Germany exactly nine years after her dad left in 1947 on one of the last displaced persons transport ships, the Marine Marlin, which goes out of Bremerhaven to New York along with 1000 Holocaust survivors and displaced persons.

The journey at the bottom of the ship with twenty-five women crammed in hammocks, one washroom, no fresh air, or places to sit is brutal and long. Finally, on March 2, 1947, at the age of twenty-one the New York harbor comes into view with thousands of people clamoring to see their loved ones. My mom stands on deck next to a woman holding binoculars and asks to use them. Here's her description of what happens next:

> "I can see a crowd of people awaiting our arrival, pushing against fences, trying to catch a glimpse of a relative or friend, whom they had thought dead or lost for years, but with whom they would soon be united again. A woman standing in front of me holds a small pair of binoculars to her eyes. I tip her on the shoulder. 'When you're done, do you mind if I take a look?' She hands me the glass and I wonder, where should I start to look at this large crowd. I lift the glass to my eyes—and the first person I focus on is Dad! I recognize him immediately. I jump up and down like crazy, shouting and waving 'Daddy, Daddy!' but, of course, he cannot see or hear me. There are too many people, and we are still too far away from the pier.
>
> We must bridle our impatience for another two hours of formalities before we can leave the ship. Mother following me, I run straight to the place where I had seen my father waiting behind the fence. The green wooden fence posts between us, we grab his hands reaching out for us, Mother taking one and I holding on to

36

the other. In spite of my eyes brimming with tears of joy, I can see that he has hardly changed. He still looks like the picture I carried around in my heart all these years. After the last examination of our papers, we finally can kiss and fall into each other's arms, never to let go again."[8]

After nine years, they are reunited and move to California where her father lives. During that time, she stumbles onto Hollywood Presbyterian Church, where she is welcomed into a vibrant body of young believers led by the dynamic Henrietta Mears. This is where she finds a reason for why her life was spared. My mom's route to becoming a Christian ministry worker in Germany is anything but predictable. She ends up spending over fifty years there and retires to the U.S. at the ripe age of eighty-seven. Her calling excludes watching her family and grandchildren grow up.

Today my mom is a nonagenarian with a relatively healthy body and mind. As she assesses her life, she tells me the pain and sadness of losing her best friend, Erika, in Auschwitz, her first love in Russia, her safety, security, trust, and childhood never go away. Tears spill out as she remembers the day in Bavaria–all alone away from her mother in Berlin–as she receives a letter from her mother affirming, "The Lord gave, and the Lord has taken away; blessed be the name of the Lord,"[9] and telling her that her home in Berlin is bombed and the valuable paintings and antiques her father had carefully procured are in ruins. The pain lives just below the surface like a swamp creature threatening to pounce in the stillness.

Know Your Triggers

My mom's story of deprivation, fear, and horror outstrips most stories. Her life is upended and nearly tossed away. Her adolescence is marked by survival against strong odds. There are no luxuries and comforts, no rest and peace, no lulls amid the storm, just a constant raging tempest. She survives the war and finds peace in America.

My mom's prodigious story of suffering dwarfs mine. Such a weighty story naturally takes center stage in a family, displacing other narratives. Add to that survivor's guilt and a story-telling communication style and you have unconscious forces that keep the attention on the survivor. Such forces are invisible and amorphous, but not unnoticed. My story of

8. Entz, *Forgive and Remember*, 130.

9. Job 1:21

insecurity seems petty next to hers, creating a reluctance to give it much credence. Like a Venn diagram, however, it overlaps in one small area with my mom's. We're both living in a country of shame. Bruised with stilled voices, we search for more. My mom wants to know why her life is spared. She's looking for purpose and meaning. I want a place to belong. Our intersection is insecurity. But it confounds me that she takes me to the place of her own insecurity, shame, and loss.

What is your debris? Working through your debris is a difficult process, but the rewards make it worthwhile. Being aware of why we react the way we do sets a solid foundation for advancing along the scary, unpredictable but ultimately life-giving journey of loss and acceptance. Let's walk a little closer to that process.

Chapter 3

Please, Unsubscribe Me
Because I Never Signed Up!

First Reactions Usually Stink, So Hold Your Nose

WHEN A DISRUPTER FIRST HITS, a natural response is to *condemn* it by refusing to deal with it. It's not a particularly effective strategy, but it is common. Before absorbing the shock, we feel its impact. Like the calm–or numbing–we feel right after a close call in a car and the shock when bad news suddenly strikes, we experience shaking minutes later or the fuller impact of bad news weeks or months later. It's common to enter a survival state with mental resources dispatched to cope instead of feel. Funeral arrangements require attention, a medical team needs to be assembled, decisions need to be made, acute pain must be endured. Young women with cancer are slammed with the possibility of infertility. Amputees convulse at the idea of losing a limb. Parents of accident victims can't reconcile the image of their active and healthy child with the casket. Reality refuses to settle in.

I've noticed two common ways people tell their disrupters, "I can't handle you! Just go away!" Some people get engulfed in their feelings–especially anxiety–and can't see their way out of the pit they're in. I call this way *attachment* because there is no space between them and the disrupter. They are too attached to the disrupter's power. Others mobilize coping strategies to avoid falling into a pit. They put off experiencing the full impact of what's happening. I call this *detachment* because there is a sizable space between them and the disrupter. They are detached from the disrupter's power.

Psychologist and author Reid Wilson uses the terms *worry* and *avoidance* for these two positions. At the base is the belief that worry and avoidance are ways to manage the anxiety, but they only increase it: "If we simply worry about an upcoming problem instead of solving it, or if we back away to get rid of our distress, we are inviting anxiety to take advantage of us, and we are on a path of suffering."[1] Both ways are automatic reactions instead of chosen responses to the circumstances. Anxiety is only overcome with resistance that walks toward the feelings of distress.

There are advantages and disadvantages to both attaching and detaching. Because *attachers* are more in touch with their emotions, they also tend to be more open and sincere about their struggles. On the other hand, they are more prone to enthroning their emotions. They wear their anxiety on their sleeves. Awaiting further news of a diagnosis, test result, accident report, or another assessment is nerve-wracking, like screaming through a Six-Flags roller coaster that someone strapped you into against your wishes. Fear spirals out of control. It magnetizes worst-case scenarios that zap resilience. Depending on the severity of the disrupter, attachers feel stuck, abandoned, and drowning.

Detachers are more adept at compartmentalizing their emotions. They put aside their worries until further notice and even experience calm and peace through the storm. That's not to say that everyone who is calm detaches from circumstances. Detachers report a surreal state of watching themselves from afar. This automatic default mode keeps them from falling into a pit of despair and readies them for the fight ahead. They have a touch of invincibility, but they run the risk of being stoic and unable to appreciate the reality of the loss. Both attachers and detachers, however, fail to grasp, own, and do something constructive with the loss. The job for both is the same: stop condemning disrupters. How? A first step is to identify their own stress responses to their significant disrupters.

I tend to be a detacher, though this time around I'm learning something from previous mistakes. My first time with cancer, I tentatively tiptoe once or twice to what Anne Lamott calls "the cold dark place within, the water under the frozen lake or the secluded, camouflaged hole"[2] to look into that hole. Then I do a quick about-face, like a pompom girl in a march. It's just too uncomfortable. It's scary still, but I'm going near the hole more often now. Disjointed is how I feel when I go there. I have my consciousness,

---

1. Wilson, *Stopping the Noise in Your Head*, 24.

2. Lamott, *Bird by Bird*, 198.

that awareness within me since birth. I have my personality, my way in the world that grows but never fundamentally changes. There's my creativity and sensitivity, that stirring in my heart for the transcendent, those parts of me that look for and bestow meaning on the world. There are my loves and passions and art. All these qualities that set me apart from the animals seem eternal. How can they just be annihilated? Dirt, decay, and grave will take the body. What takes the soul? Does it last?

Not Souls, But Wholes

I keep coming back to the resurrection of Jesus to give me confidence to walk toward the hole. Both in 2002 and 2019, I reengage the study of the resurrection begun in seminary years before. What are the arguments in favor of it? Against it? My studies reveal the preponderance of evidence for it. What else explains the fact that Jesus' body is not found despite overwhelming incentives to produce it among those who don't believe it happened? What else explains the accounts of women being the first witnesses in a misogynist culture? If you made up the story, you wouldn't entrust it to women, who were not even allowed to witness in a court of law, much less have their voices heard elsewhere. Is there a better explanation for Jesus' appearance to 500 people at different times and under different circumstances? Certainly, massive hallucinations are implausible. Is there another cogent explanation for why the early followers stop sheltering in their homes and take to the streets with surprising courage and success? Peter's sermon in Jerusalem at Pentecost results in 3000 converts with more to follow. What else explains Paul's change from persecutor to founder of the Church or the emergence of the early church and martyrdom of many in the two millennia of persecutions? Certainly, that many people don't die for what they know to be a lie. These considerations, among others, balance the scales in favor of the probability that the resurrection happened.

But what does this mean for me, for us? N.T. Wright points out that throughout history "[f]rom Plato to Hegel and beyond, some of the greatest philosophers declared that what you think about death, and life beyond it, is the key to thinking seriously about everything else."[3] From the earliest times, the church believes that Jesus' physical resurrection is the basis for the hope of receiving our own resurrection bodies, contrary to the Platonic idea of a disembodied soul that many Christians still flirt with today.

3. Wright, *Surprised by Hope*, 11.

Wright explains that the early church sees "heavenly life as a temporary stage on the way to the eventual resurrection of the body," a sort of "temporary lodging" as a "prelude to the resurrection itself."[4] Christians "realize that they are saved not as souls but as wholes and not for themselves alone but for what God now longs to do through them."[5] Shalom–wholeness–is to be a way of life.

In Jesus' resurrection, there is a coming together of heaven and earth, "the belief that that future has already begun to come forward to meet us in the present."[6] The continuity between our present and future leads to an embrace of our calling to redeem the present. It is a bedrock foundation that gives hope and motivation to change the world. It's what motivates William Wilberforce to spend twenty years of his life–including his finances and health–to end slavery in Britain. The resurrection helps me "dance around the rim of the abyss, holler into it, measure it, throw rocks in it, and still not fall in. It can no longer swallow us up. And we can get on with things."[7] That's how I feel this time around. So, I'm less detached from that hole Lamott describes.

Detach from Being a Detacher

My first reaction to a life disrupter is to mobilize coping skills. It's like I'm reaching inside a medicine chest for a calm-injecting drug. Only the drug is control. Control soothes me while the storm rages, but it wears off. I gravitate to detachment because it feels like grit, and grit is survival. Without it I fear falling into a helpless pit of despair. Sometimes I mistake denial for strength.

My first medical alarm in my thirties, a melanoma on my right calf, introduces me to that out-of-body vantage point. The words of the brief surgical report seem unreal, like they are meant for someone else. "This can't be happening!" Eventually, I come to grips with the fact that I have the worst kind of skin cancer. For a while I reflect on my mortality. Mundane concerns, frustrations, and worries shrink into miniatures, like a google earth view of your neighborhood. That bird's eye view soon fades, however, when I learn the in-situ tumor has clear margins. Tropical vacations and

4. Wright, *Surprised by Hope*, 41.

5. Wright, *Surprised by Hope*, 200.

6. Wright, *Surprised by Hope*, 122.

7. Lamott, *Bird by Bird*, 198.

sunbathing are the only things I'm denied, a small price to pay for living. I zoom in to return to my previous life. Not much about my life changes.

My first breast cancer diagnosis starts off similarly with denial, but it has an edge to it. I defiantly depress the door handle of the Tarzana Hospital where I am about to have my first biopsy in 2002, feeling certain that this is a waste of the doctor's and my time. I almost cancel the biopsy the night before, but Rick persuades me to go. I go alone, telling him to pick me up when I'm done, like I'm going to In-N-Out. I'm only half conscious that I'm really fending off the possibility of bad news.

I awaken to a harsh reality difficult to process. I have breast cancer, but it has probably not spread, so I'm told initially. That surreal feeling of dissociation, of looking down at someone else's life, takes over again. All I can focus on is the relief that I don't have to go through chemo, a dreaded fear. Chemotherapy is still a crude science with cruel effects. A string of chemo horror stories marches to the surface of my mind like fire ants disturbed by a probing stick. It seems worse than ants crawling up my legs, more like holding a tarantula, my biggest phobia.

That same day the surgeon calls back saying the news may not be good after all. There is a chance the cancer has spread, which means chemo and radiation. He orders a sentinel node biopsy that shows spread to several ancillary nodes requiring six rounds of chemo and thirty-five radiation treatments. I become more concerned about the treatment than the disease. Eventually, however, the protective shield of invincibility cracks and my life is derailed.

Seeking control–reasons and a prognosis–is my first line of defense. The internet in its infancy, I look to it for answers, for the truth. What does this mean for my future? I want to know! I feel like I am walking into the heart of darkness, a mystifying, hazardous place fraught with unknown danger. I finally realize the need to stop the internet search, take control of my thoughts, find peace. I can't control my situation, so I must accept uncertainty.

I move toward chemo with growing confidence, my thoughts and attitude geared up to fight. Friends, family, and faith make up a tripod of support. A network of survivor sisters emerges from the shadows like ghosts taking on flesh. Wendy stands out from among them. Having just finished her breast cancer treatment, she decides to take me under her wing. The first thing she says in her kind, sweet voice–an elementary teacher's voice– is, "This is going to be a bump in the road, a big one, but you will get over it." Like clockwork she calls me the night before each chemo to listen and encourage me. (Seventeen years later when I have a recurrence, she does the same, this time via texts with beautiful pictures and Scriptures curated just for me. This goes on for a year.) My mom takes a six-month leave of absence from her ministry in Germany to help our family. Worship and singing pump me up. The support feels like being carried on a litter. As my first chemo approaches, I am moving toward my fear which is like touching a tarantula, a thing I find impossible to do. I feel strong, anxiety under control, ready to go, or so I think.

I don't realize it, but I'm in denial. I don't have a port for my first chemo–a one mm titanium tube inserted in the arm or chest to transport the chemo cocktail of three poisonous drugs for a good cause. So, the nurse takes my hand and begins injecting the dreaded "Red-Devil"–Adriamycin–into my vein. She warns me not to move my hand because one drop can burn the skin. What? It can't touch the skin, but it goes right to the heart! Her warning is hardly floating in the noise space when I see yellow splotches turning black, and I faint. I hear the nurse shout "Dr. Dosik!" through the clinic as her frenetic movements kick in. They suspect a heart attack, but it turns out to be anxiety. I regain consciousness but not the nurse's respect because she brands me as nervous for the rest of my time there. Whenever I complain of nausea, she dismissively calls it "anticipatory nausea." Does she really know what it's like?

Patients put up with churning stomachs, retching, unspeakable constipation, mouth sores, hives, pain, and fatigue with meager remedies. The old world of cancer treatments–calculated, even callous–eventually strips away the last vestige of denial, and I finally begin calculating my losses. I know that the journey ahead is arduous–perhaps over several steep hills–and I have to look down, burrow through, and persevere.

A daunting hill in my recurrence is chemo. The fear from 2003, settled in a cool cave of my memory removed from the power of erosion, emerges, preserved and fresh, to greet me at the clinic door for my first chemo in 2019. Fear has a way of staying trapped in the past with memories the body remembers. Unlike 2002, this time I'm more aware of my fear of chemo and my propensity to deny it. So, I take an anxiety pill and pray! I sit in solemn silence in the waiting room, trying calm myself down. On the big screen next to me "Charlie Wonka and the Chocolate Factory" is playing. Is this benign neglect or a bad joke?

Generations of medical advances called "new agents" cajole patients to walk through the locked doors of infusion clinics. Still, entering that dreaded room triggers the old fears as I drag emotional baggage, anxiety stirred up by being taken "where I do not wish to go."

When called, I will my feet to take me to the infusion chair, each plodding step a sobering reminder of the bravery required to choose life. A friendly and voluble nurse begins the process of administering the pre-chemo drugs, a long process that catches me by surprise. So, this is what people have been saying about the new agents to help the side effects! Another cheerful nurse passes out bags of pretzels as if on a holiday destination flight. The long process of pre-chemo infusions concludes, and I tentatively settle on the realization that I'm in a new world of medical advances. The anxiety dissipates, and the fear calms down.

I'm thankful I don't have to take the Red Devil this time; he is sent to where he belongs, Wendy jokes. Chemo is still delivered to the heart in the same way and for the same reason, only now it's a more humane delivery system with the new agents that fend off immediate effects. Immunosuppression still reaps its nasty harvest, but the emotional battle–the heart of the battle–is less scary, dreaded, and formidable now.

At home that night and into the next three days, I am energized by the steroids and miracle drugs to keep the nausea at bay. I keep the anti-nausea pills ready but never use them this time. Fatigue and a series of nagging infections set in later, but overall, I'm thankful to live in a time when patient comfort matters more, a less barbaric, more humane time. The drugs are kinder on my body; I'm kinder on myself.

Two months after the surgeries and related complications, I'm recovering from surgery and the dreaded chemo is underway. I'm still stoical, unable to fully process what's going on. My son asks me at one point why I sound happy when I have cancer. I guess I'm using my mental energy to cope right now.

Then one day the robot stops, the ice melts, and feelings start flowing like the Yellowstone River in spring. I begin writing about my experiences and can't get the words down fast enough. Tears flow freely, tears of pain, sadness, and thanksgiving. It may sound strange to say but I feel a stronger connection to my own life, to God, my family, and friends. Something deep within me is stirring to life, something rich and raw. I stop compartmentalizing. I emerge from my burrow to feel the sun on my head. It feels good.

The first time with cancer two of my sons were teenagers and one was in elementary school. I was worried about them. This time, they are worried about me. I cherish the tight bond with my family, their love, questions, and listening hearts. There is so much support from our social networks that I feel my heart expanding to receive the love. This is a gift of pain.

I make a commitment to move up the acceptance scale, a process of feeling, naming, owning, assessing, and eventually embracing loss. This is a counterintuitive and uncomfortable strategy that wrestles down the anxious desire to stay in the hole and burrow, but it pulls me out into the light of day.

Detaching and compartmentalizing are stress reactions to *Lifequakes*. If a reaction becomes a habit or lifestyle, it's time to reflect and ask ourselves questions. Why do I get paralyzed by fear? Why do I compartmentalize? What am I afraid of, unwilling to face? What steps can I take to yield to the pain, to accept my situation? It's best to move to accepting and owning our losses to harness the creative potential of disrupters and to do it as often as necessary. That's when pain transforms us and connects us to others in pain.

First comes the question, "What is my default mode and why?" Then I can begin to find a way through the intense emotions and confusion to begin accepting my losses.

Part II

Overcoming Obstacles and Letting Go

Chapter 4

Loss is Multidimensional

IF WE'RE HONEST, we still get stuck at condemning even if we understand what we are doing. That's because letting go of the things we lose seems impossible. I stink at it, and I bet you do too. Why is this? Perhaps it's because we don't understand our attachments to the things we have lost. To let go—and move forward on the acceptance scale—it helps to understand the significance of our losses. That's why I want to camp out on different dimensions of loss.

We stay attached to the things lost like nouns in need of verbs. Verbs provide information and direction. Without a verb, we have phrases and fragments disconnected from meaning. In the same way, disrupters sever us from the things we depend on like reasons, remedies, people, security, and purpose. We believe if we just find the verb, then we'll be whole again when, in fact, we need to ditch the verb. To be okay with phrases and fragments for a time. "But that breaks the rules!" the inner grammarian protests.

I enjoy grammar, and I get annoyed when people break the rules to presumably sound more with-it. But sometimes, I need to question my attachment to the rules. Like here. Disrupters operate in a similar but more intense way. They sever our attachment to the way things are supposed to be. We rub and chafe against our losses and want to hold on. Moving forward on the acceptance scale, however, requires letting go of our attachments. To do this—and ultimately unleash the creative and life-giving power of disrupters—we name, assess, and own our losses. This process involves deep-level work.

Why Do I Have Such a Hard Time Letting Go?

Loss has many faces that complicate the process of letting go. *Concrete, abstract*, and *anticipatory* are three categories I find useful. Concrete loss like a job, home, loved one, marriage, or bodily function is more tangible and straightforward. People mobilize to offer practical support. Books and talks target a specific problem. A myriad of resources marshals.

Concrete loss often intersects with abstract loss. For example, a burglary is more than the loss of property; it's a violation of safety and trust. Divorce triggers a loss of hope that a marriage can improve with effort and skill. It's the loss of a dream of family cohesion, support, security, and belonging. Abstract losses are perhaps the most poignant because they run to the core of who we are. They are also harder to pinpoint and thus require more direct attention. While concrete loss is best assuaged and channeled into productive channels, abstract loss is best teased out and untangled, evoked rather than controlled, like unearthing a plant without disturbing its roots.

Abstract loss is uniquely challenging because it threatens our foundation of self-esteem, identity, and value. But, because it's subterranean, it eludes our awareness. This is especially true if the loss is symbolic, like the loss of freedom, belonging, or independence. The most enduring abstract loss is from childhood or past experiences, and it is easily triggered by a disrupter, as discussed earlier. It's entirely possible to leave these losses buried–to deny them–but we end up reacting or being controlled by the emotions they evoke. Counting abstract loss is necessary if we want to grow and flourish.

Anticipatory loss is sure-to-come loss in the near or distant future. Take the examples of hair loss from chemotherapy or a loved one with a terminal illness. Anticipatory loss is a fearful experience, and fear needs to be assuaged and channeled. The remedy is more like concrete than abstract loss requiring managing rather than evoking and teasing out. The ultimate anticipatory loss is death, a specter each of us faces throughout our lives. Some live with its presence daily.

Concrete Loss is More Than Concrete

Not all concrete losses are obvious. One of my most enduring losses strikes after my treatments in 2003. I'm in my mid-forties when premature chemo-induced menopause strikes. My chemo and radiation treatments are done, and I start eight years of endocrine therapy (ET) to suppress estrogen. Let me just say that I desperately miss estrogen and envy women who have it and those who can replace it. I often tell young women to embrace their estrogen. This loss impacts me in several ways, by far the most significant being insomnia. Sleep deprivation impacts my overall functioning, as parents of infants and young children know well.

For months, I take a natural approach with common tricks for falling asleep. But nothing works for staying asleep. In my family of origin, common remedies like aspirin are absent; they are simply non-entities. My family's avoidance of medicine inculcates an unwritten message that people who don't need medicine are stronger. A headache requires a moment of quiet, a cold needs sleep, and an ache needs rest. I unconsciously adopt this message as an adult, but it fails me when I need it most.

One day before a trip to Yosemite with Nate, I don't sleep the entire night. That is another turning point in my relationship with medicine, which starts with chemo treatments. I need a solution! I can't live this way! It's an understatement to say I try many things and seek out many health professionals in the coming months and years. The remedies offer spotty relief, but I spend most of a decade sleep deprived. Teaching early classes makes me nervous if I'm not falling asleep before midnight. I'm threadbare much of the time, like a worn-out dishrag. Bedtime makes me afraid that I will never sleep again. Then I finally find a medical solution, only to be told years later it causes cognitive impairment.

People's well-meaning advice puts pressure on me to find a solution. No one can accept the idea of insomnia as a physical impairment. Questions and suggestions like, "Now that it's summer and you have less stress, can you sleep better?" confront me. Their silence after I answer that it's not stress-related tells me they are not convinced. Natural remedies, articles, rituals, and stress reduction techniques are offered. Some preach that people who can't sleep have a guilty conscience or that sleep comes from spiritual well-being. This seems to me like telling a clinically depressed person to just pray more. Many speak of foods to avoid, foods to eat, on and on. Nothing works. The suggestions are like solutions for the common cold when I have double pneumonia. My family–some of them–and good friends sense I'm raising a wall to their advice. I'm grateful they notice.

Meanwhile Rick is next to me every night snoring within ten seconds while it takes me sixty to ninety minutes to nod off–even with pills–and then I wake up and sometimes stay up throughout the night. It's just not fair! He wakes up chipper, well-adjusted, ready to converse and connect while I'd rather avoid talking until nine. Unfortunately, my teaching day starts at 7:30 in the morning. He talks most mornings with an accountability friend. Their voices ascend. Why do people talk so loudly in the morning? Annoying! It reminds me of the proverb: "Whoever blesses his neighbor with a loud voice, rising early in the morning, will be counted as cursing."[1] Sleep deprivation makes me cranky. Can you tell? On weekend mornings Rick reads the paper, completes the crossword, and finishes a vertical climb on his mountain bike before I consume the first sip of coffee. So, I live with tiredness for many years, but somehow–with prayer, God's grace, and taking control of my thoughts–I bungle through it.

This goes on for seventeen years and intensifies after my recurrence requiring another regimen of estrogen-inhibiting drugs. I finally meet a new GP who says she has several patients who can't sleep given my condition and the new round of ET. She gives me something I can use without concern. Her words feel like a mother shushing a colicky baby; they soothe and settle me. She gives me permission to simply accept that I have an incurable sleep problem. It's an affirmation that I'm not crazy or lacking in skills to make it go away, something I often feel when talking about it with others, even medical professionals. It's a way of owning my loss after many years of fighting it. I take her prescription, but I slowly build up a tolerance. The old fear that I'll never sleep creeps in again.

Naming my loss leads to accepting it. Mysteriously, the bad news that I have no control over this issue liberates me from the pressure of being a solutions-person. I do my best within the limitations and look for smaller aspects of the problem that I *can* control. The biggest challenge is my rampaging brain that magnifies problems and fears in the wee hours when I lie awake–sometimes for an hour or two. Thoughts veering toward doubt and negativity take over, like an out-of-control shopping cart pushed by a kid looking for trouble and bumping a new car in the parking lot. These vexing thoughts turn into harmful ones like criminals breaking out of prison. Soon, I'm doubting God, my relationships, myself, my life. I impugn nefarious motives into everyone, especially myself! When I reach the level of self-loathing, I know it's time to pull out the weapon of prayer and "take captive" my thoughts, a life skill for negative thoughts in general.

---

1. Prov 27:14

There is also a release of creativity in the night. I often rewrite a piece I'm working on or think of a new idea. I don't like insomnia, but I'm learning to manage it, and that makes it bearable. I may not be able to control the insomnia, but I can control how I react to it. This is a lesson that translates to other problems of everyday living.

Concrete Loss is Porous

Concrete loss bleeds over into abstract loss, like the loss of control and normalcy during cancer treatment. I often feel trapped in my body, like I want to escape it. It's like the time I contract chickenpox in my thirties, wishing to be suspended in mid-air not touching anything. During chemo I am pestered by dogged discomforts; I squirm, groan, and complain. Tautness in my chest, irritation from the PICC line tapping my nerves, bulgy bloating, not to mention the effects of chemo, wear me down. My fifth UTI in less than three months with more antibiotics and news of possible abdominal surgical complications bring me to the edge of a long-delayed cry. I try to walk it off or move to a more comfortable spot, but there's no relief. I feel raw, tense, oversensitive. Several months after my surgeries, still wedged to vexing pain, I struggle to find my balance. More tests are ordered. Worry of secondary cancer creeps in.

A pile-up of small stuff–unforeseen and invisible–erodes my defenses, opening up a floodgate of bottled-up emotions and pushing out hot tears, quietly at first, then in-full-force. Until this point, the battle is so intense I fear not being able to cope if I give into the tears. But if I'm honest, it's because I don't want to lose the only hair I still have, my eyelashes. Now I can't hold the tears back any longer.

I struggle with unexpected stomach issues: bloating–no, distension–and pain. Isn't it enough to have cancer? I'm on a strict diet called FOD-MAP where each letter is a type of food to avoid. It pretty much eliminates most healthy and enjoyable eating. I'm always hungry and want to sink my teeth into a maple-glazed donut, or two. I sometimes feel like crying in the grocery store as less than five percent of the foods are options for me. For nine months, I experiment with different foods, supplements, specialists–traditional and functional doctors–but my tests and scans show nothing is seriously wrong. I have SIBO, a silent killjoy that only the few who have it understand. I join Facebook support groups, but the conflicting information and lack of cures discourage me. Can I figure out how to live with constant stomach pain?

A hike with my friend, Lori, who has food challenges shows me how to count and accept this loss. We discuss ways to make our own food by adding tasty ingredients ourselves. I'm not usually interested in recipe swapping. I've always said that I eat to live not live to eat, but here I am, one of those picky people who make others uncomfortable cooking for me. As Lori and I hike and talk, I feel encouraged that I can make tasty and enjoyable food. Our conversation opens a window into not only what is lost but also what remains. That's where I need to focus my thoughts.

Concrete loss is more than concrete. Added to these concrete losses is the vast gap between expectation and reality, how I appear and how I feel. There's pressure to *be* fine when I'm *not* fine, pressure from people and myself. From the outside things may look fine, from the standpoint of time removed from surgery, things should be fine. People often remark how "good" I look for what I've gone through. I appreciate the compliments, but they also frustrate me. People forget I'm tethered to my body, focused on pain. They naturally expect and hope for improvement and progress, not intending to apply pressure, but their expectations breed a fear of moving into the category of "chronic," a place of non-healing, a purgatory of pain. There's also the pressure I put on myself. I dislike being dictated to by my body and expect to feel better by now. I don't want to be a complainer who others gradually avoid. Happy, healthy people are more fun to be around. I need to give up that expectation for now.

Breaking up with My Boyfriend

Anticipatory loss triggers anxiety and fear, like hair loss from chemo or the loss of femininity and attractiveness after a mastectomy. I'm attached to my hair and fear losing it for a second time. Two weeks into my chemo, I look at my pillow and brush, wondering when the process will start, the slow and sad process of hair loss after the first chemo. Memories from seventeen years ago are vivid, at first a few hairs sticking to my pillow and clinging to my clothes at work. I remember the kindness of my colleague, Dave, picking off stray hairs from my shoulder and back in the teacher lounge before class. Suddenly hair starts falling out with a vengeance, in clumps, making brushing and shampooing a delicate exercise. I start looking like a zombie with random wisps of hair. My then nine-year-old youngest son tells me I look scary. During a shower one morning, my eyes closed and shampoo running down, I feel something big glide down my leg. Is it shampoo? When I open my eyes, there's a large clump of hair, the rest of my head, lying defeated near the drain. I sob. I remember the sadness of waking up each morning for nine months with a bald head, a melancholy reminder of the disease even when I no longer feel sick.

As I anticipate my second hair loss, I decide to take preemptive action. Cold caps are an option, a process of freezing the scalp to retain most of the hair. I even set up an appointment, but I put off scheduling it. Waffling between my options, I ask Lori to help me arrive at a decision. After talking to her, I realize I don't really want to do it. I wonder if, generally, dislike is cloaked as avoidance.

Still recovering from five surgeries, anxious about chemo, and uneasy about the pain of freezing my scalp and the time it takes—four extra hours for each infusion—I'm not up for the additional challenge. I yield to baldness. Maybe I'd choose cold caps if my body wasn't battered, like my friend JoAnn during her second and third chemo treatments. She doesn't want the constant reminder, the well-meaning questions from others; she wants to maintain her business and keep her life as normal as possible. Cold caps make sense for her, hair loss for me. I will, however, choose my method! I decide to have my hairdresser, Terrie, shave it in defiance. It's the defiance of Sisyphus, but at least it's something.

The day of my shave, I'm buying some lingerie. The salesperson asks how my day is going, which I answer superficially, "Fine, how about yours?" What if I tell her what's actually going on is that later on my hairdresser is coming over to buzz my head even though I'm not really losing my hair yet. Why this preemptive step?

Preemptive shaving is like having a boyfriend you're fond of and want to keep around until a trusted friend informs you that he is going to break up with you soon. Why not beat him to it and break it off before he can? This time I refuse to let hair loss happen to me. I want to make a clean break and avoid the slow letdown of watching, wondering, and whining. It gives me a little bit of control, a small choice, which ends up being more significant than I know at the time.

I imagine honestly telling the clerk about my day and realize that I often make assumptions or judgments about strangers, even friends. They look good, say the right things, so I think they must be fine, even good people, or they look or act badly, and I make bad assumptions. Appearances may just be appearances. Not far below the surface of a seemingly normal day shopping for underwear, layers of deep feeling reside. I'm reminded that you never know what someone's day is really like so it's best to reserve judgment.

Terrie arrives at my house for a private appointment later that day. With the earnest look of someone who is about to do something daring and unusual, Terrie pulls out a specially consecrated bottle of holy water from Lourdes and dabs my head and shoulders multiple times in the sign of the cross, invoking Jesus' name for healing and blessing. She then gives me three cozy caps to wear around the house. She asks me how I'm feeling to which I reply, "nervous, but excited to do something preemptive."

A hairdresser at a high-end salon, Terrie has come for a home visit to shave my head to a short buzz. She tells me each one of the twenty-five women she has shaved, which sadly includes young women, many with long hair, reports being nervous and anxious. She then offers an emphatic and empathetic pronouncement that cancer "sucks," repeating it several times.

As she applies the razor, I catch bunches of hair in my hands, holding and stroking their softness before releasing them. I tell her that I would only want her here. Each woman, she says, wants it that way. We are in a sacred space together; she is entering a painful moment, doing a defacing, not enhancing act, but with grace, solemnity, and healing. It is an odd ceremony, a liturgy of loss, a ritual of bitter beauty.

When done, she takes a step back, looks at my head, then back at me with a gush of compliments about the shape of my head. She tells me it's perfect and that I look like a model. Apparently, it's a fashion statement at the time to buzz one's head. Her words have an unexpected effect on me, soothing, assuaging, and hushing my worries. I feel affirmed and loved just as I am.

Terrie runs into the garage for a broom, sweeps up the head of hair under the kitchen stool, and deposits it in the trash. Last time I sobbed when I saw my clump of hair in the shower. This time there are no tears, there's no sting of sadness, just a quiet acceptance and defiant triumph. She then shapes my wig to make it look just like my hair. I look in the mirror at my buzzed head, then at the wig and smile. Peace arrives like the bouquet of flowers delivered to my doorstep earlier in the day.

I hand her my credit card, but she refuses to take anything. She hugs, kisses, and blesses me, packs up her tools, and sprightly walks out the door.

She is my "Shave Angel" whose special touch leaves me strangely empowered, even buoyant, grateful for a priceless gift of love.

Later that day, my friend Nancy calls me asking if I broke up with my boyfriend.

Memento Mori

The ultimate anticipatory loss is death. I brush up against it more than a month into my cancer recurrence. The plastic surgeon sits on his green vinyl office stool, rolls it toward me, and starts, "I probably shouldn't tell you this . . . " He grabs my attention. In English class this is a rhetorical device called Praeteritio designed to get the audience's attention, like saying "I'm not going to talk about" but in fact talking about it. He informs me that he will not do the reconstructive surgery on the left side until six months after treatments due to a considerable chance of cancer recurrence. What? My heart sinks, but I don't want to reveal alarm for fear he might stop his insider's revelations. The shock palpable and appointment already long with other patients waiting, I fail to ask clarifying questions. I leave wondering why I didn't learn this before. For now, I'll let it sink in; I'll sort it out for myself.

Later that day, we take my mom to see *The Art of Racing in the Rain*, a story from a dog's perspective, including the death of a young woman from brain cancer. The story agitates my mom. When I walk her to her door, she passionately instructs me not to think about the movie. Her discomfort is understandable for many reasons: the fact that I'm her daughter, the background noise of being in her nineties, the childhood trauma of hiding from the Nazis.

I don't mind the subject of death in the movie; in fact, I'm surprised at my willingness to let it breathe, to consider it a worthwhile object of reflection. I recall a sermon by Rankin Wilbourne from Ecclesiastes on *Memento Mori* (remember thou art mortal). It originates in ancient Rome when a servant is given the task of saying these words while standing behind a victorious general as he parades through town. The term morphs into a medieval Christian theory of considering the vanity and transient nature of earthly goods and pursuits. Much of Christian art encourages *Memento Mori* as a valid and useful practice. The book of Ecclesiastes circles the idea again and again. I, too, need the servant's whisper "Memento Mori" in my ear.

Like most people, I have an approach/avoidance relationship to *Memento Mori*. During my first bout with cancer in 2002, I only consider it existentially once or twice because it unnerves me. Avoidance feels safer. Now the barrier is less impervious. The close juxtaposition of life and death is like riding a motorcycle, something I enjoy immensely. No wonder Harley riders like skulls. It's the adventure, thrill, torque, speed, and adrenaline next to the possibility of danger. It might be a flirtation with death, the thrill of living on the edge. Slowly pulling the throttle of my Harley on an uphill turn in the Santa Monica Mountains is among my favorite thrills. Listening to the roar of the Vance and Hines pipes, leaning into the curve, my body crashing into the warm air, muffled wafts circling in the helmet, and accelerating as the curve straightens make me feel alive and rebellious.

Perhaps riding motorcycles is not so far removed from *Memento Mori*, but still, I'd prefer to choose my adventures in the context of a secure and stable life, not to drop the bike or disrupt a pleasure ride. One time I rode through a cloud of bees on a ride to Ojai. I stopped, wiped the splatter from the face shield, extracted a stinger from my thigh, and moved on. I wish it were more like this with cancer.

Memento Mori demands intention and effort; it hurts and unbends me, but it feels important, even propitious. The thought of being with Jesus when I die secures me, but the real possibility of my own death unfastens me. After hearing the surgeon's words, I'm moving toward instead of away from it. My first campout on death sparks some initial realizations: This is not the time to figure out my future. It is the time to jump into what compels me, to do the little I can right now, to write, appreciate, enjoy, store up treasures in heaven, invest in something that endures. It is the time the Westminster Catechism enjoins to glorify God and enjoy Him forever. It's the time to seize the *kairos* moments—where time stops, the sacred is unveiled, the eternal enters—moments surpassing chronological time. It's the time to affirm and cherish people. Perhaps these campouts aren't so scary after all.

The day after the movie, my friend Janet and I meet Andrew at an upscale fusion restaurant in Culver City. The conversation quickly drops into deep waters ranging from spirituality, philosophy, and theology to sharing our hearts while savoring flavorsome menu items. I'm immersed in a mystical world of relational wonder, another "God moment," a blessed visitation, a divine stirring of earthly waters, a *kairos* moment.

Memento Mori sifts the valuable from the vapid, the eternal from the ephemeral.

Why Counting Loss Matters

Moving forward on the acceptance scale has to do with how attached we are to the things or people we lose. A loss that removes a pillar of our lives like a parent/child relationship ranks highest for most people. The loss of a child is compounded by the loss of future hopes for that child. There will be no more milestones, no grandchildren, no one to keep us company in old age.

The less tangible the loss, the more deeply rooted and difficult it is to examine at its roots. Abstract loss is particularly hard to sort out, especially if it has a symbolic quality, like the loss of freedom, a dream, or a plan. For older people it might be the loss of driving connected to independence and agency. An example for me is the loss of my retirement dreams–at least temporarily–as I get sick on the eve of my retirement. My plastic surgeon jokingly states that he has never operated on a person on his or her first day of retirement. I round out his list.

Amid acute loss, we lose sight of the task of loss–naming, assessing, and feeling it–because it seems like participating in a pity party from which it's hard to emerge. It interferes with a positive attitude desperately needed to keep fighting. What if we become self-absorbed? What if we sink into a hole of sadness? What if we lose our fighting spirit? The fear of entering a pit of sadness and anger, however, extends and compounds these negative feelings. Depression and anger result from trying to push loss underground. Like a beach ball under water, the feelings are hard to keep submerged. Dealing with loss is much like grieving, the product of which is a willingness to let go and live without what is lost. Shortcuts simply short-circuit the process and delay–even inhibit–future flourishing.

Naming a loss leads to an awareness of our attachment to it—a crucial step in not short-circuiting the process of healing. I learn this from Rick, my resident shrink with a reservoir of knowledge on loss and depression.

The psychology of depression is that it is a function of loss. The ten symptoms we associate with depression are:

1. Depressed mood

2. Problems experiencing pleasure

3. Low energy

4. Disrupted sleep

5. Diminished/increased appetite

6. Mental/physical agitation or slowing

7. Feelings of worthlessness, guilt, negativity

8. Difficulty concentrating

9. Thoughts about escape – mild to severe

10. Isolation

When therapists think about depression, they add up six to eight of these symptoms to constitute an episode, and a very depressed person usually has all ten.

Picture a green line going straight to represent a person's life. A loss event (or a series of losses) is a U-shaped curve that goes down, bottoms out, then climbs back up to the line and then extends out. When we lose something of value, we are built to have an experience like the U to recover and get on with life.

The depth and length of the U are functions of attachment. The more we are attached to what we lose, the steeper and deeper the U is. For example, when a parent loses a child to death the length and depth of the depression U seem to go on indefinitely. That might be the kind of loss you don't fully recover from, even if you work at it. This is arguably the toughest kind of loss. With other kinds of losses, we can influence the shape and depth of the U curve.

Counselors often talk about grief work, which includes verbally and emotionally exploring the dimensions of loss. Actively grieving pays dividends in terms of recovery and the shape of the line in the U. Ignoring or suppressing the loss–what Rick calls short-circuiting the grief process–is like a red line running through the U. Instead of going to the bottom of the U and then back up again, short-circuiting cuts off the process and the healing. This short-circuiting actually extends the duration of the recovery.

When Rick first starts doing therapy, he thinks his job is to get people to leave the session happier than when they arrived. He soon learns that if someone is in his office because of significant loss then his job is to help that person frame the experience as such and face the loss with courage, openness, and integrity. Allowing the feeling of pain puts the symptoms in the context of loss. The work is talking about the attachment to the person, job, reputation, wealth, hope, dream, etc. that is lost. This normalizes depression. By actively letting ourselves grieve, we get to the bottom of the U, start climbing out of the pit, and then put the loss in the larger context of our life. Tennyson's quote about it being better to have loved and lost than never to have loved at all turns out to be exactly right!

Attachments are forged through years of work and dedication, like an education, career, business, or organization. Hopes and dreams we dedicate ourselves to, like family cohesion, the emotional and spiritual health of children, or career dreams are hard to relinquish. Years of intentionality, effort, and prayer go into identity formation, making us highly invested in the outcomes. Such losses hit at the level of our identity. Identity loss is perhaps the hardest to let go of, especially when our identity is set over years and decades. When a disrupter threatens to nullify our efforts, it feels like our foundation has cracked and shifted. Naming and processing this kind of loss requires self-awareness and courage, but it is crucial to flourishing. We learn to let go and live without what is lost. Shortcuts prolong and complicate the process.

Naming our losses leads to owning them. Owning loss propels us upstream toward a new destination. It releases us to accept–and in some cases even appreciate–the disrupter and the gain it brings, the way it enlarges our hearts and our understanding. We have a new identity, a new purpose, and we are freer to be ourselves and to tell our own stories. These are deep stories of loss and survival, stories that belong to us and are ours to tell. The statement purportedly–not conclusively–ascribed to Dr. Suess, "Be who you are and say what you feel, because those who mind don't matter and those who matter don't mind" is still worth following.

Is it fair to say that most people refuse to let go of their deeper attachments? Perhaps they just want to be safe and secure, but they miss out on a great discovery. Those who do find a vibrant life beyond loss, a life of surprises. Just when you give up on ever having the thing you lost, you are surprised by the gifts that come, unbidden and free. That's because grace happens, and gifts are dropped in our laps, even in the darkest of times. Once we discover the paradox of losing our life to gain it, we understand that letting go is essential to flourishing.

We gain courage to engage in the deeper work of growth, character formation, and rediscovering our purpose. Life with less investment in outcomes is a profound discovery few are willing to make. It's for explorers, pilgrims, and adventurers.

Chapter 5

Shelob Won't Jump on Me

Turn Expectations into Wishes

How do I stop condemning my disrupter and start to *endure* it? Two things that stand in the way are expectations and fear. Humans waste a tremendous amount of energy holding on to their expectations even when they get dashed. What starts as a wish becomes an expectation, and soon the expectation becomes a demand. It's like the "precious" of Tolkien, the cherished ring Gollum can't live without. The ring consumes him because it's a part of him or he of it, but it corrupts him. What is the mechanism that turns a harmless wish into a toxic expectation? Coveting: wanting things to be different than they are and wanting another story than the one we've been given. Relinquishing our expectations is hard to do because letting go of our precious feels like capitulation, but it's necessary in times of disruption and change.

Accepting the reality of a situation is key to enduring it–and flourishing again. It's like pulling a magnifying mirror out of the drawer and going into the backyard to look at your face. The mirror shows the nasty chin hairs, out-of-control eyebrows, or nose hairs that get worse with age. We can pretend they are not there, but that doesn't make them go away. We may not see them, but others will. We can hold onto our expectations, subjecting ourselves and others to a pretend reality, or we can train ourselves to let go. It's better to live in reality than in pretense. Pretending something is true doesn't make it true; it just makes us miserable.

Accepting reality starts with an attitude adjustment. When expectations rise, I find myself using the annoying but useful cliche, "It is what it is!" Then comes a useful statement I discovered years ago. I say to myself and perhaps another person, "I wish this would happen (my expectation), but I can live without it." I neither abandon my dreams, nor turn them into demands. This downgrades the expectation into a wish and reduces the pressure I put on myself and others to meet my expectations. I am an adult and don't have to have my way.

A sense of freedom takes hold and helps me breathe through my distress. Others also relax around me because they don't feel the pressure to make it all good again. Strangely, becoming skilled at releasing my expectations reveals new opportunities and gifts I don't expect. I discover an enduring secret to a full life veiled by the need to hold my precious and control my life.

Face Down Fear

A second barrier is fear. Fear slows progress on the acceptance scale. The key to reining in fear is walking toward it instead of away from it, but this is neither direct nor heroic. Small, incremental steps do the job. Shifting my focus away from the fear is key. A strategy I call "Look down!" helps me buckle down and endure the onslaught of negative emotions and push through the acute phase of the disrupter. As a short-term strategy, "Look down!" still falls short of full acceptance, but it's crucial to regaining my footing in times of extreme distress and pain. More on that later; first the fear.

Much of our fear is imagined and irrational, eluding rational interventions. My symbol of fear is a tarantula, that hairy Theraphosidae I can't even bear to look at. As a child, I am close to my older brother, Rich. He mostly dotes on me, but sometimes he caves to the primal urge to tease his younger sister. Once when we are still living in California, he calls excitedly from the bathroom, "Sheri, Sheri, come here!" and I run toward his playful voice, thinking there is a happy surprise at the other end. He grabs my neck and sticks my head into the bathtub near a spider. There are other, less dramatic incidents, but this one sticks with me.

Growing up in Germany, I often have spiders in my room because there are no screens on the windows. For years, I follow a bed-time ritual of looking under the bed and on the walls and ceiling for dreaded arachnids.

Still, before nodding off to sleep, I imagine spiders crawling toward my bed. Tarantulas are my Hieronymus Bosch symbols of fear.

Disrupters evoke powerful imagined fears. They jar and dislodge our lives with what-if questions like: "What if I can't handle this?" or "What if I don't get back to normal?" or "What if I lose my purpose?" or "What if I die?" Questions like these magnify our fear and lead us to condemn our disrupters. We become helpless and overwhelmed, denying our agency and resilience. We get stuck. Or we dive into denial by ignoring the fear, shutting off our feelings as a facade for coping. Fear is a repulsive emotion that's hard to tolerate. Enduring, however, shifts our mindset from "I can't handle this!" to "I think I can." It's like the determined train that keeps talking to itself. A new what-if question begs to be asked: "What if I *can* handle this?"

How do I endure fear if it is impervious to rationality? I can't simply think my way out of it; I must slow its momentum. I often hear the logical voice of a friend telling me tarantulas are harmless, and I say sarcastically to myself, "Wow, thank you; that's what I needed to hear! I'm over it now!" When I saw the series *The Lord of the Rings,* I turned my eyes away from the towering spider Shelob. Why? My mind confused looking at the theater-sized arachnid with it crawling on me. It was as if looking at Shelob meant she would jump from the screen and into my life. Fear jumps from perceived threat to extreme conclusion faster than a Tesla reaching sixty miles per hour. The key is to find a way to inhibit the jump so that fear doesn't drive me.

Fear must be addressed indirectly. It starts with faith in a personal God who sustains me in life and death. This is a sure safety net. Faith pivots my anxious thoughts away from the future to the present. Doing this corrals fear. Once fear is penned in, I shift gears from avoidance to surrender, which is anything but passive. Surrender is a conscious willingness to accept the disrupter's presence and trust it will be okay. Surrender is like a bug spray used to slow the spread of disease. Over time, green foliage returns to bless the gardener.

Surrender demands a tremendous amount of exertion. Let's change the metaphor from spiders to barges. It's a jump, but there is a silk thread between the metaphors–pun intended. Growing up on a hill overlooking the Rhine River, I watch long transportation barges depressed with coal and other goods float close to the water. They ferry up and down the river day and night. Sometimes a barge reverses course to go upstream. As it turns, the length of the barge is almost the same as the width of the river.

The rest of the river traffic must come to a halt. Meanwhile, the sound of labored engines churning in the murky water dominates the noise space. For a long time, despite the grating exertion, it appears like nothing is happening. The turnaround is fraught with anxiety and fear. What if a downriver barge doesn't see me? What if the effort is for naught? What if I crash on the rocks? Then, slowly, the whirring engines still and slow, and the barge belches forward against the pulling current, a wide path of white water trailing behind it. The barge is on its way, much more slowly than before, but steadily. The effort of the turnaround requires the pilot to keep focused on the goal.

It's like this when disrupters hit. We are forced to change course. We covet normalcy but must push against the currents that entice us back down the easy flow to the expansive sea. We give up. We try again. The exertion is hard because it seems to lead nowhere. Revving the engines without obvious results makes for a precarious float. Laden down, sideways, and exposed, the barge is vulnerable to potential hits. "Maybe I won't turn this thing around," we wonder. "What if I get stuck?" Finally, we start to labor upstream. Occasionally, our barge catches some junk in the river it wouldn't have caught going downstream. The junk creates drag. It seems so unfair, so utterly taxing and draining! "Isn't it enough to have to change course?" we protest. "What will I find up ahead?" We fear the future is more treacherous. It's hard to stay optimistic when our efforts aren't bearing fruit and when it looks like our circumstance is chronic. Regardless, we push ahead because we must.

Secrets of the Chronic Club

Fear of being in the chronic club keeps us stuck in condemning our disrupters. Nobody wants to be in that club. It's a purgatory with no clear exit. The biggest challenge for the chronic club is to stay optimistic. I read many stories of advanced stage cancer survivors. They have no sweet perfume, no pretty bows to tie up their stories, and yet many are brave and full of hope. The aforementioned Kate Bowler calls herself an incurable optimist. Her life is marked by scans–a perennial reminder of mortality–but much more. She discusses this juxtaposition: "Our society finds it especially difficult to talk about anything chronic–meaning, any kind of pain, emotional or physical, that abides and lives with us constantly. The sustaining myth of the American Dream rests on a hearty can-do spirit, but not all problems can be overcome. So often, we are defined by the things we live with, rather than the things we conquer. Any persistent suffering requires being afraid–but we hang our fears in the balance of our great loves and act, each day, as though love will outweigh them all. Life is chronic. Fear will always be present. I can only make those brave, soft choices to find my way forward when there is no way back."[1]

We don't normally associate the word brave with soft but with words like plucky, daring, foolhardy, audacious, fearless; we associate brave with active, rebounding, rebellious words. I don't know why she uses soft, but it fits the idea of absorbing and enduring a disrupter. To me a soft choice is the decision to yield, and this is the least expected but most important choice in overcoming disrupters.

There's something true and genuine about the chronic club. We gain insider's knowledge about the way the world really works behind the curtain. Here are those who understand a true secret to flourishing through lowering expectations and accepting limitations. People on the other side of the curtain celebrate success and triumph. Fix-it people with solutions and methods to improve others' lives receive kudos there. These are members of a club of happy overcomers inside the Compaq Center gravitating toward the myth that problems are all within the control of the mind. Extinguish negative thoughts! Fill your mind with good ones! Instead, the chronic club fixes on where we are and what we can do with where we are.

"Look Down!" is a Life Strategy

This mentality creates a healthy headspace wherein we create short-term strategies for coping. Let's get off the river for a land metaphor of a hurdling race. The athlete looks down to get into position at the beginning of a race. Are my feet positioned right? Is my body poised for the starting gun? Am I set to hurdle the gates ahead of me? A strategy for endurance I call "Look down!" may not be the subject of a motivational talk, and it doesn't win accolades for bringing cheer like "Look up!" but it's a prescription for healthy headspace in times of fear and distress. "Look down!" is a tool I discover on a first-generation mountain bike–a ponderous clunker compared to today's bikes, especially E bikes like the one I currently ride–as I pedal up the steepest hill in the area, doubting if I can get to the top. A particular moment is seared in my memory. Instead of looking at the steep hill ahead,

1. Bowler, *Living a Chronic Life*, WP.

I decide to zoom in and look only at the ground below me. Shifting to the lowest gear, I resist the urge to look ahead, and after a few minutes, I reach the top. The experiment works! As I fix my eyes on the ground below, it appears level. It takes concentration and intention, but only for a few minutes. This type of exertion is possible in small, finite spurts. I actually trick my mind into believing the ground is level, just long enough to reach the top. My lungs, of course, tell another story, which is almost silenced by the flat earth narrative I'm spinning.

The essence of "Look down!" is to stop looking at the future–to live day to day, even hour to hour–which is easy to say but excruciatingly hard to do. "Look down!" initiates a training process of the mind, a skill for when fear first spikes. The skill is reining in fearful thoughts like a lasso on a wild horse. "Look down!" is a dependable gizmo in my mental toolbox that I polish up again and again.

I grab it in extreme times when questions like, "Will I make it to the top?" or "How much longer?" press down on me. This tool unlocks the secret of intense focus on the now, of fixing attention on what's immediately underneath, the current, not future path. What happens when we look down as we plod up our hills? A sudden awareness startles us: "I'm actually in my worst-case scenario, my nightmare, and I'm handling it! I'm crushed but not destroyed by it." What a powerful discovery this is! Perhaps this tool is also useful for everyday life.

Chest Jabs and Hot Plastic Mattresses

I first put this tool to the test in 2003. I'm just finished with chemo and radiation treatments–a harrowing experience. I'm building up strength and enjoying life again. Curly chemo hair is sprouting, and I'm anticipating a trip to Hawaii with the family. Alex, my athletic sixteen-year-old son, stops me in the hallway of his school where I teach, complaining of chest pain. It's finals week. His pain not severe enough to keep him from taking his second final, so I set up a doctor's appointment after school. The pediatrician looks at him and orders an Xray at the hospital.

The next thing I remember is gasping from shock while fixed in place in the hospital's radiology department after being told that his left lung is completely collapsed. That's the moment I decide to look down. There's nothing like a child's illness to motivate a parent to buckle down, muster strength, and be there for the child. I am thankful my cancer treatments are over and that the lung issues don't happen sooner. Perseverance is the word I cling to as I look down and will the ground to level out. The next part seems surreal and inexplicable even today: The pulmonologist tells us to go home! Does he think the lung will inflate by itself? It doesn't, and a day later, Alex is admitted to the hospital where he would spend a total of fifty-seven days on three separate occasions. The confinement, pain, discomfort, and uncertainty of this experience is a life disrupter for Alex.

Alex's story is long and complicated, but after eighteen months of lung issues, including additional partial collapses on both sides, numerous tubes jammed into the chest cavity,–the first one without drugs–tests, procedures, and surgeries with still no clear solution, we end up at Children's Hospital Los Angeles. The local doctors can't help us anymore. We start in the oncology unit undergoing tests for cancer. The doctor suddenly exits the examination room after a cryptic, "This might not be good," leaving us suspended in shock and alarm. Alex's fear magnetizes the worst-case scenario.

Waiting for the doctor's return turns out to be Alex's most fearful experience of his life. All the tests are thankfully negative, and we end up in the pulmonology unit where a skilled doctor takes care of him until he is healed. I think of the families in the waiting rooms whose worst fears *were* realized, and I cannot grasp the gravity of it. I see the nobility and love of a mother who pushes the stroller of her eight-year-old daughter with lung problems and the colorful bows she ties in her hair. There's something deeply moving about the cheer and dignity of patients and medical staff in a children's hospital.

The diagnosis of spontaneous pneumothorax caused by blebs on the lung–blisters that spontaneously pop without provocation causing air to leak into the chest cavity and displacing the heart–is a condition which has a fifty-fifty chance of recurrence. Alex has to manage the anxiety of his prognosis. As difficult as this is for a seventeen-year-old, it ends up being a formative, character-building experience for him.

It's not pretty going through these challenges with Alex. Seemingly endless days in excruciating pain confined to hot plastic mattresses with countless setbacks push him to the limit. He is in pain–lungs are hypersensitive–and takes out his anger on me. It's to be expected; he's an active teenage boy. The pneumothorax is an all-out trauma affecting his life. Along with the loss of health, there is lost time in school, a baseball career in jeopardy, and the shattering of his peace of mind. This time of testing, however, increases his inner capability and builds compassion for others. Today his health is excellent, and he is even number two on *Strava*, an app that tracks times, on his favorite mountain biking hill. Maybe he'll become king of the hill soon. He has his own production company, which represents hospitals as a major focus.

Winning the Mental War

I grab this tool again more recently throughout the surgeries and treatments. It becomes a lifeline during the unexpected fallout–both physical and emotional–from the entire cancer experience. The stretched-out days in bed with pain coming, it seems, from all directions and the emotional battles clubbing me into submission are my cancer war.

Sometimes it's not the big crisis of cancer that gets me down, but the small stuff. It is then that the journey feels incredibly long with no end in sight. Faith flickering and patience thinning, I get sucked into a vortex of spiraling negativity. Like Macbeth I am "cabined, cribbed, confined, bound to saucy doubts and fears."[2] I appreciate the climax of these carefully crafted words by Shakespeare. The anthimerias (the rhetorical device of using one part of speech as another, a noun as a passive verb here) combined with the hard "c" of these three words quickly hammer the nail to Macbeth's confinement. I too feel hemmed in, closed down, and shut up. "Hope deferred makes a heart sick."[3]

And yet sometimes it seems easier–at least more straightforward–to fight the battle of chemo than the war of cancer? The Pyrrhic victory of winning the battle but losing the war is a famous mental model. Is it possible that we are better equipped for battles because they are well-defined, measurable, and limited in scope? Maybe we feel like we have more control over battles. So, we prepare and marshal our resources for a concentrated effort. While fighting a battle, however, we underestimate the scope and demands of war. Wars cover more area and involve more foes; sometimes wars drag on without an end in sight. We can win the battle but lose the war.

So, how do we win the battle and the war? By recognizing that the war of cancer–and of everyday life–is a war of the mind, a war of fear and expectations. By tolerating discomfort and a loss of control. By knowing

2. Shakespeare, *Macbeth,* III.iv.26.

3. Prov 13:12

that war will surprise us with unforeseen foes. By being prepared to fight and never give up. By accepting the reality that most of our troubles stem from the mental toll of small, recurring, persistent, and insolvable puzzles and troubles. By learning not to covet.

This mindset allows me to filter out toxic thoughts and desires, the most noxious being questions about the future, like whether I'll get to see my granddaughters grow up or hold future grandchildren. "Look down!" helps me pull myself back to the moment, the hour, the day as a way of embodying the imperative, "Give us this day our daily bread." Living a day at a time becomes more than a cliché but the most important coping strategy. I look at the tasks and gifts of each day and refuse to look ahead. The tasks are my daily burdens, puzzles, and problems and the gifts are the small blessings, unexpected and fresh, that rain on each day. This strategy helps me wrestle with toxic thoughts, take control of my responses, and live with gratitude. Paradoxically, this battle strategy also helps me fight the war.

From the cancer patient to the everyday person with everyday problems, we all share a similar challenge of coping with the incessant head noise of aggravations that nag, sap, rankle, and deplete us. We are earthen vessels. Will we crack or hold up under fire?

After my recent treatment battle, I assess the damage. There are cracks in my vessel, but the vessel is intact. Like a battle-scarred soldier, I don't like what I see. I don't like how I feel–the numbness, pain, limited mobility–and I have a hard time coping with my losses. Rick's affirmation gently nudges me on to acceptance. My mind fixes on Lt. Dan in *Forrest Gump* who transforms from a bitter amputee to a man with wounds and purpose. I look at my scars, take care of them, and gradually start making peace with them–though I continue to struggle with this. My scars now belong to my story, and I want to tell that story. Endurance sets me off in a new direction, like the quiet swish and glide of a train leaving the station. I'm on the way to a new identity and purpose.

Control is a Drug

The final result of endurance is that it enables letting go of control, so easily said but difficult to do. At first, it is a stubborn choice born of necessity, but eventually, letting go of control becomes a portable habit and practice for everyday life. Letting go of control is probably the biggest human challenge. We see the desire to control everywhere, in society, institutions, and

ourselves. Just think about what happens when there's a global crisis, trag-
edy, accident, health crisis, personal betrayal, or failure of any kind. In our
craving for certainty we pounce on answers, even irrational ones, and we
are quick to blame because we want to have some control over the situation.
What's most needed, however, is humility and patience, but we moderns
lack these qualities. Is it any wonder that our lives are filled with stress and
rancor? It doesn't have to be this way. It's possible to endure a disrupter with
a modicum of peace.

At the start of the pandemic, anxiety chases away sleep at three in the
morning. My stomach is in knots. I'm swimming in that familiar ocean
again with my head barely above water. This time it's not the cancer that
casts me adrift, it's the worry over my sons. Two of them are in the film
industry, which has shut down; two own businesses–one in the wedding
industry–with responsibility for others. They've all been struck by a wave,
pulled out to sea by currents they can't control. Stories like theirs proliferate.
A woman in line at Armstrong Nursery tells us she is losing her restaurant
after forty-five years. Will ordering take-out more often be enough to turn
the tide? I feel like we are on the cusp of loss and devastation.

We're experiencing cognitive dissonance. One moment we are living
in an age of control. From on-demand viewing to customized purchases,
we believe in choice and self-reliance. We are competent, efficient, and re-
sourceful. The next moment we're hit with the coronavirus and respond
in predictable ways: search the internet, stay glued to the news, repeat the
same talking points, shop, hoard, you name it. Why is online shopping,
even for Clorox wipes, so satisfying? Am I losing my mind? Our response
is shallow and hollow, but it's human to meet the unpredictable with behaviors of control.

Inevitably, we get knocked off the tower of control. A news flash on
my screen announces: "The DOW plummets more than 1,300 points, wip-
ing out gains since President Trump was inaugurated." How do we cope
with the plummets, knocks, and waves?

From ancient times to today, a common response to being out of control is to do something: placate the gods, consult fortune tellers, develop
piety, save up for a rainy day, etc. My dad, born in 1916, endures The Great
Depression, which stays with him his entire adult life. He is both extremely
frugal and an occasional binge shopper of sales. A favorite memory of
growing up as an American child in Germany with limited resources is the
quarterly visits my dad makes to the American PX, the tax-free grocery

store on American military bases in West Germany. The kitchen table is laden with the plenty of American food and candy before being stocked in the pantry and my dad's closet. He places boxes of Charm suckers in shiny wrappers and Mounds bars that I can almost smell high in his closet. If I climb on the bed and reach up, I can get them.

These moments of plenty fulfill our longing for American goods in a foreign land of pork, potatoes, and marzipan. As a child, I have a little toy grocery store which I endlessly stock, organize, and rearrange. I love the satisfaction of plenty, and to this day I enjoy stocking up on essentials. Stocking up offers a comfort-feeling of being prepared for the future, but this control is a short respite from the terror of the untamable.

How Beasts Tame us

How do we deal with the untamable beasts in our lives? I love bears, especially grizzly bears. I remember buying a book called *The Mark of the Grizzly* after trudging along the trail to Granite Lodge in Glacier National Park. Right there in the store I read about an attack on that same trail of a photographer who stepped into the forest to relieve himself. Reading about bear encounters both scares and fascinates me because of the unpredictability of bear behavior. I read to find a pattern, a pattern to protect myself from danger.

I remember visiting Brooks Falls in Alaska with Alex on a float plane through imposing mountain passes in the middle of a rainstorm. It's a unique place with viewing platforms of grizzlies in close proximity to people as they watch the social hierarchy of bears hunting salmon swimming and jumping upstream. Alex and I spend hours observing and nicknaming the bears. On our way back to the plane through a forested area inhabited by bears, we are caught in a close encounter with a mama bear protecting her three cubs from an opportunistic male sniffing out a shortcut to the hard work of fishing for salmon. Alex snaps the encounter on a camera lifted high over his head. That day ranks as a favorite day in our lives. The fear, mystery, and awe we experience shift my perspective and sense of place in life, reminding me of the uncontrollable power of nature. It's humbling and good to know one's proper place in life.

Control is a posture of pride and pretense so common today. It's born of modernity. We are used to it and expect it. C.S. Lewis makes a fascinating connection between the magic of the sixteenth and seventeenth centuries and modern science which also developed during that time, claiming "[t]here is something which unites magic and applied science while separating both from the 'wisdom' of earlier ages. For the wise men of old the cardinal problem had been how to conform the soul to reality, and the solution had been knowledge, self-discipline, and virtue. For magic and applied science alike, the problem is how to subdue reality to the wishes of men: the solution is a technique."[4] Tim Keller comments on Lewis's connection: "Instead of trying to shape our desires to fit reality, we now seek to control and shape reality to fit our desire."[5] Modernity is about dreams of power and control, which are realized in times of normalcy but not when a catastrophe strikes.

I hear the whispering reminder: "Be still and know that I am God."[6] Endurance tames the fearful heart long enough to push through the pain and realize we are not in control. At best, it's a short-term solution to propel movement upstream. But it's a crucial step toward the deeper work of character formation and flourishing. What is your "Look down!" type of strategy?

4. Lewis, *The Abolition of Man*, 77.

5. Keller, *Reason for God*, 71.

6. Ps 46:10

Chapter 6

What do Mennonites and Jews
Have in Common?

Pushing Through Pain

LOOKING DOWN HELPS ME push through pain. It's good in the short term, but it has downsides in the long term. My family tree has deep roots in persecution and suffering. My dad, from a Hutterite clan, a group of Mennonites that fled persecution in southern Russia due to their religious and pacifistic beliefs and set up communal farms in South Dakota and elsewhere, is shaped by his heritage. Mennonites are a tight-knit, exclusive group that intermarry. My mom has Jewish roots from Berlin. Her survival story of enduring the horrors of the war, emigrating to the U.S., and returning to Germany for five decades of ministry–after vowing to never set foot on German soil again–is gritty and inspiring. She knows a little about not being overcome by her emotions.

Mennonites keep alive their sad history of persecution; Jews pass on their stories of centuries of oppression, especially in World War II. Persecution is a part of their identity. Free from the need to create triumphalist narratives devoid of suffering, these two communities suffer well together. It's a beauty to behold the support and comfort such communities often offer members in adversity. In her cancer memoir, Kate Bowler describes her husband's Mennonite family as they come around her and "how wonderful they are at suffering together" and how "they insist that suffering never be done alone."[1] Their history supplies sustenance in times of drought and stress.

My mom keeps the painful parts of the Holocaust locked up deep inside her. She walks around the periphery of the horror. She's nineteen when the war ends in the Bavarian village of Pfaffenhofen thirty kilometers from Dachau where her mom found a place for her to hide from the Nazis. There she meets American military personnel who recruit her as translator. Her dad's encouragement to learn English pays off, but the payoff is bitter. She is promoted to the Central Intelligence Core (CIC) as a translator of mini-Nurnberg trials. These are interviews of Nazi concentration camp officers. At age nineteen, following a youth of fear, death, and loss, she is not only listening to these men describe the details of their horrific exploits, but she's also writing them down and translating them. The gruesome facts pass through her twice. They say writing makes information stick more. These facts stick so closely that she feels unable to talk about them the rest of her life. Most Holocaust survivors choose silence. But at what cost to themselves and others? What if she had brought the truth to light more? Could this have released her from the horror she did not deserve? Could it have allayed some of the anger?

Being a Holocaust survivor is noticeably debilitating; being the child of one is less noticeably so. Children unconsciously pick up their parents' ways of handling adversity. In my family and in the German culture of the time, children's emotions aren't evoked, teased out, and given the chance to breathe. Children are seen and not heard. But if you don't hear a child, you also don't see it. There is no psychology; there are no self-help books, no counselors. It's a given that everyone copes with the circumstances dished out. There's no suggestion otherwise, like living in a poor area without rich people anywhere in sight to punctuate the grind of poverty. We simply do the best we can with limited resources. In this way, feelings and motives are pushed under the cold ocean waters.

Over the years, unvalidated feelings settle like a question mark in my heart. I question my perceptions and judgments and feel unsure of how to act in the world. Feelings submerge and take a deep dive. They surface from time to time for air, looking for someone to say, "Look at that!" But no one sees. My voice is muffled, like a dream where one tries to talk or scream but can't get the words out. The question mark punctuates the confusion in my mind.

1. Bowler, *Everything Happens*, 62.

Pain Blinders

The first time I seriously submerge my feelings is after the aforementioned overnight move to the U.S. in sixth grade. In the summer after that wrenching experience, I'm living in Van Nuys. My neighbor, Paulette, the daughter of an Academy Award winning actress now in faded glory past her prime, is my ticket into a cohort of teenage rebels. She is a girl with power, who kids secretly dislike but follow for unknown reasons, a bit like Angelica on Rugrats, but more unpredictable–and mercurial. Her cohort is lightyears removed from the German innocence of walking arm-in-arm with my girlfriends at an all-girls school.

Normally, that's all I tell of my junior high rebellion story. I quickly seal it up in an underground sea cave. It's safer that way, but is it wise and good to leave this story in the dark? I'm beginning to think it's not because truth has a liberating power. In a way, I'm a textbook case of early adolescent acting out. A wrenching cross-cultural move in a time of life when belonging feels like survival leaves me wanting a place to belong. My dad is far away in a distant country, and I need attention, so I get it from a coterie of boys and girls also looking to belong. That should fit nicely into the file of cause and effect for teenage rebellion. External forces influenced me. End of story.

But there's more to it. Yes, there are drugs like the blue pills I steal from my grandpa's medicine chest to sell to friends. There are hallucinogens with long and frightening trips I desperately want to end. There are the boys I'm too weak to deny, like my boyfriend Paul, a fifteen-year-old who matter-of-factly tells his thirteen-year-old girlfriend of a couple of weeks, "I make love to every one of my women!" I go along with it because he asserts it like a rhetorical question demanding only one answer. It's a warm summer afternoon in a modest and unkempt ranch house of a divorced father living with his son. A lasting memory is the white curtains in the bedroom. White curtains in bedrooms are romantic, but these are shrouds of death. I remember the pain, the disdain, and the shower to wash it all away, like Lady Macbeth scrubbing stains from her guilty hands. Then comes the fear, the aloneness. I've just begun my monthlies, but now they are delayed. Desperate, I sock my stomach more than once. I have nowhere to take my burden. After a few weeks and to my great relief, the monthlies return, but shame remains and sets up a permanent residence in my heart. The nameless shame of non-resistance pulls the deed underground and perpetuates blame.

I blame myself. Alone with no one to process my confusion, the blame settles as an indictment on me, not on him. I'm unaware there are names, labels, and categories for my experience. Because I lack a name, I don't understand the immensity of the violation. If only there were a MeToo movement or another name for what is, unfortunately, a common experience for young girls! In the absence of a category, I deny the impact of the deed, but the wound festers and grows. I'm not aware of the pus until many years later, though I get occasional whiffs of the putrid odor. For four decades the billowy white curtains blowing in the California sun and the dreadful events in that room invade my heart, preserving the pain, fear, and violation of my dignity until I undergo a special kind of psychotherapy for trauma called EMDR (Eye Movement Desensitization and Reprocessing). After that, not only do the memories fade, but more importantly, the sting of the memories disappears. As I look back, I wish there was someone to cut out the wound, to shed clear light, blame the perpetrator, and show me how to be strong. But I'm forlorn in my pain.

For now, at least there is belonging–for a while. Then comes my first experience with bullying. I'm home alone at the beginning of summer with three months of fun stretched out before me. A knock on the door calls me. I am excited; friends are visiting. I open the door to Paulette, who is my close friend by now. Before I comprehend what's going on, she barges in, her posse trailing her–also my friends–and they begin to ransack my house. Drawers emptied, closets pillaged, clothes and household items strewn in wild disarray throughout the house, I withdraw to a kitchen corner. As quickly as they come, they bolt, leaving the door open, but my heart closed in shame. I never find out why I am chosen on that particular day, and maybe there's no logical reason. That's often the case with hateful actions. We search for reasons to explain the inexplicable. All I know is that Paulette brings another disrupter into my life that starts a downward spiral.

Jerked and Kicking

It's the summer before high school. Paulette's bullying leaves me dejected and defiant, and I tell my mom that I refuse to go to Van Nuys High School in the fall. Helpless and invisible is how I feel, a microcosm of the universal experience of estrangement. All I know is the pain of losing my friends in one hour and my stubborn refusal to feel that kind of shame again. Ironically, I end up getting the very thing I set out to avoid.

My mom sends me to a nearby private Christian high school, another new start, but a happier one. After three days, I meet a couple of friends to ease the lunch anxiety, and I begin to settle in. But then another disrupter jolts me, another abrupt move back to Europe. My dad has remained in Germany for the three years we are in California, except for occasional visits. Now it's time to join him again. Joy and Rich stay in California where Joy gets married and Rich goes to college. My mom remains long enough to sell the house. I'm sent ahead immediately to a boarding school in Loerrach, Germany on the three-country corner of Germany, Switzerland, and France.

I pack my bags and return to Germany. My dad picks me up at the Frankfurt airport and deposits me at a Mennonite missionary boarding school for the start of high school. I continue to keep my feelings to myself. Even if I were aware of how hard my situation is, there would be no one to help me process my feelings. So, I keep my voice muted, but my body talks. Acting out is a pattern now.

I feel alienated in the strict boarding school for missionary kids, and the commute is monotonous. Every day we drive from the French apartment where the dorm is through the Swiss border and into Germany where the school of about fifty kids is–elementary through high school. The border guards often wave us by and smile at the minibus of expatriate kids. From the outside looking in, we seem like sophisticated globe-trotters, but we are all children away from home in three strange lands.

On my first night at the dorm, the house mother, Velma, a severe Mennonite missionary from Morocco, apprises me as a rebel with unacceptable clothes. She dresses in light cotton belted dresses with abundant pleats descending to the calf. It reminds me of prairie clothing from a bygone era. Meanwhile, the world of fashion embraces sculpted hip-huggers and miniskirts with go-go boots. I embrace fashion. My colorful hip-hugger jeans, sewn in at the crotch to wear low with a hefty Mexican leather belt, offend her sensibilities. I especially love my purple jeans. On my first day there, she takes out the seams with efficient disdain, and the contrast between the faded and unfaded parts makes it look like I peed in my pants. I shed inconsolable tears alone in my room that first night. I feel lonely and angry. Subsequent nights end the same way.

Strict rules, regimented schedules, and a pervasive joylessness run through the days, weeks, and months there. A highlight of the week is the delicious Sunday bread pudding we make from humble French breadcrumbs that we meticulously save throughout the week. Talk about being frugal! Nevertheless, the bread pudding is a French culinary delight, but it doesn't keep away the hunger for a different kind of life.

On one occasion, I am overcome with a laughing fit during a prayer meeting, the type that gets worse when you try to stifle it. My punishment is writing a Bible verse about obeying one's elders over and over. As I watch my pen mimic these words in detached repetition, a bitter resolve to be done with that school at the semester break sears itself into my heart. I make a choice to flunk out of that school.

I find another ill-fitting student to go out into the field behind the school where I've stashed a blue and red striped airmail envelope in straggly bushes. I've waited for just the right moment to retrieve it and use the contents. Inside are two joints from my brother in America. We furtively light them, and no one notices. My grades dipping precipitously, I reach my low aspiration of flunking out by Christmas. I'm elated to be released from that prison! It's my way of kicking back to the jerking. But what about my first semester of high school? What will happen to my record? Thankfully, the entire semester is expunged, a small victory in the quest to find my voice.

My Gray Font Needs More Black

The question mark that casts doubt on my feelings punctuates my life up to this point. My mom notices something is wrong but doesn't know how to help me. She fears she has lost me. I, too, feel lost. If only I had someone say, "Tell me more about what you're feeling." Getting to my story would be hard, but a skilled advisor could help me turn the gray font of my emotions into something more defined and readable. Black font is much easier to read than gray font. Black and white is bold and asserting, whereas gray is shy and receding. Counseling resources are not available at the time.

While my own narrative is gray, my family narrative is more black-and-white and singular. Family narratives often override kids' stories, and that's how it is with me. It's hard to find my voice in a home that insists on a singular viewpoint, that everything is going according to God's plan. Tucked into this is the story that all things work together for good to those who love God, my mom's life verse from Romans 8. Questions and dissent impugn the family narrative. I don't understand it at the time, but my rebellion is a way to turn my gray into black and my family's black into gray. As

I get older, however, I get frustrated by my family's unwillingness to see the narrative as a mixture of successes and failures. Why? There's the little girl whose narrative isn't heard, a girl who becomes an adult with a longing to be heard far into adulthood when she should have gotten over it. I'm on a quest for nuance and honesty. Can the narrative adjust ever so slightly? I prod and probe, but there's more of the same, even stronger. God prepared every step into a marvelous plan. The language of regret is absent.

My gray area is unspecified and murky, like stirring up a riverbed with a stick. How does "all things work together for good" work in bad circumstances from unintended consequences? There are my siblings who have their own difficulties. Our experiences are not cases of intentional harm, which further confuses the process of ferreting out our feelings and theology.

The brain pretzel question of Christianity is: How do you reconcile human free will with God's sovereign and effective will? Affirming the existence of both is not easily resolved with logic, and it requires living humbly with a mystery. God somehow transforms bad into good, but it's helpful to recognize the bad, like Joseph in the Bible. He acknowledges that his brothers intended to harm him, but that God worked in and through their mistakes. But how do you acknowledge unintended harm? Most families don't, either because it feels like an indictment against the parents, or it is a muddled process. Thus, the stick that stirs the dirt is tossed and the river flows placidly along keeping the murky feelings on the riverbed well into my young adulthood.

I'm still tempted today to return from *endure* to *condemn* or denial, but in so doing, I delay growth and future flourishing. It's easy to get stuck and move backwards on the acceptance scale. Over the cancer treatment year, I lose many of the pillars of my life beyond my health. I'm stretched to the limit, sometimes to the breaking point. One day it hits me: I feel bullied, like the girl who opened the door to Paulette many years ago. I'm tired of things being taken from me. I want normalcy. I want control. No more quiet submission. What's the use of being good at taking it and a compliant patient who nods at doctors' prescriptions? Resist the thieves; stand your ground!

Defiance feels powerful for a time, but it proves ineffective. Several days later, I'm like a runaway teen returning home in need of a better perspective. It comes from a book and a conversation with friends who also face loss. This community of mourning validates my pain, and that validation breaks up a logjam in my heart.

Loss is universal. We can't avoid it. Strangely, accepting our inability to change our circumstances releases freedom. Inability is not a popular concept today, but it contains a secret to flourishing because it makes us humble and turns our face to God. Yes, I am tired of all the losses, but it's a part of my story now. I can deny the story or embrace it as God's story in my life. And then the thought comes to me–actually, a prayer–that God will use my story to help others.

But a big job lies ahead of me. I want to figure out how to assess and name my losses. This feels more genuine to me, more auspicious. Naming loss requires insight, work, and prayer, but there's a way to get there, which I want to share with you next.

Part III

Live in the Moment for More Than a Moment

Chapter 7

Obnoxious House Guests

Are Dead Ends Really Dead?

ASSESSING LOSS HELPS ME move forward on the acceptance scale to *tolerate* the feelings the disrupter brings. I come from "Make it go away!" to "What if I looked at my fear?" to "I'm actually handling my worst-case scenario!" and finally to "Why not me?" My pastor, Shawn Thornton, proposes this question to me in the hospital, and it becomes a source of strength for me. Why? I view distress more objectively. Wilson advises: "Don't wait until you believe you can handle whatever Anxiety might throw at you . . . Act as though you can survive"[1] the distress of your disrupter. Tolerance builds marathon endurance, and this helps me settle into my new life. The revving engines turn the barge around, the upstream course sticks, and the labored journey starts. To change the metaphor, I'm starting my trek up the second mountain.

Becoming a Second Mountain Trekker

In his book *The Second Mountain,* David Brooks describes first and second mountain people. First mountain people are achievement-oriented, following individual goals and the pursuit of personal happiness. Then something happens; a disrupter knocks them off the first mountain, either a failure or the disillusionment of reaching the top and the question,

1. Wilson, *Stopping the Noise,* 337.

"Is this all there is?" Second mountain people undergo a change of perspective because "[s]uddenly life doesn't look like a steady ascent up the mountain of success; it has a different and more disappointing shape"[2] and they now get a look at "something bigger than personal happiness,"[3] "a person or a cause or an idea"[4] that they fall in love with and dedicate their time to. Brooks believes the life of second mountain people is a committed life of investment and fulfillment.

Before climbing the second mountain we often face a void. We're aimless and unproductive. What do we do when we're confined–to a bed, a house, or a circumstance–unable to make plans or reach goals, when we want that sweet feeling of accomplishment? Before cancer I endure an occasional day in bed fighting the flu; during cancer treatment I lose track of the days. Background noises mark the hours as I lie on my bed: mastiff howls, traffic roars, street sweeper scrapes, mailbox clangs, delivery rings, the neighbor boy's commands. The end of the day is signaled by slamming car doors, departing workers' trucks, and creaking garage doors. Recovery is months of these days, but in that void, I find a voice through writing. Before retirement I spend my energy on my students, but as I enter retirement, I'm not sure how to spend my time because my main job is simply to heal. Before the pandemic, I buzz around all day; during it I wake up to anxiety and days of solitude. The second mountain is a place of freedom where we get to forge a new identity.

Second mountains pose questions of worth that challenge our very identity. Disrupters unsettle our lives with agitating questions like: "Who am I?" or "How do I fit in, find my worth, my purpose?" Most people think their worth is acquired, not innate. Performance pressure drives especially younger people to curate images on social media to stay in the social loop. Poses with the right voice, gestures, hair, friends–mistakes removed because they take ten pictures and choose the best one–declare, "Look at my awesome, amazing life!" As a high school teacher, I know star student athletes thrown off balance by debilitating injuries. Some get depressed and flounder. Others discover new talents, passions, even career paths. What makes the difference? It's stepping into the freedom of taking risks.

To take risks, it's good to learn the art of self-forgetfulness. This means not judging ourselves based on what others think of us or what we think of

2. Brooks, *The Second Mountain*, xii.

3. Brooks, *The Second Mountain*, xiv.

4. Brooks, *The Second Mountain*, 53.

ourselves–we often don't see ourselves accurately–but what God thinks of us. We take ourselves less seriously because the ultimate verdict is rendered by Jesus' sacrifice on the cross, and we are released from the prison of our own egos. What is human value? Human beings are made in the image of God, flaws and failures notwithstanding. A full grasp of our inestimable worth decreases performance pressure as soulfully captured in Lauren Daigle's song "You Say."

The second mountain is a place of invention where identity flows from passion more than ambition. I've had more than one second mountain in my life. Among the reasons I move from pastoral ministry to education is my struggle as an American kid in Germany and a German kid in America that draws me to teaching, especially students lacking confidence. I love one-on-one conferences over projects or rewrites. Watching students who doubt their abilities accept the struggle needed to improve–an inescapable ingredient in learning–and build confidence and excitement over obtaining a new skill is especially satisfying. "Can't" becomes taboo. I encourage students to adopt a growth mindset–not a fixed one, as psychologist Carol Dweck delineates–the willingness to fail and improve through hard work, grit, and lots of edits. Tolerating discomfort not only makes us better people, but also nurtures a better society and world; these are big effects from small steps.

A fixed mindset interrupts the trek on the second mountain. The rigidity of seeing intelligence–and adult development–as fixed and unchanging over one's lifetime leads people to avoid taking risks. They fear failure because it confirms the limits of their IQs and innate giftings. They tie failure to their worth and value. A growth mindset, on the other hand, sees the brain as malleable and changing but individual value and worth as unchanging. These people have learned to uncouple their self-esteem from failure. They know failure is both necessary and advantageous to learning. This sets them free to take risks.

Life disrupters initiate us into the second mountain club. Initiation is involuntary, but here we are. Soon we realize that this club is a hinge opening a door to new possibilities. Granted, the possibilities aren't as exciting as *Let's Make a Deal*, but they are more promising. They are possibilities of becoming a certain kind of person, a person of character who can tolerate the discomfort of abnormality, anxiety, fear, and shame, all universal human experiences we strongly dislike.

These feelings are like obnoxious guests at our doorstep. They bang on the door so loudly we fear the door might break down. Do we run and hide, or do we cautiously open the door to receive them? Each of us faces a decision of whether we are willing to tolerate discomfort or leave the door closed. Here it helps to remember that "Great things don't come from comfort zones" as Roy T. Bennett succinctly states in an Instagram story.

Building Discomfort Muscles

Tolerance is not a happy process because it means putting up with something I strongly dislike. It's like a boot camp at an elite gym, only I'm there involuntarily. My job is to build a "discomfort muscle" good for marathons. The starting gun is a perspective change to resist the allure of the normal. Living one day at a time sets the pace. As we learn to tolerate the "chronic," our expectations lower and we can focus attention from where we want to be to where we are. This helps us see the benefits of the disrupter. This kind of tolerance is chosen, clawed out, hardscrabble.

How do we tolerate the discomfort of leg cramps, side aches, and exhaustion in the latter parts of the marathon? Like a cheering crowd at the sidelines, a well-tested theory supports us along the way. This theory states that challenges requiring more discomfort, effort, and even failure–making one question the gains–create greater benefits than challenges we feel more competent mastering. Struggle and failure are surer indications of improvement than comfort and ease. I understand this theory, but it's still hard to accept. It's like traveling on a Swiss cog train that chugs up steep mountain passes. The effort is great, and the progress is slow. It's easy to conclude I'm getting nowhere, until I spot the sweeping views up high.

The best learning happens when we are uncomfortable and full of doubt. Take the experiment of Cal Poly SLO's baseball team with how to improve batting skills cited in a ground-breaking book on learning called *Make it Stick*.[5] Half of the team practiced the conventional way of hitting forty-five pitches in three sets. Each set was one kind of pitch thrown fifteen times. For each set, the learning seemed easy as the hitters saw more of the same pitch. The other half of the team faced three types of pitches randomly thrown for a total of forty-five pitches. At the end of the forty-five pitches, the hitters still struggled to connect, calling into question their proficiency

---

5. Brown, *Make it Stick*, 80–81.

compared to the other half of the team. It turns out, though, that the perception of proficiency is unrelated to skill development.

After twice a week of these extra practice sessions over six weeks, the players with random pitches, who felt less proficient, showed significantly better hitting skills. Hitting a baseball is arguably one of the most difficult skills in sports. This is especially interesting because all the players were already skilled before the experiment. This experiment underscores how comfort not only skews our perspective but also hinders learning and growth. The same applies to disrupters: tolerating discomfort is a winning strategy for the long haul. When the disrupter ends, the victory is satisfying.

I'm pushing myself to embrace struggle and incompetence, like the pickleball workshop several friends and I take from a pro. As my body rebounds from treatments, I have high hopes for playing with my friends, but while everyone else progresses, I regress. Why am I going from bad to worse? Many of my friends know tennis and pick it up easily. My hand-eye coordination stinks. I hear "good try" and "almost" so much that I'm back on the playground in in sixth grade gripped by the same loser-feeling. My eyes glaze over as the instructions mount, and I decide this sport isn't for me. Why bother? I want to do something I'm good at like soccer and skiing. Nonetheless, later in the day, I remember what I learned from the book *Make it Stick* with the baseball story above. Can it give me a breakthrough in pickleball? It's so much bigger than pickleball; it's about living with discomfort and failure. It's about improving myself even if it doesn't feel like I'm improving.

A couple of weeks later, I play with friends, and again I'm the worst one on the court. Then Dolly starts dinking and volleying with me. No score, just back and forth, back and forth. She offers me tips, and slowly I start to progress. Her kindness helps me decide to stick with it. A few months later, I take another course, and I see myself making progress. Then I learn that undertaking a new skill–especially one involving new information and moves like ballroom dancing–can prevent Alzheimer's. That gets my attention!

When comfort rears its seductive head, I'm learning to chase it away, like a rodent in the vegetable garden. I need a mental sonic fence against this sly intruder. Embracing discomfort leads to discovery and healing. Like the 2020 World Series–this is for the four men in my life–the gain is worth the exhausting fight and long wait.

The Pesky House Guest of Normalcy

Three obnoxious house guests pound on my door to gain entrance. The first one is the sweet and seductive knock of normalcy. As a one on the Enneagram, I have a hard time tolerating a lack of normalcy and open-endedness. Forces from deep within drive me toward the status quo. I'm in the first part of my thirty-five radiation treatments for the recurrence. A fever pitch of anger sends me out of the hermetic radiation chamber on an Indian summer day. I gun the car's accelerator, even shift into sports mode for extra oomph. Speeding past the mall, I consider retail therapy, but that won't cool the heat. I need an outlet for my shock at the news that trickles from the radiation therapist, so I let it rip. Why didn't I know five months ago that the surgeons left alone a suspicious, stealthy lymph node in front of my heart? Was it lost in the post-surgical haze, left out, or only discovered later as the physicists prepared the radiation mapping?

I try to put the pieces together, the tearful concern of the oncological surgeon, being the subject of the monthly tumor board meeting at the hospital, the plastic surgeon's worry over recurrence, and now this! Why aren't the doctors more upfront? I have the feeling of being the last one to know, like a woman finding out about her husband's long-standing affair. And now I'm stuck waiting a week to ask the doctor.

Fumbling for reasons, I question my self-advocacy as a patient and hit a dead end. Am I a compliant people-pleaser, who doesn't want to be "that patient"–a demanding diva–or a slow learner of doctors' methods to wait for the patient to ask the right questions? But how can I ask about something I'm not even aware of? Why do I allow a gastroenterologist to send me home after two months of severe bloating for two more months of healing on my own? He bluntly remarks that an atom bomb went off in my stomach–chemo and excessive antibiotics–possibly causing permanent damage.

Deciding that returning my stomach to normal is up to me, I develop elaborate strategies to decrease the symptoms, which ultimately fail. One evening it hits me with force that I have a compliance problem, so I insist on seeing the GI doctor right away with the mission to get a solution without being a b****. My newfound assertiveness, however, leads to an office visit with no solution. The road back to normal is off the map. I'm stuck in a reality many people experience daily–especially the underserved and marginalized–that our best efforts sometimes turn up little. In a rush to normalcy, even a new normal, I grab simple solutions based on thin truths, but life–and health–don't always comply. How do I stop skirting complexities in favor of instant answers?

The pandemic highlights our culture's desire for instant answers. At the beginning of the pandemic, the world languishes in the vacuum–and acceleration–of knowledge about the virus. People pounce on binary choices, conspiracy theories, anything to avoid the discomfort of not knowing. In our need for certainty, we blame and damage other well-meaning–and equally lost–people. Why do we refuse to dwell in the land of in between? As popular culture moves from vision-casting and goal setting to mindfulness and living in the moment, it needs to make peace with reason-deficits and human limitations without losing hope. Perhaps it's time to dust off, polish, and mount the ancient virtues of humility and patience on our mantles. These will season and deepen us as modern humans.

Reasons may come in time, but if not, humility and patience offer rich rewards. They restore poise and peace in our posturing and fractious world. They build appreciation and grateful hearts. Patience is long-suffering, a decision born of humility to be long or large in spirit and delay anger.

The week after testing the limits of my car's torque, I learn it is standard procedure for surgeons to leave behind disease in risky areas for hematology and radiation to kill and zap. The killing is done, but the node still lights up under a scan, so now comes the zapping. The radiation oncologist flags the suspicious node–and thirty to forty neighboring ones just in case–with erudite mapping and a Sharpie-X on my chest. He tells me that more radiation treatments are ordered, special agents for an extra surge. Dedicated and kind, he is my clean-up hitter to sweep up the bases, the most crucial hitter in the lineup. His extra surge may be the biggest shot I have right now, my last chance, to destroy that daunting foe, shrunken by chemo, but still lurking as a menace. I tell him my life depends on his excellent work.

In the purgatory of waiting for normal, my eyes notice the good things and people around me: the steady progression–and purification–of science through the excellence of experts. In this progression lies the hope of future remedies for people with incurable disease who fear they might never find normal again. My radiation oncologist is such a person of excellence. His work is a product of passion, and passion is birthed by pain. At age sixty-five, he maintains a noticeable passion for his work because it is a calling, a personal mission. He is the only doctor from my cancer seventeen years before who is not retired. On our first visit, he spends twenty-five minutes in his office piecing together my old and new stories before meeting with us for ninety minutes. He makes connections others don't make. He does not project the pedantry of "I've heard this story before" or "that's a dumb question." He engages, teaches, and makes me feel valued.

Wendy, my friend and fellow cancer survivor, reminds me of the origin of his passion in an email: "He was an engineer. His father developed cancer back when the radiation and treatments were so devastating to patients. As Dr. Miller said, the modern technology was too late for his father. But then his mother was diagnosed with breast cancer, and the science/technology/medicine had come so far that she survived. It changed his life as he sought to help others as she had been helped. He said he applied his exacting engineering mind to the science of zapping the right bad cells. He saved my life. The only doctor among five to push for radiating the super clavicular nodes. And after one week, my tumor markers were finally down." I share Wendy's gratitude.

Several months later, when the radiation is complete and I anxiously await news of my first post-treatment scan, the phone rings. It's the radiation office. My radar attuned, I scan each tone and inflection. The voice is chipper. Good sign. Time is arrested. Then come the words "no visible signs of cancer," the seed of life in five short words, a message of a few seconds that changes everything. I stand still in awe and appreciation for this doctor's excellent care and for all the doctors, nurses, and technical support I am privileged to have.

We must go through darkness and pain in this life with normalcy as a chimera, but hardship leads to passion, passion to hope, and hope to endurance. "Flowers grow out of dark moments" hangs on my wall as a gift from Nate and Mady. This is one certainty to cling to in abnormal times.

Dead ends are not actually dead. As the Apostle Paul encourages us: "we rejoice in our sufferings, knowing that suffering produces endurance, and endurance produces character, and character produces hope, and hope does not put us to shame, because God's love has been poured into our hearts through the Holy Spirit who has been given to us."[6] So I say, "Bring it on!"

6. Rom 5:3–5

Pesky House Guest Two: Anxiety

The second obnoxious house guest at my door is the persistent, grating pounding from anxiety. What remedies are there for tolerating anxiety? A good place to start is to read the anxiety messages my body is sending. Heading to my first post-treatment PET scan, I adjust my shirt as I strut with brisk–no, officious–steps from the parking lot to the radiology office, like a professional late for a business meeting. I wear my anxiety before I know it. It leaks from my body.

As I shove the door to the building, I flashback to the Tarzana Hospital. My brain gathers up other pictures from the "denial" folder before I realize what's happening: My snappy stride belies anxiety and fear. The body knows something the head denies. It's called *scanxiety*. We've all experienced the roller coaster of test anxiety, and medical tests are no exception, though perhaps more nerve-wracking and serious.

Scanxiety births two unhealthy offspring: to control or be controlled, denial or acquiescence. Another healthier outcome is needed. Switching to a clothing metaphor, denial is like dressing for success in business attire, which confers control and empowerment. This coping strategy is the fruit of hardship, and it has its rewards, if not taken too far. My pattern is to keep life normal and exercise control over what I *can* manage. Often before scans and tests, I decide there will be plenty of time to deal with bleak news, so why ruin my fun now? I carry on confidently until my anxiety pushes through, like a mouth revealing contempt. Then my anxiety breaks through the mental dam. It's scary to lose control of my resolve to keep things calm. That's when I need a change of clothing. Maybe a soft robe will do.

Another option is putting on dark funeral attire by imagining the worst-case scenario and immersing myself in what ifs. A month before the PET Scan, I undergo a different scan for colon cancer due to persistent intestinal issues. As I ponder the dark possibility of two primary cancers, my mind fixates on dark thoughts, and I consider the things I would miss in this beautiful life: the smell of rain on a dust-caked path, my granddaughter lifting up her arms to be held, fast cars and motorcycles, the family at Thanksgiving, velvet pants, and a thousand pleasures of this embodied life. These thoughts make me so depressed that I change back to business attire. I can't dwell in the land of what ifs very long. Thankfully, this time both scans are negative, and I have a new lease on life.

What's a better way of riding the roller coaster of anxiety? Surrender and scream. Every year, when Nate was still in school, we would celebrate the end of the year at Six Flags Magic Mountain, roller coaster heaven. The annoyance of hour-long waits vanishes after the adrenaline rush of thirty seconds of raw thrill, a perfect price to pay for epinephrine saturation. I feel intensely alive during those seconds. There's a trick to riding a roller coaster: go with the flow and scream. You can't be rigid. You *ride* it and scream to release the fear–and increase the delight. Fear is a close cousin of delight.

The trick to riding test anxiety is similar, surrender and scream, trust and feel. It's an intense ride, like the first time you see bad test results on a printout and your world becomes those words. Priorities come into sharp focus in an instant. The clarity–a grounding like some people feel when they help in crises and emergencies–stays with you for a long time, and you don't want to lose it.

Brittany, a former student of mine, knows this intensity well. She is a beautiful and intelligent lawyer, who is newly married and has endured bouts with lymphoma. Hers is a story of two bone marrow transplants before reaching the age of thirty. Her descriptions sting, but her wisdom as a roller coaster rider heals. She ties up loose ends at work preparing to undergo her second transplant with her brother, Michael, a medical doctor, as the donor. She will be in isolation for a few weeks, away from her new husband, enduring the familiar ravages of chemo. She'll be unable to keep food or drink down, pasted to the floor by the toilet too weak to rise. The fear of the transplant not working will whir in the background. She'll worry about getting graft vs. host disease and other unknown side effects. She emails me saying, "I've never truly made it to long-lasting remission. My longest was not even one year." Although she is exhausted, she continues her valiant fight with animated defiance.

Brittany understands what it means to own, but not enthrone her feelings, to allow them room but not take over. She recently inked the two words "even then" on her wrist from the song "Even Then" by Micah Tyler. The song was released right before her original diagnosis three and a half years before and she felt like the lyrics were speaking directly to her: "Even when it feels like my world is shaken, Even when I've had all that I can take, I know, you never let me go. And even when the waters won't stop rising, Even when I'm caught in the dead of a night, I know, No matter how it ends, You're with me even then."

Brittany attests that "this message and feeling has gotten me through a lot in the last three and a half years. It reminds me that no matter what is going on, no matter how desperate things may seem, He is with me, watching me, and loving me. He shares in my pain and celebrates my victories." About the tattoo she adds that "my husband and I have a rule that you have to want a tattoo for two to three years before getting it on your person, so when I found out about my second transplant, I knew I wanted to get it beforehand as a reminder."

Even then is a choice she makes; it's a bold declaration and a settled conclusion. *Even then* stakes out her mental landscape. She knows firsthand that, ultimately, God's presence is her greatest gift and comfort in this fragile and beautiful life on planet earth.

Brittany's bravery inspires me. Her words jolt me in an instant out of my pity pit. I want to stand with her in her fight, firm-footed and steady, not letting my disrupters wrestle me to the ground. I want to be strong for her. This is how our journeys touch others, how we draw strength of character from one another. Like trees in the forest drawing sustenance from vast root systems, we infuse strength in others when we stand together.

Brittany is sadly too familiar with test anxiety, but her lessons on anxiety are profound:

> "I've always had test anxiety, especially with standardized tests in school. I've taken my SATs and LSATs more than once because of it. I'm sure everyone does to some extent, but medical exams are their own beast. Worst case scenario for a standardized test is an F or retake. Worst case on a medical exam could point to literal death. I don't say that to be dramatic (although if you ask my husband, I generally am). I say that to really give perspective on how this type of fear is so different from other kinds.
>
> It's not something I wish on anybody. The fear. The despair. The waiting what feels like forever to actually be told the results. The dreaming up of the worst-case scenario while trying to bargain with God, promising Him you'll be more X or do more Y if He just makes the results positive. All of these negative thoughts and emotions swirling in your brain, while also trying to remain as upbeat and positive as possible. While also trying to go about your "regular day," if any semblance of regular even exists in your life anymore.
>
> Talk about exhausting! So how do I deal with it every few months? It is by no means easy, but I find peace in the surrender. Truly accepting that my situation is out of my control and, most importantly, was not caused by me. I think cancer patients often blame themselves for getting cancer in the first place. 'If I had just

eaten less sugar or worked out a little more consistently, maybe I could have avoided it.'

The reality is, a lot of cancers are genetic, or the cause is unknown. I could drive myself crazy always trying to figure out what caused the cancer. For goodness sake, there are THOUSANDS of scientists who dedicate their entire life's work to just trying to figure out what causes a singular type of cancer and I'm sitting over here trying to Google my way to an answer?

I believe in being a positive person, but I think it's equally as important to allow myself to really feel the hurt–feel the upset and to know that those feelings are valid and okay. If someone asks how I am doing, I'm not afraid to say, 'You know, not great but I'm okay with it.' It's okay to feel the negative feelings as long as you don't let them consume you completely.

Cancer has given me numerous bad things. And yet, it's also given me some great joys I might not have experienced otherwise. It's connected me to old friends and new ones. It's shown me relationships not worth putting my time into anymore. It's given me another support group living in a city away from my hometown. It's given me the encouragement to be more understanding of others and to help out in any way possible.

It's reaffirmed what I believe spiritually. I don't know how people go through this type of life event without the presence of spirituality in their lives. It reminds me of Proverbs 16:9, "In his heart a man plans his course, but the Lord determines his steps" and Psalm 37:23-24 "The Lord makes firm the steps of the one who delights in Him; though he may stumble, he will not fall, for the Lord upholds him with His hand."

You can't find peace by excessively planning or trying to control this thing or how it will affect your future. Trying to control the uncontrollable is a form of disbelief. Allowing your mind to make multiple plans is a recipe for disaster when something takes those plans even slightly off course. Just when you think you've made a roadmap for every possible scenario, something unexpected occurs and brings all of the confusion on again. By bringing God all of my hopes and fears, I can turn from a path of planning to a path of peace (although I'm only human and will still make plans in my head)."

Surrender orders Brittany's anxiety like the raked rocks of a Zen garden. This is the balancing act of faith and fear.

Brittany writes this as she awaits test results from her second bone marrow transplant to be delivered on Christmas Eve. Christmas is her favorite time of year. She is buoyed by the decorations and parties, but she can't silence the background groan of the terrible. Her Advent anguish pierces my heart.

On December 27, this email greets me: "Merry Christmas! I have great news! My 100-day scan was completely clear! HUGE relief." She has a new lease on life. Five months later she's enrolled in an MBA program, gets a puppy, and buys a house. Months later, she gets another puppy and plants a garden. She's now wearing a princess dress and tiara.

Fast forward to the Covid shutdown of medical procedures deemed elective. Brittany waits two months for her second belated scan and must wait even longer after that. Each scan is like a Chinese college entrance exam with only one chance, only much worse. High stakes. I tell her I'm posting the reflections she generously shared on test anxiety on my blog next week. She is struggling to find surrender again. She rereads her own words and is helped, but fear is a mosquito bite craving another scratch.

Fears, halts, stops, starts, celebrations, dreams, decisions, fears, halts, stops, waits. Lots of waiting. Lots of clothing changes. It never leaves, the anxiety, the fear. How do we cope with fears that won't go away? Stand up to them. That sends a strong signal to our brains: there's power in standing up to our fears.

It's easy to be fearful when a person is between the familiar and something different and daunting, whether it's between student and professional life or college graduation and an uncertain job market. In the medical world, it might mean being between a biopsy and the results, a procedure and its efficacy, the end of chemo and beginning of radiation, or the last treatment and the rest of your life. We all live in the Land of Between, but can we travel from there and thrive?

Stepping over anxiety and fear is a sound strategy. I like to imagine fear as a scrawny creature with sharp fangs yipping at my feet. I greet and name it; then I taunt it. I envision taking a high step over it; I hurdle it. Rick instructs patients to look anxiety in the face and say, "*Bring* it on! Bring it *on!*" It's as counterintuitive as leaning on the downhill ski, but it works. Our instinct to avoid it only breeds more anxiety. Selective shut-down of the anxious brain–Rick calls it the birdbrain–is a mechanism for thriving. Just one small decision each day to greet the awkward and uncomfortable is all it takes. Before long I feel more alive, more in charge of my happiness. This applies to ordinary and uncommon fears, routine discomfort, and worst-case scenarios. I must ask myself how much do I really want to thrive?

We only thrive on the other side of fear and anxiety. I enjoy adventures with my family. The night Andrew asks me on the spur of the moment to go lobster diving at ten at night, I agree before really thinking about it. I wiggle into the wetsuit and glide into the black Pacific Ocean. Admittedly, I only skim the surface of the water guided by his bright flashlight while he dives to the bottom to catch the critters. Then the thought of nocturnal threats enters my mind. I need a bold counter to chase it off, so I say to myself: "If I die on this adventure with my oldest son, I'll die doing something crazy with someone I love like crazy." Okay, the last part is true, and I only half-believe the first part, but the thought slams the fear for a few minutes. Sometimes you have to engage the stupid to override the fear.

Riding motorcycles requires a full-scale stepping over fear for me. Before each ride, the file in my brain labeled, "Well-intended stories of crashes to serve as warnings" pops up. I develop a pre-ride ritual to hide the file: the traffic is cleared, the glare gone, the temperature warm, gloves snug, helmet tight, shield wiped. I don't ride because I'm fearless; I ride for the magic of the throttle reverberating in baffled pipes and the torque and wind tossing my hair. I ride for the freedom, the vitality I feel. Many of our friends and family don't understand why Rick and I like motorcycles. They see it as a prefrontal cortex suppressor that downgrades you to a caveman state. I see it as an exhilarating dance between fear and pleasure.

During college breaks I go out with Nate through local canyons. He looks like a guy from *Easy Rider*, sans chopper handlebars, with his beard and long hair waving under the helmet and his relaxed bike-handling skills. My ride is slower than his, but he is patient with his mama. One Mother's Day, on a ride with Nate and Andrew, I think I am the luckiest mom alive to spend two hours trailing her boys through California canyons. We lean; we turn; we gun it; we feel alive together.

The problem with fear is that it keeps us stuck in the Land of Between with our eyes on the obstacles instead of the possibilities. Prepositions like "between" are banal parts of speech that define a location or position. Between is stuck in the middle–a grammatical purgatory–a position over "under" but on the downside and "above" or "beyond." The only way to travel from the Land of Between is to budge anxiety with the defiant taunt, "Bring it on!" somewhat like Macbeth's challenge to fate, but not as foolhardy: "Rather than so, come fate into the list,/And champion me to the utterance!"[7] Macbeth calls fate to come into the arena to fight him to the

7. Shakespeare, *Macbeth*, III. I. 70.

bitter end. Up against long odds, he sees himself as a knight, going bravely into battle against fate itself. The analogy ends there, but we, too, must defy fear–a crazy and counterintuitive move–to keep progressing.

The Third Unwelcome Guest: Shame

The last guest at the door is shame. Shame is quieter than the others. Disrupters often evoke shame because we tend to blame ourselves for something broken or lost. Whether it's the shame I feel from my internal critic–the conductor–telling me I'm the cause of the disrupter, from my helpless and exposed state, from dislike of my bald head and scarred body, or from becoming more assertive as my own health advocate, shame makes me want to withdraw and hide. Why? Shame exposes my vulnerability, and vulnerability is hard to tolerate. But tolerating–and acting against–shame propels growth, even new identity formation. Most of us know the experience of being pushed to do something we'd rather not do only to discover surprising benefits. We must learn not to run in shame from shame.

Shame is universal. My examples of dealing with shame may not be yours, but the lessons are universal. Hair loss is a laboratory of shame–especially for women–offering insight into the creative potential of a disrupter. The benefits of hair loss come unexpectedly. A few weeks after my preemptive shave, as I'm embracing my baldness more, I'm learning about the inner workings of shame. On a surface level, I enjoy having a soft face, like an expensive facial or wax job. Also, there's nothing quite like hearing my kids say, "You're cool and hip with a buzz." They might change their minds when I'm completely bald, but I'll take the compliment. Then there's the freedom of not having to shave my legs, or shampoo, cut, and style my hair, not to mention the savings.

On a deeper level, hair loss bumps against a sense of embarrassment which casts a long and familiar shadow over my life. It's hard to strip the layers of shame from my childhood. Shame is an unconscious part of my inner framework; it creeps into my perceptions and relationships; it steals joy, stifles spontaneity, and leaves regrets.

It's time to emerge from the shadow of shame. I don't want to conceal my baldness like my first bout with cancer when I never shed the wig. After all, it's summer and wigs are itchy. Not ready to go out with a balding buzz, I'm experimenting with straw hats and caps. My mom jokes about my having an *Armeisenkopf* (head of an ant) when I pick her up at the curb wearing a bucket hat for the first time. I like the feeling of flaunting embarrassment. I've spent too much of my life trying to blend in, look right, be right.

Shedding my wig is exhilarating. No one stares at me as I go out wearing the baseball cap my friend, Tracey, gives me with "FOX" on the back. It's a small daily act, but I feel strangely empowered by it. I'm not sure I would feel that in Germany. Unless you live in another country, you may not notice American politeness and the space people allow for individual expression and that people don't stare and try not to offend. Freedom is imperceptibly embedded in American culture. It's not the same in many other parts of the world. Americans may have good reason to complain about civic rudeness, but there's also much to celebrate.

Just as shame builds incrementally, I suspect it diminishes incrementally. What makes it diminish? Moving away from my comfort zone toward awkwardness and vulnerability. It's possible to create patterns of avoidance where discomfort crowds out our better selves. We communicate indirectly because we'd rather not face the discomfort of dealing directly with a person in conflict; we avoid speaking our minds, tell lies, curate an image, say what's expected, do what everyone else does, and ultimately create a false self. Before too long, we are cut off from ourselves, our true feelings, our voice. Just as avoidance of shame feeds it, so small daily movements toward shame dismantle it. I make a decision to take bigger and bolder steps once my hair grows back. Starting a blog would certainly be a step–no, a leap–in the direction of discomfort and vulnerability! Or writing a book. So, I'm hitting the road in my cap and not looking back.

Disrupters destroy, but they help us discover something new. We find a strong and true voice, our true selves. It comes to us when it feels like all we are doing is letting go and losing. But then we discover the inside workings of the paradox of Jesus, "Whoever finds his life will lose it, and whoever loses his life for my sake will find it"[8] on the other side of the door.

Sometimes I need a push, a shove, a kick of the door to leave my comfort zone. So, I say, "Bring it on!"

8. Matt 10:39

Chapter 8

I'm Finding My Voice, Sort of

MUCH OF MY HIGH SCHOOL EXPERIENCE is about the aforementioned obnoxious house guests. I have a hard time telling them to "Bring it on!" After the bumpy start of high school, another disrupter smacks me, another new school, community, set of challenges, but this time I have some say, some control. The only option left for an American education–I am now too far into the American system to return to the German one, and I prefer it–is to attend a Department of Defense school near Bonn, the capital of Germany at the time. It's an hour from home, but it takes longer to get there. An extended commute is a part of the new arrangement, but it's better than the boarding school. I agree to it with mixed feelings. My daily commute starts in a small, chartered bus for business kids and other expats who live in our area near Koblenz and takes us to school in Bad Godesberg. There I meet Lee Ann, who becomes a good friend. At the end of the semester, the bus service is canceled, and I am left alone to commute by train.

Grinding and Growing

I drag myself out of bed at five in the morning to wake up my mom, who drives me to the train station. On several occasions when we are late, we see the train in the distance, and she speeds up to catch up and drop me off just in time. My mom loves driving fast. I do too. Much of the time, however, I'm waiting on the platform freezing despite my warm coat and boots. Cold, tired, and alone, I put one foot in front of the other. On the train, I constantly nod off but somehow never miss my stop. Once I arrive at the station, I board a bus that drops me off near school and walk the rest of the way. My commute takes three to four hours every day. In winter, I do it in the dark, a sad and lonely routine.

At Bonn American High School, the kids are smart and urbane, diplomat kids from all over the world who speak two or three languages. I spend time with an Israeli friend who lives behind a gate secured by her own guards. I interact with an Ethiopian boy who aspires to become a leader in his country. There is the boy who aces tests without studying and the girl whose dad works for the CIA. Wendy becomes a close friend, and I often spend the weekend at her house. She lives in Plittersdorf, the American *Siedlung*, a neighborhood of homes for American diplomats and officials provided by the U.S. government. She's my reprieve from the drudgery of the long commute.

BAHS opens my world and unlocks a desire to learn, which lies dormant in six years of severe German education and three years of American education in four schools. Energized by the new environment, I start to invest in my own learning, and I love it! My learning gaps are wide—and embarrassing, but avoiding shame has a way of motivating me to play catch up. I become especially interested in English taught by my favorite teacher, Mrs. Geyer. I start to write again, which I had dropped after the first abrupt move to the U.S. That school ends up closing after the German government moves to Berlin, but its influence continues in my life until this day decades later. BAHS births my life-long love for learning.

After the setbacks at the boarding school, I learn that failure is not final. In fact, it is often a gateway to something better. Failure is one of the most effective teachers because it unearths latent desires, clarifies priorities, and holds out new dreams. If we refuse to take risks and fail, we stunt our growth as individuals. Most disrupters eventually end, and we're left with ourselves and the question of who we will become. What will we do with our failures? Will we fall forward or back?

My social life follows a familiar teenage pattern. Pubs and parties break up the monotony on the weekends. Without a legal drinking age in Germany, teenagers drink together in public. I notice how kids become transparent with alcohol and how it seems like they're best friends. But the next day, we're strangers or mere acquaintances again. The false allure of alcohol only deepens a growing sense of sadness. Once when Wendy's parents are gone, we have a party at her house where I drink my first vodka and end the night throwing up. My disdain of vomiting leads me to shun vodka from that point on. Why is disdain such a strong motivator for me?

During school we sneak down to the banks of the Rhine River, tuck ourselves in a safe foxhole and smoke hash in gigantic bongs. How do we get away with this? We even smoke in parks of the nearby capital of Bonn. In a culture defined by rules, these rules are surprisingly lax. A highlight of school is when a streaker–a fellow student–runs across campus. But the void of aimlessness increases, leading me to search for my life's purpose.

The scenery of the commute fails to divert the tedium. Here I am riding trains along the Rhine River, arguably one of the most beautiful places in the world. Steep banks of vineyards in dramatic descent, barges and pleasure boats plying the waters, and endless green hills dotted by ancient castles that attract countless tourists delight and excite most people. I feel hollow and alienated.

German culture contributes to the alienation. Operating by an unspoken rule that says, "Don't talk to strangers," communication is the hard stares I remember from childhood, the critical eye locking on your face and lingering awkwardly, then gliding on the entire body to the feet. It's the quiet hurling of an insult. Communication is also the pedantic instructions from adults to children, like the time I sit on the side of a wide concrete staircase at a train station and a man insists on walking exactly where I'm seated. He yells at me with moralistic instructions impugning my character. German is a great language for this. It's called *schimpf* (scold), a guttural nastiness that deflects anger disguised as advice onto someone weaker and smaller. Experiences like this are not rare.

I officially target the abiding German stare as an offensive game and enjoy the rebellion of this sport. Dressed in colorful hippie clothes unsuited to the conservative German attire at the time, I stare down strangers with the temerity to stare at me. I shun conventions like not sitting on stairs, walking on grass, and many other verboten activities. Blending in like I used to do is no longer an option. Perhaps I'm finding my voice, but it's a shriveled, angry voice. Underneath the anger is sadness, which is harder to know and express, especially in the German culture at that time.

Still, the drudgery of the commute wears me down. I start reflecting on existential questions like, "What's the purpose of life?" and "Why do people go to work, have families, and engage in the expected rituals of life?" These questions, along with a deepening depression grip me. I'm also gripped by guilt and shame over my life as it is. Shame is a feeling I disdain.

Jesus Freaks in the Streets

That's when I meet a group of American Jesus People in my mom's tea house. My mom has a Christian ministry in the inner city of our town, called the *Teestube* (teahouse), that invites young people to talk about life over tea. Atheists, Marxists, agnostics, believers, drug addicts, straight edge, disenfranchised, those looking for company, and those prepared for a knife fight, everyone is welcome. My mom is a tough middle-aged woman who talks to anyone. If they are open to it, she suggests giving Jesus a chance. Once she even finds herself in the middle of a knife fight between two visitors. To this rough and tumble place, a group of American ex-druggies who have found Jesus comes to minister. They have started living in community at the nearby Hahn American Air Force Base and are planning to form a commune. Their kindness and understanding reach my teenage angst.

Finding this group coincides with reading authors like Francis Shaeffer and C.S. Lewis. Together they till the crusty soil of my heart and make it receptive to a message I rejected–though never completely–since middle school. After a few months of thinking and reflecting on my life, a moment of decision arrives. I'm watching a parade in Belgium with the group, and I decide then and there to follow Christ. There are no fireworks, just a love that displaces the guilt and sadness. It starts small and grows into a full-scale change and a commitment to full-time Christian ministry, though I don't know what form it will take. I've met students like myself over the years, the ones who experiment early only to hit a dead end in the middle of high school. They become sold out for Christ and don't look back. They find a something important they lost along the way.

A sense of purpose propels me to share the experience of love I have with others. I make a red brochure with a heart and a short gospel message called "All You Need is Love." Totally out of character for me, I boldly hand out flyers on trains, and I am surprised at strangers' willingness to talk. Germans enjoy deep conversations. They see Americans are superficial and pride themselves on their critical thinking skills and philosophical depth. Passing as a German, I learn something new about the culture in general, that they are afraid to be the first to reach out but are more than willing to engage in deep conversation if prompted. All that talk of not speaking to strangers is really fear. For the first time I have a real voice–though it's not yet a full-throated one–and I like the feeling of initiating meaningful conversations with strangers. It's like a salesperson discovering the skill of selling for the first time, though for me it's more like sharing. I want to share the good news that has changed my life.

I take that evangelistic fervor into my high school with conversations and Bible studies. A few friends become Christians. On a choir trip to a divided Berlin, a choir member decides to trust Christ with her life in a noisy train car. It's one of the happiest moments of my life. To see someone be receptive to change and find hope boosts my decision to go into full-time ministry. I have a sense of purpose far beyond my small teenage life.

Evangelism, which is just sharing the good news without coercion, is also important to the commune. On weekends we go into the streets in our long flowery dresses and bell-bottoms to engage people in conversation. Prepared with pamphlets, first-hand experience, peace, and love, we go to train stations, parks, and downtown areas to witness to the power of Christ. For a shy person, I'm surprised to feel at ease talking with strangers.

Harry is the charismatic leader of the group stationed at the Air Force base less than an hour away. His former life of sex and drugs is turned around by Christ, whom he ardently follows. He leads his community of American converts to form a Christian commune. I start spending weekends with them. Harry tells us he is going to London to pick up his sister Eva and bring her back to live with them at the commune. He asks me and my mom if I can come along.

I'm surprised that my mom agrees, and I think it is because the joy she feels over her lost daughter's return eclipses her better judgment. Granted, Harry is upstanding and promises to take good care of me, but I am barely sixteen and he is twenty-two. Nevertheless, we set off on our road trip through Germany and France to the English Channel. At the border into England, a guard stops us with skepticism. What is a military serviceman doing on a trip with a teenage girl? I feel sheepish. After a delay, he lets us through the border, and we pick up Eva in London. On that trip, I secretly fall in love with Harry. I fall hard because I am young and trusting and he is older and trustworthy, I surmise. To his credit, he honors his commitment to my mom.

Back at home, I become the girlfriend of the commune leader. On weekends he picks me up in his old Opel. His lead foot and relaxed style of leaning back with his right arm casually draped over the seat stand in jux-taposition to the caution required for the winding mountain roads to the base. He likes to push the limits with speed. When it's warm, he picks me up on his motorcycle where we wind and lean through forty-five minutes of curves.

An unconventional German who looks and acts like Doc Brown in *Back to the Future* offers his home to the group. This is a Franconian half-timber-work structure in disrepair with clay and straw walls and errant pieces sticking out here and there. Once there, we join the others in making the commune habitable with a low-budget DIY facelift. These are American baby boomers repairing a German home made more than a millennium before they are born.

The finished product is scruffy. Separate bunk rooms for the genders covered with green military blankets, sagging sofas, chairs in semi-disrepair, and colorful rugs create a shabby Bohemian look. Against the cheap vibe, a vibe of earnest worship and Bible study makes it seem like we are rich and powerful. The group prays, studies the Bible, and prophesies. Once someone prophesies that God wants Eva and her boyfriend Ron, another service member, to get married. They do, and we celebrate with a roasted pig in a nearby forest glade.

All I know at the time is a tinge of unease with this prophesy. (They eventually divorce after having twin girls back in the U.S.) Other life decisions are made through prophetic fiat. They call on the Holy Spirit to baptize them with tongues, and they cajole me to "just start speaking and the tongues will come." I tentatively give in but stop midway. I don't like the pressure, and I don't think the Bible supports the idea that everyone receives tongues. This is just one of the various spiritual gifts. I know this from reading doctrine books since I was young, a long-standing interest of mine. My rebellious streak might be tamed, but it's not extinguished.

In the summer of 1972, we prepare for an exciting opportunity, the Olympics in Munich. YWAM (Youth with a Mission) provides a castle they own outside Munich for fellow evangelists. The scene at the castle is a Christian Woodstock but smaller and without drugs or alcohol. It's a social movement of Jesus People in long flowered skirts, loose clothing, headbands, and guitars to gather and prepare to engage the Olympic village. A short time after our stay, the Munich Massacre, the infamous terror plot of a Palestinian group against Israeli athletes, shakes the world. We narrowly avoid it.

A moment during that trip is frozen in time. Our group is in a restaurant, and I leave the table for a moment. Upon my return, Harry comments on my stiff gait and lack of arm movement. He doesn't say this, but it feels like I'm almost catatonic and uncomfortable with my body, dissociated from the confusing emotions of adolescence. Why does this stick with me? I see myself from the outside and the outside matches the inside feelings of inferiority, weakness, and dependence. I still have a quiet voice showing itself in a constricted body.

A negative pattern of behavior develops between Harry and me. He is the kind of person who evokes attention and respect from others. His advice is sought. In our relationship, he sets the course and I respond. It's a classic dance of one person withholding and the other wanting more. Crumbs of affection keep me nibbling. I'm like a gambler fixed to a slot machine by intermittent reinforcement. In a state of constant insecurity, I look to him for something indefinable that I never fully receive. Power differentials are common in relationships, but this one widens and expands to create serious consequences.

A Toxic Brew

The summer before my senior year Harry flies home to Minnesota on furlough. I plan to meet him there a couple of weeks later along with Eva and his brother Kent. From there we plan a road trip to California where the home my mom inherits from her parents needs a new renter. I'm excited to spend time with him outside of his responsibilities as commune leader.

As soon as I arrive in Minnesota, a terrible blow hits my lovesick teenage heart. He's gone back to his high school girlfriend, Paulette. They have sex. How easy it is to relapse into old behaviors. Several thoughts randomly race through my head like, "I only know two Paulettes in my life, and both are jerks! Who names a kid Paulette anyways?" Another thought is, "We kept ourselves from having sex all this time, and now this!" and "How can I sit in the car with him for a week?" Breakups happen all the time. Why am I so hurt and devastated and so wildly jealous of Paulette? Inconsolable tears and hurt overwhelm me.

A week or so later we head West along with his siblings and a friend. That long trip through dry landscapes with dried out tear ducts stretches out like the time between a death and the funeral. I must simply cope. There's no girlfriends' trash-talking session. No chance for them to tell me what a jerk he is and that I don't deserve it. No chance to throw a temper tantrum. All I can do is endure the misery and try letting go of him. But I don't let go.

I foolishly hold on. The approach-avoidance dance has shifted. He usually withholds and I approach. But now he approaches, and like a proverbial doormat, I don't avoid him. There's no chance to reflect, no unearthing of the roots of our dysfunction, just emotional stuffing and minimizing, though it's hard to suppress the hurt I feel. I let him come back to me because I need him, and we reconcile and revive our relationship. Back in Germany, the revival becomes an awkward toe-stubbing dance. Unable to shake the hurt and my desire to be with him, I deceive myself into thinking we can forge ahead into the future.

My mom's validation of my pain sustains me in the last year of high school. At night she sits on my bed for hours to hear my sadness. She understands the depth of a child's hurt because she has been there herself. Those hours of quiet listening spread out over months to soothe my pain. She hears the pain of the damage inflicted on me, but what about the root causes that keep me tethered to a man who is not good for me? These remain buried and unexplored.

Harry and I hold on for the rest of senior year, but it's actually I who do most of the holding on. As I make plans to attend Westmont College in Santa Barbara in the fall, he assures me he wants to get engaged to me at Christmas. With excitement and hope I say goodbye and leave him for three months, or so I think.

A tearful goodbye with my parents sends me from Frankfurt to L.A. where a family friend picks me up to deposit me at Westmont College. All alone a continent away, I'm a poor student on a missionary scholarship excited at the possibilities of a new life with pastel-dressed and well-to-do kids. My roommate Carol turns out to be from the Central Valley, a farming community where my dad's relatives live. What a godsend!

Westmont is like a summer camp with a strong academic focus. Somehow, I miss the pre-registration deadline and end up with Religious Studies–starting with ancient *Koine* (Biblical) Greek–as my only option. Because language is a strong suit and theology an interest since childhood, I quickly declare myself an R.S. major. I'm the youngest female student to take Greek, and I love the professors who teach us how to conjugate verbs through song. Greek is my initiation into a new group to belong to, a group of learners not unlike those generations before us. My other classes integrate faith and learning, offering interdisciplinary connections. Here my newly found love of learning comes alive, but it takes a lot of effort and library time to prove myself fit to belong.

The long commute over, I delight in living in the dorm and walking to class. It's not just the classes I enjoy but the environment, kids, and activities. Anyone who visits Santa Barbara knows the invigorating power of that place. My new friends have a winning wholesomeness that I want to emulate. Fun activities break up the hard academic work, and I do some platonic dating with a California surfer boy and others, but I don't let anyone hold my hand or kiss me. After all, I have big plans for Christmas.

Christmas rolls around with no place to go. Silence from Harry. I'm all alone without money, and my family is 6000 miles away. What do I do? More silence. Then Carol's family invites me to spend time with them. We go skiing–I've only done that once–and have an American Christmas together. They take me in as their own and generously provide a home throughout my college stay.

Why don't I talk much about Harry to anyone during that Christmas break? Am I ashamed? Do I know deep inside that something is wrong?

Mid-January arrives and still there is no word. I call Eva to find out what happened, but I only receive a veiled response. I take a road trip with friends to Colorado at Easter to see her, but still, there's nothing. My hurt floats in mid-air like a gas leak with no one to shut off the valve.

Then suddenly, almost overnight, I find the tool to shut the valve. It's as if my life stops. My barge stops, belches, and turns around. Like a beam of light penetrating the darkness, truth breaks through, and I suddenly see myself as I am. I see the truth. I am weak, dependent, and insecure. A trodden-on doormat. And this is when I discover my true voice.

A Glaring Light

I view the beam of light from two directions, retrospectively and prospectively. Both views carry different emotions, one anger over what a fool I am and the other appreciation for how God spared me from a bad future. The stronger emotion is anger, and its intensity casts my teenage self in stark relief. How could I be so blind? So weak? So needy? I will never again allow myself to be controlled by a man! I will never feel this kind of shame again. I will never date a self-centered person again. With ruthless force, I turn my anger on myself and begin the cleavage between my childhood self and my newly emerging identity. My disdain of shame leads me to commit to another radical change. Like the song "When I fall in love" I decide that the next man I kiss will be my future husband. I fall one kiss short. No one is perfect, but the vow seems perfect to me.

Instead of arriving by blunt force like anger, a sense of appreciation for a brighter future arrives in waves, delightful waves. I feel God's protection, how I'm spared physical harm, how I'm spared from my own destructive desires. My social world is exciting, and my academic world widens as I take on a second major in English, which takes me on a semester abroad to England with a month in Israel. My group is led by a favorite English professor, Dr. Delaney, who is gifted in Socratic discussion–at times he's intimidating but always challenging–and takes us to plays in London. Spending nearly a month in Jerusalem at the end of our trip reveals a new horizon of study and interest for me. I have never enjoyed learning as much as I do in the three weeks there. Excited by new interests and capabilities, I look forward to the future. My old self in the rear-view mirror, I feel little need to look back.

In all, my college years are invigorating. Social life exceeds my expectations as I immerse myself in wholesome activities. I feel no desire for the partying associated with today's college experience. I've been there and done that. During this time, I'm enjoying friendships with different guys and stick to my no-touching dating vow for two years until I meet a guy I like. During this time, I'm also getting to know Rick. I first notice him as a freshman in his wide striped-blue tee shirt that screams homegrown in America, stability, and confidence. He has a girlfriend, so I tuck away the image until junior year when he is single again. I'm on a group date with friends and Rick is among us. It's a casual event. Rick's confidence stands out to me as he leans over to me to start a conversation with the statement that he wants to get to know me better. Whoa! I like that! We start a friendship in which he becomes a confidante to talk about my interest in a guy I like.

At a school dance with this guy on the Queen Mary, I notice Rick having a blast with another girl. Meanwhile my date's rather lifeless demeanor is a stark contrast. Does he not like dancing? Or maybe he doesn't want a relationship with me. The latter possibility triggers me! I never want to be in the position of wanting someone who doesn't want me again! Instead of waiting around to find out, I screw up the courage a few days later to ask him directly, but my blunt question scares him off. He probably thinks I'm eager to graduate with an Mrs. degree. When you're trying on new ways of being, it comes out awkwardly at first, like trying a new skill. No matter;

at least I'm in charge of my relational life this time. I won't trade that for comfort and ease.

One evening when I have a black eye from heading a soccer ball into a teammate's jaw, I get permission from my RD for Rick to be in my room–it's the seventies in a Christian college–to read the book of Acts aloud to me, which is an assignment in a Bible class. That's when I start to notice Rick more. After six months of being friends, Rick and I make it official, and in less than two years we are engaged. My vow to marry a man who wants me, who is safe, and who encourages me is fulfilled. And he is what I want, an athlete and academic who loves Jesus. Love is supposed to make you stronger and better. His love turns up the volume of the voice I muffled for so long.

Rick applies to several grad schools, and we put our wedding date on hold until he decides to go to Fuller Seminary where I am also headed. We marry in the first year and scrape together enough finances to get by. My dad pays our rent, and we each have one or two jobs to pay the tuition and expenses. We furnish our apartment for five dollars from mostly castoff furniture. But we are happy to grow up as adults together and wouldn't want it to be different.

Sometimes God protects us from ourselves. He spares me from a bad marriage with Harry. As Aesop reminds us, "Be careful what you wish for, lest it come true!" so we often fail to consider what might happen if our wishes come true. But when we let go–or are forced to let go–we discover something good on the other end. It turns out that I needed to lose my life to really find it.

Part IV

ACCEPTANCE IS A PROCESS OF OWNING LOSS

Chapter 9

Lament is a Posture of Devotion

The Mysterious Intimacy Between Mourning and Acceptance

Accepting our disrupter means living at the confluence of sorrow and joy. I grew up at the confluence of the Rhine and Moselle Rivers, where the smaller Moselle flows into the Rhine. It's a beautiful spot marked by a large monument called *Deutsches Eck* (German Corner) made of dark stone with an equestrian statue from 1897 of William I to commemorate his role in the unification of Germany. The statue was destroyed in WWII and rebuilt in 1993 to remind Germans of their newly forged unity.

Unity is hard to maintain. This is true of societies and individuals. Within each of us resides a tendency to splinter ourselves and our experiences. The Bible calls this a divided heart. Integrity is an integrated self in which the different parts work together in harmony. This is what we discover once we give up the need to control the outcomes in our lives. Incorporating the horrible and wonderful into our lives–the things that make us sad and grateful–marks this progression, which starts with accepting our disrupters.

Here's how we know that we're inching toward acceptance: We discover the good things *in* hardship, not only *after* it. It's the fall between chemo and radiation when I drive to my favorite nature preserve on the western-most point of the Santa Monica Bay. My body is feeling a bit stronger, but it will be hit again by radiation. Thighs and lungs burning, calves stretching, I relish the splendid pain of exercising as I huff up the hill that used to feel like a walk. My heart wells up with gratitude, and I can't stop saying "Thank you, Lord." On the top there is a bronze plate commemorating the discovery of Pt. Dume by George Vancouver in 1793 on an expedition to determine the extent of settlement of the northwest coast of America. The expanse is ringed by a 360-degree view of ocean, cliffs, and mountains. I feel a connection to travelers on arduous journeys who journey beyond the Land of Between to moments of discovery.

What if down the road you realize you're living out the worst-case scenario and you are surprisingly okay? You discover there are good things *in* hardship, not only *after* it, glimpses of the terrible and the beautiful, anguish and delight, living side by side. I realize this on the one-year anniversary of seven surgeries—including one more reconstruction surgery and an emergency appendectomy on the eve of the COVID shutdown–and cancer treatments with a host of setbacks. There is both pain and awakening; I feel more connected to myself and others, more in tune with God. For some, the Land of Between is a Sahara, with only faint glimpses flickering in the distance, but they are enough to keep you moving. You discover a strength you didn't know was there.

This is a common experience of people with cancer. Abigail Johnston, a young woman with Stage IV breast cancer (MBC) writes in her blog about the difficulty of living with a terminal diagnosis. "First of all, I've realized that learning I have MBC broke me. It broke my sense of self. It broke how I viewed my body. It broke how I viewed the world. It broke how I view God. It broke my view of love and caring. It broke my view of fear and resilience. It broke my sense of justice and fairness. It broke my relationships, and it decimated the career I'd spent nearly twenty years building. Acknowledging and facing that has taken me a lot of time, work, and reflection.

"In the beginning, I thought being broken meant I was weak, meant that I had failed somehow. I now understand that to look closely at the experience and my brokenness is how I move forward. I now understand that being broken doesn't mean that I'm no longer whole. I now understand that to be broken just is. I now understand that we often must be broken to heal. To me, being broken means I have the opportunity to put my life back together in a different way. To rebuild from the ashes of a life I thought I wanted, into a life of meaning, a life of purpose, a life I actually want. Being broken is an opportunity to make something entirely new."[1]

1. Johnston, Abigail. "Strength." *No Half Measures.*

The Legitimacy of Lament

But how do we get to that point? Tolerating a disrupter helps us put up with it. We don't like and would rather avoid it, but it's here to stay, so we'd better let it be. This leads to *accepting* the disrupter, but it's hard because accepting feels passive. This is because accepting rubs against a common tendency to be fix-it people who improve situations. Yielding to a disrupter is anything but passive because it requires a countercultural punch. Anne Lamott's claim that acceptance is something we're taught not to do is verified by our experience. "We're taught to improve uncomfortable situations, to change things, alleviate unpleasant feelings."[2] We must challenge this mentality. But how?

It's counterintuitive, but I begin by lamenting the loss. Not lament! It's messy, inefficient, and too wrought with sadness! Yes, lament because it releases something from deep inside us that helps us own the loss.

Lament is a legitimate posture of devotion. Lament is often cut off before it has an effect, but expressing sorrow or regret connects us to God and others. Lament starts with acknowledging a disrupter. For Latasha Morrison, a Black woman dedicated to racial reconciliation, it involves acknowledging the 1921 Tulsa massacre and other events "intentionally buried in the archives of American history."[3] The kind of lament Morrison seeks is lament *with* not lament *over* or *for*. Small prepositions have outsize impact. She invites white people to unleash the power of lament *with* Black people.

Walking through the one block memorial to the murdered Jews in Berlin is another form of lamenting with a group of people. The memorial is made of hundreds of concrete sepulchers of uneven height and size, creating confusion when walking among them. It creates a symbolic experience of disorientation for those who visit. Doing so connects the visitor to a suffering community.

We need communities that suffer well together. When Kate Bowler is diagnosed with Stage IV colon cancer at age thirty-five, she is engaged in an academic study of prosperity gospel churches. She recalls attending Lakewood Church on Good Friday in the former Compaq Center arena, home of the Houston Rockets. Greetings of "Happy Good Friday!" pepper her numerous times on her way from the parking lot through the escalators and into the arena. "To the Osteen's credit" (pastors Joel and Victoria

2. Lamott, *Bird by Bird*, 178.
3. Morrison, *Be the Bridge*, 45.

Osteen) she comments, "Jesus stayed dead for about three songs in the opening worship set . . . Then Victoria appeared from backstage, her stiletto heels clicking as she entered with a toothy smile. 'Isn't it great we serve a risen Lord!' she asked rhetorically. On a day and at an hour during which, historically, Christians refuse to speak the word Alleluia (Christ is risen) in song or prayer, Victoria loudly skipped"[4] that somber moment in the tradition. Why is this?

One might argue that the resurrection is the hinge point of the early church as people move from fear to courage and shift worship from Saturday to Sunday, as ancient documents attest. Shouldn't we set up our church communities on this foundation? So, what's wrong with the above scenario? The problem is that it is a springboard for a preferred message more pleasing than suffering and death. It gives people what they want: success and a happy, healthy life of wholeness. What's wrong with that? Nothing, except when it crowds out suffering, a vital aspect of the Christian experience.

We need to make space for lament and anguish as legitimate expressions of piety. I reflect on a concert I attend during my treatments of *The Sons of Korah*, a group that puts music to the Psalms, the honest and passionate songs that have consoled people throughout the ages. The first hour of the concert–and more than half of it–is spent on Psalms of lament. They begin with the Babylonian exile and even Psalm 88, which does not have a happy ending. They create room to feel sadness and disappointment. The music is doleful at times, emanating from Mike Follent's ancient Middle Eastern guitar reverberations. One song is strung onto the next without break or applause, allowing the audience to give itself to the experience without the pressure to be upbeat. The musicians' refusal to entertain the audience in a "rah-rah Jesus" way or to make sure the audience is happy with them allows the music to wrap around me like a soft blanket. It is rare. It is beautiful.

In the quiet of this concert, I feel a door to my feelings of struggle, sadness, and disappointment turn on its hinges and creak open. Instead of closing the door, I allow the cool breeze to waft in and clean out the stale air. There's no need to sensor my feelings; there's no shame or push-back; there's no interior judge instructing me in the way of triumphalist faith. Sadness becomes a welcoming friend, warm and cozy, just as joy is. I realize that there is a lot about American culture, and particularly evangelical culture, that is built around a Starbucks caffeine high. The message is, "Don't

4. Bowler, *Everything Happens*, 131.

slow down too much to feel emotions that might derail you, or if you do, be sure to pick yourself up again really soon." Sadness might be allowed, but only for a short period of time.

Lead guitar and vocalist Matthew Jacoby–who also has a doctorate in philosophy/theology from the University of Melbourne–offers an apologetic for the devalued imprecatory psalms (songs that invoke judgment), stating that though they seem harsh to us, we still need them. We still engage enemies, calamities, and injustice. Jacoby proposes that the psalmists, in bringing their pain to God, express genuine and strong faith, which looks to God for help. Instead of lowering their expectations of God like many modernists do, they expect God to act on their behalf. The faith of the psalmists is a dogged, persistent, and buoyant faith.

I want to belong to a community that suffers well together, like my Mennonite and Jewish forebears. Their stories give them the capability to suffer well together. Communities that suffer well together are life-giving. When we cannot explain why everything is happening as it is, we have the posture of lament as we seek God during an uncertain time.

Many fear that lament turns them inward when it may have the opposite effect. Our lament connects us with the laments of others. A community is forged that otherwise would not have come about. As we listen to stories of lament, we witness the pain of others with us and those who go before us. I need these stories when I curse my disrupters, wishing they would diminish, fade, and vanish. We all need these stories to expand us, build empathy, and see the central role of suffering in human experience.

Who is Uncle Tom?

The languid months of recovery draw me into literature of struggle and injustice. My journey starts with David McCullough's *Pioneers,* a story about settling the Northwest Territory starting in 1788, a wilderness northwest of the Ohio River which would develop into the states of Ohio, Indiana, Illinois, Michigan, and Wisconsin. I'm fascinated by Manasseh Cutler and his son Ephraim who together labor–and at one point almost lose the struggle–to keep the territory free of slavery. Theirs is a far-reaching legacy.

Harriet Beecher Stowe's 1851 book *Uncle Tom's Cabin* belongs to that legacy. Her composite stories heard from Black servants during the seventeen years she lives in Cincinnati where slavery is illegal make the characters personal and their suffering relatable. The sensational success of the book leads to it being said that "Mrs. Stowe made more converts to antislavery with her book than all the preachers and lecturers combined." That catches my attention. I want to read the stories of this woman whom Lincoln allegedly greeted in 1862 with this flip comment: "So you are the little woman who wrote the book that started this great war."[5]

So, I read *Uncle Tom's Cabin*, an extensive, gut-wrenching account of families caught in slavery, stories of children ripped from their mother's arms, mistreatment, violence and oppression, unimaginable horror, stories which vivify slavery. Why do I put myself through such an emotional wringer when I'm struggling through my own pain? Perhaps it's because I'm looking for a way to cope through a story far worse than mine; perhaps experiencing pain increases my capacity to enter another's pain. I'm riveted to these stories.

Stories of benign and beastly owners, they make the point that even the benign ones, who treat their slaves kindly to assuage their consciences, are equally complicit in the system of injustice because they don't use their power to end it. I learn of human depravity and the importance of just laws. Stowe lets no one off the hook, neither the North nor the South, calling slavery America's problem.

What comes to mind when you hear the name Uncle Tom? Probably not a strong, self-possessed man but an abject sell-out. No one wants to be an Uncle Tom. So, how does he inspire me? The answer is that before Uncle Tom becomes an insult, he is a martyr, a slave who sacrifices his freedom and life for his fellow slaves.

I'm fascinated by the complexity of Tom's character. Tom has a hard life of oppression, loss, and grief. Clearly, there's something to the sycophantic association with the character, especially when he lives in the South under the indulgent master St. Clare. When his owner dies, Tom is sold farther north to a cruel owner named Simon Legree. After a life of struggle and pain, it is almost unbearable to see him end up there. Legree lets his fury fall on Tom over the escape of two slaves, Cassy and Emmeline. He resolves that if the hunt with neighboring plantations, dogs, and guns does not produce Cassy and Emmeline, he will break Tom down to find out where they are. He hates Tom because of his independence of mind, even though he is faithful.

When the hunt turns up nothing–the women are hiding at the plantation until an opportune time for escape–Tom steels himself for an assault

5. McCullough, *Pioneers*, 255.

from his despotic master. Knowing the details of the fugitives' plan, he resolves not to betray his fellow slaves, even if it means dying for it. Stowe ties Tom's resoluteness to a moment of inspiration: "[A] higher voice there was saying, 'Fear not them that kill the body, and, after that, have no more that they can do.' Nerve and bone of that poor man's body vibrated to those words, as if touched by the finger of God; and he felt the strength of a thousand souls in one."[6]

With virulent anger, Legree tells Tom he will kill him if he doesn't reveal the whereabouts of the slaves. Tom refuses, but Legree commands him to speak while striking him furiously. When asked if he knows anything, Tom responds, "'I know, Mas'r; but I can't tell anything. *I can die!*'" Impassioned, Tom urges his master to consider his conscience, "'Oh, Mas'r don't bring this great sin on your soul! It will hurt you more than't will me! Do the worst you can, my troubles'll be over soon; but, if ye don't repent, yours won't never end!'" Then after one "hesitating pause, the spirit of evil came back, with sevenfold vehemence; and Legree, foaming with rage, smote his victim to the ground."[7]

Stowe's description of Tom's death stops there with the poignant comment: "Scenes of blood and cruelty are shocking to our ear and heart. What man has nerve to do, man has not nerve to hear."[8]

Tom stands on the non-negotiable decision to protect life, the life of his friends, who are also two of the most disadvantaged members of society, female slaves. He knows what's worth dying for and dies on his own terms. His choice and his autonomy are the things that no person, no weapon, no authority can take from him. His martyrdom ultimately becomes the defining moment of his life, which shapes how we view this character.

When I finish the book, I'm curious about the origin of the derogatory association with Uncle Tom. Shouldn't literary characters, or anyone, be considered by the arc of their lives, instead of a part of it? Doesn't the climax of a book and character ultimately determine how the character is viewed? This disconnect removes us from an inspirational character who still encourages us today. Uncle Tom represents a triumph of the will and heart, that even in the face of certain death, he commands his response. To some extent, his character tells us we too can choose how to respond to our disrupters.

6. Beecher Stowe, *Uncle Tom's Cabin*, 637.

7. Beecher Stowe, *Uncle Tom's Cabin*, 638.

8. Beecher Stowe, *Uncle Tom's Cabin*, 639.

I find out that the epithet emerges years after the book is published as minstrel shows–usually performed by white actors in blackface–depict him in a negative light. These shows are pro-slavery, changing Uncle Tom from a Christian martyr to a fool. At the time of publication in 1851 Stowe's stories reject the racial stereotypes of minstrel shows, though clearly Stowe weaves her own sentimental racial stereotypes into her characters. While she deserves criticism for this, she, like each of us, is also a person of her time, bound, to an extent, to its zeitgeist. Imperfect as her book may be, it propels the abolitionist cause like no other force at the time.

One way to lament is to read. *Uncle Tom's Cabin* leads me to stories from Frederick Douglass's autobiography and contemporary stories like Isabel Wilkerson's *The Warmth of Other Suns* about the migration from 1918-1970 of millions of African Americans out of the south. Wilkerson points out that "[t]he term *narrative* comes from Greek for the word *knowing*. And I think that that's a powerful message because it means you cannot tell a story until you know the story."[9] Her fifteen years of research involved interviewing more than 1,200 people to make three composite characters in her narrative about the sixty years between World War I and 1970, when more than six million African Americans migrated out of the South. Wilkerson's book draws me into the personal stories of people chafing under Jim Crow laws. I feel a fraction of their anguish and degradation. The book expands and remodels my interior house and rearranges the furniture.

Remodeling one part of the house often leads to other rooms. Colson Whitehead's historical and imaginative stories *The Underground Railroad* and *The Nickel Boys* and Toni Morrison's *Beloved* characters and narratives pull me further in. I'm riveted to these stories. Somehow witnessing their subjection to hardship increases my capacity to empathize. Isn't this a key purpose of reading? I'm reminded that suffering is a universal human experience.

I regret that in some circles my even writing about this as a white woman is verboten because it removes us as humans from one another. It splinters our identities into isolated groups without universal connections. Building empathy is a way to attend to our house, which contributes to becoming more curious and desiring to learn from others who have different experiences. Jalen Rose, retired NBA player and ESPN analyst, calls for engagement when he invokes that "[w]e need people who aren't black, we need people who aren't brown. When you know these things are happening

9. Wilkerson, National Endowment for the Humanities.

in your society . . . have a voice, a legitimate one, lock and step with us, protest with us, not just when it's convenient, when it can be uncomfortable."[10] Witnessing unites us around universal human stories. It's a way to be incarnational, as Christ was.

Be a Witness

The costs of remodeling can be high–going out of our comfort zone, setting aside cherished viewpoints, admitting wrong, becoming agents of change–but the costs of doing nothing may be higher because an unattended house eventually succumbs to dilapidation and decay, both morally and personally.

Why should we care about stories of lament? They are stories of people who chafe under sorrows and burdens, who, like us, don't choose their disrupters. They show us how to cope and persevere and what's worth living and fighting for. These stories validate our stories and connect us with the universal experience of estrangement then and now. They lead to solutions and progress in the march toward justice.

My friend, Lauren, chooses the word "witness" for the power of seeing and validating another's pain. By paying attention, listening, and allowing another narrative–not our own–to breathe, we give it air and allow it to move inside and affect us. Then, instead of telling people to move beyond the past, we acknowledge that they carry their pain and with it their story, even a responsibility to their forebears to remember. Validation–empathy not sympathy–communicates, "I see you. You and I are not the same, but you are not alone." This is a part of the solution and not an insignificant part because of the exponential power of love.

Witnessing leads us to stand up for others. Rwandan genocide survivor Jacqueline Murekatete coins a compelling term as she reflects on the genocide: "People make choices and choices make history . . . people made choices to be bystanders and . . . to be upstanders . . . if more . . . Hutus had stood up and become upstanders—rather than perpetrators and bystanders—I have no doubt in my mind that the genocide would not have happened."[11]

10. Rivera, "Jalen Rose's Passionate Plea After the Death of George Floyd." *Sporting News.*

11. Murekatete, "Facing Today: A Facing History Blog."

The whole world regretted its silence on Rwanda. Are we bystanders or upstanders? Upstanders are "wise as serpents and innocent [harmless] as doves."[12] Upstanders know the power of love as Martin Luther King Jr. persuasively argues: "When evil men plot, good men must plan. When evil men burn and bomb, good men must build and bind. When evil men shout ugly words of hatred, good men must commit themselves to the glories of love."

Lament validates suffering and validation spurs acceptance. When is the last time someone listened to your story as it is without distraction, editorializing, or advice? How did you feel? A first step toward acceptance is to lament loss for ourselves and others.

The Courage to Change

The ultimate reward of lament is that it propels change. It's a mystery how validating pain enables acceptance of the pain. Somehow, this acceptance sparks a motivation to change. Maybe it's because you don't have to keep trying to be heard, and the cloud of lament has lifted to reveal the next step. This is, of course, not always the case because it's easy to turn lament into blame and get stuck there. Change requires courage, and courage requires honesty. Am I willing to acknowledge I need to change? Can I admit I'm wrong? These questions have the potential to make us second mountain people.

People who have the guts to undergo significant change fascinate me, like the Apostle Paul after the Damascus Road experience. I often ponder his state of mind after he gets knocked off course. One moment he is fully committed to persecuting Christians–motivated by a justifiable desire to preserve Judaism which he thinks is threatened by Christ followers–and the next moment he is stopped in his tracks by a blinding light and a voice that pleads, "Saul, Saul, why are you persecuting me?"[13] It's the voice of Jesus after his resurrection and ascension. How does he handle this disruption?

I think about the three days he lies blinded on a stranger's bed without food or drink. Withdrawn from everyone and everything he knows, what goes through his mind in those three days? Does he ask, "Why is this happening to me? Does my blindness mean God is rejecting and punishing me?" Does he know he's wrong? Does he despair of the harm he's caused?

12. Matt 10:16

13. Acts 9:4

Does he wonder if he can face his victims? Does he fear for what's next? Does he worry about his reputation? Does he save face in a culture that values honor? His emotions swirl in the dark chaos.

Perhaps he gets distracted by worry: "What if this blindness is permanent?" Or by guilt: "I'm beyond redemption." Or by defenses: "I did it to honor the Lord; I had the support of the Sanhedrin [government]; I did it preserve our way of life; I had a moral mandate." At some point during those three days, he intuits a radical change is in store for him. But he can't possibly know the extent of his shift from zealous upholder of tradition and murderer of Christians to member of that community and eventually founder of the Christian church to the Gentiles. Everything is about to change, his motives, desires, assumptions, and beliefs. But will he allow it?

Paul's life stands as a witness to an intervention that can't be explained by natural causes. Even if we don't buy into the story itself, we need to explain how the change in his life and the exponential growth of the church happened. These are historical facts in need of an explanation. At this point, however, he's a learned and zealous Jew who is willing to own that his motivations, actions, and devotion are completely mistaken. He finally denies his pride and enters a new life. His story forms my bedrock foundation of the existence of a personal and loving God. Nothing else explains such a change, and even if this is not granted, one is still faced with the question of why Paul changed.

After those three days, Saul is healed of his blindness and baptized by Ananias. Losing his eyesight symbolizes he's bereft of knowledge and so he leaves Damascus–he barely escapes alive–and withdraws to the Arabian desert to learn and reflect. There this learned and zealous man unlearns and redirects his zeal. He views himself the chief of sinners called by God's grace to bring the good news of salvation to the Gentiles. Incorporating loss into one's life allows a person to forge a new identity.

The Christian community needs to change as well. Ananias needs to face his fears about visiting Paul in Damascus and Barnabas his fears to introduce him to the Jerusalem Christians who know his chilling reputation. The other apostles and members of the Christian community must take a risk as well. But the risks pay off and soon they make inroads into communities of the Pax Romana.

Disrupters invite change. At times they invite us to face the consequences of bad behavior. We can fight for the status quo and deny change like an alcoholic or drug user. Moreover, the older we get, the more threatening it feels because more is at stake. It's not until we hit a wall or the bottom and run out of options and excuses that we are open to change. But, actual change is another story which only a few can tell.

It's easy to let disrupters stir our emotions and clarify our priorities and then pull back. Take the example of Chris Cuomo's disrupter, reflection, and next day back-pedal. He is working from home after being diagnosed with COVID-19 at the end of March 2020 when he bumps into the existential part of quarantine. Cuomo expresses major frustrations with his role in journalism, politics, and what it means to be a celebrity on his SiriusXM show in an article on his momentary crisis: "I don't like what I do professionally. I don't think I mean enough, I don't think I matter enough, I don't think I can really change anything, so then what am I really doing?" He further explains that his experience with COVID-19 has made him rethink his values and question what he does. "I don't want to spend my time doing things that I don't think are valuable enough to me personally," he continues. "I don't value indulging irrationality, hyper-partisanship."[14]

The next day, Cuomo takes it all back saying he loves his job. I don't know what changes and what it's like to be in his position. But it's common to have an insight that we don't act on. It's common for a moment of clarity to abut the barricade of the status quo. Perhaps it's too demanding to act on moments of clarity, too destabilizing. But seeing disrupters as opportunities to live better, more open and expansive lives, moves us toward change. Moving toward acceptance has to do with resisting the things that pull us back to the status quo, back to the pulling currents of the river.

Not Having to Have the Last Word

Sometimes change requires admitting we are wrong. Admitting wrong makes me feel ashamed, and I have a hard time with failure. The reasons abound, but regardless of the reasons, I miss out on opportunities to grow and improve, like the time I refuse to watch preaching tapes of myself in a homiletics course in seminary, even though it is a requirement. In my fear of facing the possibility of failure, I deny myself the possibility I might be doing a good job. I do this in other areas of my life. The result is that the accusing voice isn't muffled because I'm not giving myself the chance to update how I view myself.

14. Midkiff, "Chris Cuomo Had a Major Existential Crisis," *Yahoo News.*

I lament that I wasn't trained to deal with failure. What if I heard, "I may have misjudged" or "I may have been wrong about . . . " more often? What about the cliché, "Failure is for learning" or Thomas Edison's famous lines claiming he had not failed but found 10,000 ways that didn't work. Would these things have helped?

What helps me now is to see my therapist again and to accept the good and bad in my own journey. Sadness and joy, failure and success coexist, and ultimately God works through it for our good. I will no longer white-wash, omit, overlook parts of my journey. I know the map of my journey, the roads, the land, and the open spaces where there is no road. I'm responsible to make my own road and to stop the blame. I fold the map and put it away. I feel free. With that freedom comes a love that fills the potholes and paves the broken roads because love "covers a multitude of sins."[15] This is a good start, but I still need a way forward beyond the shame of failure.

A short and unforgettable statement by a person long on insight comes to mind. I take out the journal in which I wrote his lecture notes and pore over them like I'm looking for a lost treasure. The statement comes toward the end of one of Dallas Willard's last conferences in February 2013, three months before his death. Dallas Willard is an American philosopher and influential voice in Christian spiritual formation. A top-grade thinker and debater, he is competent in the art of persuasion. The rare kind of speaker I can listen to for hours, he plumbs depths and makes connections like few others do. His teaching reframes failure and offers me a new perspective.

In an interview-style presentation with Dallas Willard, John Ortberg refers to a story of a student in one of Willard's classes, who challenges him with erroneous statements in a combative style. He pauses and tells the class that that's a good place to end their discussion. Somebody asks him afterward why he didn't counter the student's argument and put him in his place. "I'm practicing the discipline of not having to have the last word" is the professor's response. Thin and frail, Willard expands on this point at the conference with muscle and force, and I never forget it.

Having to have the last word involves gaining superiority. The term applies when a person makes up for the deficiencies of a case, exerts power, makes the final decision, or when something is the most advanced, up-to-date, or fashionable as in "the last word in sports cars." It's neutral, even beneficial, if it engenders competence and expertise. It's harmful, when

15. 1 Pet 4:8

applied to relationships as it seeks to shape the behavior of another person. The harmful effects are far more common than the beneficial ones.

Having the last word is more than just having the final say; it springs from a deeper, more disguised motive, the desire to control by pushing away uncertainty, a dearth of reasons, disorder, or chaos. Some personality types like the Enneagram one experience unique struggles in this area. Ones are called improvers, reformers, or perfectionists; they instinctively see what needs fixing, and they tend to have a strong moral conscience; some call a strong justice gene. Solutions that erase doubt, statements intended to provide stability, and emphases on truth and precision are second nature to ones. They think that saying the right thing is a way to help and improve lives. The motive of control lies submerged in murky waters and is thus hard to detect.

Statements like, "You need to, I'm trying to spare you more pain, I want to show you a different perspective, I'm just telling the truth!" or "I have a special cure" disguise the motive of control. In the cancer world, it might be the certainty of purveying foods to avoid recurrence or the more sinister conclusion that cancer is your fault because you didn't avoid the foods you loved or the stress you put yourself under. Many people create businesses based upon stoking fear in the cancer community. They try to sell people on just about anything. They peddle their products and viewpoints with a force more definite than scientists whose conclusions are based on lifetimes of research and treatment.

In the realm of relationships, having the last word is corrosive over time, but it is often discovered after the corrosion has set in, like the rusting splendors of the Titanic. Is it possible to release its objects from their watery grave and polish them up again? I bump up against the negative effects of having to have the last word on those I love during my recent cancer ordeal. My family tells me that I'm not just a teacher by profession but by personality. I wish this were a celebration of the nobility of the teaching profession. They also tell me why they don't adopt some of my beliefs.

After many deep and difficult talks, I feel anguished and depressed at my failings. I'm angry that I'm left to deal with this hurt in addition to the cancer. It would be a lie to say I accept my failings easily. But I also know that I can't wish away my kids' feelings and that I want to do my part to keep their anger from becoming bitterness. Eventually, I realize I want a better legacy with my children. Thankful that they trust me enough to be honest, I absorb their perspectives and over time there is a fresh love and respect to replace the failings. We are more connected than ever before! Letting go gives me more than I expect. This is the beauty of life on the other side of pretense and control.

Most weaknesses intersect with strengths. I'm a teacher at heart. Teachers correct–better, improve–what's wrong. We've all had teachers. Bad teachers are legendary like Ferris Bueller's Mr. Lorensax, but what are the good qualities? Teachers see what's wrong and apply themselves to make it right. We run a tight ship. We improve our worlds. The "justice gene" within us targets bullying, unfairness, and cheating. We are organized and know how to meet objectives and break down our communication into clear steps. We work against "I can't" and "I don't" and encourage our students to aspire, struggle, and achieve. We connect learning to life and preserve what is true, beautiful, and good. We nurture tender shoots that grow toward the light. Developing these strengths without the weaknesses is an arduous process. How do we change a fundamental part of ourselves? Behavior modification won't work. What works? I return to the thirty pages of notes I took at that conference to find a better way.

Willpower alone is weak; my heart must change. Winning over the heart is more than getting ourselves to believe certain truths, working hard, or making something real by willpower. The will is bad at overriding habitual attitudes and behaviors, and it often leads to defeat. Instead, God first gives us a new heart, as God says to Ezekiel: "Moreover, I will give you a new heart and put a new spirit within you; and I will remove the heart of stone from your flesh and give you a heart of flesh." After this we can change our parts.[16]

Dallas Willard explains that if we take care of the parts, the whole will take care of itself. Romans 12:1 says to present your bodies as living sacrifices through the renewal of the mind. Here's how it works. The heart is the executive center that sets our will toward what is good, the mind sets the scene for what to choose, and the body works by habit. Spiritual practices interfere here: they enable us–ultimately without thinking–to grow into good habits and out of bad ones. Heart change comes through small and sustained tangible practices.

So, what does this mean practically? It starts with prayer and a plan to gradually replace bad practices with good ones. The list includes listening, empathy, not giving unsolicited advice, seeking out people who disagree with us, stating the merits of the opposite side; the list is only limited by the

16. Ezek 36:26

imagination. I don't abandon my principles; I abandon my control only to learn I never really had it in the first place. These tangible practices begin to weaken the old habits, train me in new ones, and build an atrophied muscle that withstands the urge to have the last word.

Are the disciplines just human activities? No, they are designed to meet the grace of God. The soul, the deepest part of the self–best accessed by solitude–brings wholeness and restoration as I place the dimensions of the self under Christ's control. In time, I figure out where the desire to have the last word comes from, and I become willing to not want what I want. That's how the roots of our desires change.

Perhaps the most basic practice is the straightforward word, letting "your 'Yes' be 'Yes' and your 'No,' 'No.'"[17] Yes and no are indicatives, not imperatives; they describe, not prescribe; they don't *sell* a product or viewpoint, but they *share* a state of mind–genuinely. Statements like "I swear to God" added to the simple yes and no are designed to control a response. A person may even succeed in convincing someone for a short time. Ultimately, however, most of our words aren't heard, much less the last word. Not having the last word honors another's freedom and knows that heart change is a personal responsibility. The straightforward word is simple, unencumbered, and sweet.

I hope the sweet water of not having to have the last word stops the corrosion. Maybe in time some of the lost objects can be brought to the surface, even polished up a bit. I'm beginning to see glimmers of hope, new sprouts on a pruned tree.

Accepting my disrupter reveals new possibilities, but I must maintain my focus and not get distracted. As my barge chugs against the currents, I come across enchanting vistas that tempt me to stop, like the siren Lorelei with her bewitching hair. The myth of Lorelei is associated with a steep rock on the Rhine River where fishermen were enchanted by a siren who lured them to their ruin. River travelers of old, hypnotized by her song, crashed on the treacherous rocks. I will not look up at the golden hair that entices me to abandon the arduous journey. I will not listen to the bewitching voice that charms me with empty promises. I will not abandon my journey to accept my disrupter. Somehow, I maneuver safely around the rocks.

Ancient castles and vineyards beckon with their beauty and plenty, and I begin to relax and enjoy my new journey.

---

17. Matt 5:37

Chapter 10

In Defense of Private Ownership

Will-Power Won't Power Me

ACCEPTING MY DISRUPTER LEADS to owning it, but owning my story is not a straightforward or easy process. Distress triggers my defense mechanism of denial, and denial results in compartmentalizing my life. Unable to acknowledge the distress I feel, I minimize and suppress it. This is a useful strategy in acute phases of loss, but it becomes toxic as a habit or way of life. Why? Compartmentalizing eventually compromises integrity. If integrity is a wholeness, like a bridge, in which the parts of yourself are united into a sound structure, then the lack of integrity is a fragmented self, a hypocritical self. Hypocrisy is not just saying one thing and doing another, but it occurs when a person makes a prescriptive statement of something he or she believes but the person's actions show otherwise. Like a bridge lacking integrity, a hypocritical self eventually falls into disrepair, and those crossing the bridge witness its ruin.

Strong-willed parents practiced at compartmentalizing unwittingly pass their practices to their children. I have already described my father's iron will. When he sets his mind on something, he is unstoppable. When he becomes a Christian, he stops smoking and gambling from one day to the next—his way of getting the girl. He even pays restitution to old acquaintances. It's a clean break. Denial has some good effects like turning our lives around and helping us stay strong during hardship. We can detach from our circumstances and figure out a game plan. Denial feels like control.

Will-power does not, however, keep the truth under wraps. As an adult, I discover my dad's pattern of denial in key events of his life. I am in my mid-twenties when my brother lets a casual comment slip in a conversation, "That's probably because dad was married before." In disbelief I ask, "What did you just say?" His statement jolts me because my father inculcated the belief that divorce is wrong and damaging even to the point that I shouldn't date boys from divorced homes. Learning that he was previously married is a shock to my system. I find out that his previous marriage lasted seven years, but it was childless. Never could I imagine divorce to be a part of his life.

It takes me months and years to understand this crack in our family foundation. I never talk about it with my dad out of deference to an unspoken family rule to keep bad stuff under wraps. There's often a feeling of shame over airing family secrets, especially in ministry homes where family dysfunction might end a ministry. Rich, Joy, and the extended family all know about it, but I guess the baby still needs to be protected. How do I process such a profound lie? I simply accept the reality and move on. But deep in my heart I tuck away a theme that well-intended motives have unintended consequences. Keeping information from loved ones to protect them harms them when it comes out.

Years later in the spring of 1984, at the age of sixty-seven, my dad seeks out medical help in Germany for pain he's experiencing. The doctor suggests he might have cancer. What does he do? Ask questions? Schedule tests and biopsies? No, he makes a beeline out of the doctor's office and goes on a vitamin regimen to treat himself. He doubles down on a vitamin called Neutralite, which he took to fight polio back in the 50s. Neutralite features prominently in our family narrative as a miracle drug that slowed the paralysis in his stomach. Highly energetic and determined, my dad wills himself into health once again, and it works, or so it seems.

Six months later, when my dad's body begins to break down, he and my mom come to the U.S. to stay with us for medical treatment. My 6'2" father, defined by unbounded exuberance, is now restricted by whatever is going on in his body. Hunched over the kitchen table, he is barely able to consume the needed calories into his thinning frame. He is listless and quiet, a shell of himself. And still, he drags his body on a two-block walk every day. That is the spirit I admire and want to emulate.

The doctors suspect pancreatic cancer. Just before his exploratory surgery in January 1985, he returns to Germany to take care of his office and put things in order. He is concerned about his work there, he tells us. During that whole time, he is taking one aspirin at a time for the pain. Returning to California, he prepares for surgery. The doctor opens him up only to sew him right back up with the sad news there's nothing he can do. Pancreatic cancer has spread everywhere. Three weeks later he leaves us. Up to the surgery, he doesn't know he has cancer and takes no pain killers! Talk about denial! Denial has a certain kind of power to help him burrow through the pain. It's also a model to others watching. Years later, I tap into his strength when I have my first cancer. "If dad can do it, I can too" I tell myself. His strength inspires me.

Grieving the loss of a loved one can be a rich experience of recognizing the qualities to emulate. It's a clean process of sorting through someone's life and holding onto what is good while also recognizing the bad. But secrets and moral compromises complicate the process of grieving. One day I learn the sad truth about my dad's walks. Instead of merely exercising, he drags his defeated body with a pocketful of quarters to a phone booth. Why? To have final conversations with someone in Germany. Six months earlier, my mom reveals to me she has discovered my dad is in a relationship with a German woman. She doesn't know who it is or for how long, but we suspect it's been many years, perhaps back to my junior high days when he stays in Germany for his work while my mom and the kids are in California. When she confronts my dad, he convinces her it's not an affair, just a friendship. This leaves my mom in limbo for months, not knowing what to do.

My mom is by his side in the hospital following his terminal diagnosis. We kids are there too. It's a rich, meaningful, and intimate time as we share our love, pray, and read Scripture. Each of us has a chance to pay our respects and affirm my dad. Then something inexplicable happens. As my dad's condition worsens, he becomes anxious over something. What could it be? Is there a loose end we need to tie together before he passes? Did we do something to make him uncomfortable. Finally, it comes out in a conversation with my mom. My dad asks my mom if she will continue supporting the woman when he is gone because she is a poor person who needs help. He says it in the tone a preacher uses to convince his congregation to give to missionaries. He feels sorry for this unnamed woman and wants my mom to help her. Incredible!

What do you say to such a request? My mom is simply too incredulous to formulate a coherent response. The fact that he asks this of my mom shows the ridiculous spin he tries to wrap around her. What mental mechanism enables him to carry on a double life as a Christian leader and role model? What web of rationalizations explains the request to help this woman? What is the mind capable of? His death leaves us with questions, confusion, and anger that complicate the process of grieving.

I have regrets. I never talk to my dad about his girlfriend, but I wish I had pressed the issue like I wish I had discussed his divorce. I always felt his unconditional love and acceptance of me, but now I'm left with the impossible task of reconciling these conflicting parts of him? At this point I am seven months pregnant with Andrew. What would I tell him and my future children about the grandpa they never got to meet? How was I to tell of his love, generosity, verve, how proud he would be of them–and now this? Sad stories of duplicity and hypocrisy in Christian leaders leave stains on the church or organization, but what about the family? How do the children process this kind of betrayal? How do they look back on their fathers? How do they hold on to their faith?

On a Scent Like a Hound

I tell this story to illustrate the complicating variables of grieving my father and the long fallout in my life. But there are also benefits that enable me to remain faithful in my walk with God. The experience with my dad leaves me circumspect, mistrustful, and sensitive to hypocrisy. My radar picks up on posturing and self-promotion, on people who tell stories to make themselves the heroes. I question people who claim to have a special relationship with God, say they hear God speaking to them, and offer glib and overly spiritual answers to complex questions. I scrutinize speakers, preachers, teachers, and leaders. I vow to never be a hypocrite and a poser. I cannot, of course, keep that vow as I would wish. Someone once said that if you want a church without hypocrites, you had better leave the church yourself because we all have some hypocrisy in our lives.

Over the years two head pastors betray a congregation I'm in. Both are charismatic leaders of large churches, and both are caught in sexual misconduct. Each experience is like a sock to my stomach. Each one makes me question my judgment of character, especially the second pastor, a member of my small support group whose purpose is to live life together transparently. None of us suspects the problem until it's too late to confront. With shaken confidence, I feel like a fool for being tricked. My boys' faith is also rocked by this experience. I know people who leave the church to go elsewhere and some who leave church altogether. The ranging destruction is hard to take in.

Ultimately, however, the benefits of my experiences with betrayal eclipse the fallout. I learn the value of character over charisma. Leaders must be in their proper position as sinners in need of grace under the headship of Christ. To allow a leader to take me off the path of discipleship is to give that leader too much power. Added to the leader's betrayal must not be my betrayal. That is doubly destructive.

Fortunately, there are other ministry leaders in my life who understand their vulnerabilities and proactively avoid temptation. They keep me invested in the church. I'm drawn to leaders with self-deprecating humor who don't take themselves seriously, people who aren't the heroes of their stories and put aside their pride to point beyond themselves to Christ. These are people like Dallas Willard, John Ortberg, Gary Demarest, Dave Wilkinson, Shawn Thornton, and Rankin Wilbourne, who understand the long and difficult process of spiritual formation. I want to be more like them.

But still the scent of self-aggrandizing reaches my nose too quickly, like a dog sniffing out a substance. Unfortunately, such leaders proliferate in American culture, charismatic people who manipulate others with their oversize egos. Congregations are to blame as well because the results–reaching people for Christ–obfuscate the dysfunction they know is there. Pragmatism compartmentalizes character and results. Compartmentalizing is a difficult pattern to unlearn, but it can be done with practice.

Making integrity a core value in my life requires me to face my own shortcomings. As previously illustrated, I have a hard time owning the failures and weaknesses in my own story. If my integrity is impugned, I immediately defend myself, my ego. That's why I need more than a desire to emulate good leaders; I need ego-denying practices, like not having to have the last word and being vulnerable in front of others. The task of "work[ing] out your salvation with fear and trembling," is, however, God's work, "for it is God who works in you, both to will and to work for his good pleasure."[1] I'm not left to my own devices–or will-power–to complete the process of sanctification. This gives me the courage to be honest about myself.

1. Phil 3:13–14

Owning the Shadow Side

There are two aspects to owning our stories. One is taking responsibility for our shortcomings, and the other is accepting our story as our own, failures and all. For much of my adult life I live with a dissociation between my childhood and adult selves. This is like Jung's shadow self–the repressed content with undesirable qualities one pretends to cut off–which still exists in the self even though we think it is gone. During two major changes in late adolescence–my faith experience in high school and new identity in college–I cut myself off from key parts of my childhood self: sensitivity, shame, conformity, shyness, and ethical lapses. Isn't that what it means when Paul argues, "Therefore if anyone is in Christ, he is a new creation; the old things passed away; behold new things have come"?[2] Yes and no.

When Paul explains his "forgetting what is behind and straining forward to what lies ahead"[3] the context is attaining the resurrection from the dead. He's aware that looking at his past accomplishments is the wrong stance for a runner who wants to win a race. So, he looks ahead. Rather than disowning the past, he lets the past remind him of God's grace. Elsewhere Paul states, "For I am the least of the apostles and do not even deserve to be called an apostle, because I persecuted the church of God. But by the grace of God, I am what I am, and his grace to me was not without effect"[4] as a demonstration that his past failures are a conduit for future success. Instead of losing sight of his past, Paul allows it to remind him of his abiding need for grace, which is something a man of his rigor and devotion easily forgets.

That's not the spirit in which I deal with my past. My second semester in college, I lock my past into a hermetic chamber and look ahead. Determined to never be a doormat again, I turn my anger into action. Isn't that what the experts advise to do with anger? I immerse myself in all the good stuff college life has to offer, and I am happy. Or am I in denial? This lasts through college, graduate school, and my twenties. I'm becoming a more confident person, kind of.

2. I Cor 15:9–10
3. Phil 3:13
4. I Cor 15:9–10

A Pilgrim's Progress

Marrying Rick at the beginning of graduate school is a great blessing. He sees me not as I used to be but as I am now. He helps me turn up my voice when old insecurities surface as I step out to take risks. Speaking and preaching in front of groups unnerves me, but his support blows wind in my sails. There's some truth to the idea that that we choose partners based on past experiences with the parent of the opposite sex. My father's affirmation of me leads me to a person like Rick. Harry is an aberration in this view, and I'm deeply grateful for escaping that anomaly.

With a double major in English Literature and Religious Studies I try to figure out how to make the commitment to full-time ministry a reality. Is it teaching, ministry, or journalism? I take a stab at teaching. I enter Fuller Seminary for an MA in Theology and start a PhD program in Historical Theology. Rick also enrolls there in a PhD program in Clinical Psychology, and we get married in December 1979. We begin the first five years of our marriage as students making ends meet with various part-time jobs while my dad pays our rent in a run-down bungalow. We love it!

I spend time on the basement floor of the library surrounded by theological tomes–many of them in German which is good when the books written in English are checked out. The bad thing is the prodigious sentences of German theologians that run up to a page. Among the stacked up dependent clauses, my mind wanders to my future. Do I want to spend the next five years down here or do I want to be outside in the "real world" ministering to people? Or maybe I should follow the English route and get a degree in journalism. I apply to USC for an MA in journalism and get in. But I'm drawn to theology because it feels familiar and fitting. An intense tug-of-war and time of soul-searching ensues. Uncertainty about women's ordination initiates an intense examination of the Bible's view on women in church leadership. I conclude that I can make a good case in favor of ordination, but I am also aware of the merits of the other side. It's not a foundational subject like the Trinity but a secondary one people can disagree on, I decide.

This decision culminates with suspending my PhD studies and pursuing an MDiv with the goal of ordination in the Presbyterian Church. I apply for a two-year process of being under care of the Presbytery, a requirement for ordination. After graduation, I give birth to Andrew while finishing a part-time internship. I then move into a part-time ministry as singles pastor until giving birth to Alex, after which I stay at home for three years.

My ordination process complete, I stand behind a hefty lectern for my ordination trial in 1989. It's the first time I discover the thrill of fear. As a candidate for ordination in the Presbyterian Church (U.S.A), I give my first major talk to a governing body on why I feel called to the ministry. I am so nervous my body is shaking–I haven't shed my childhood shyness at that point in my life–but the hefty lectern disguises the shaking legs. A few minutes into the speech, my fear disappears, and I look out at the congregation suspended in thought: "This isn't so bad; I'm *actually* enjoying this!" This is a completely new experience for me. Instead of timidly looking up at my fear, I'm confidently looking down on it. As time expands, I hear a beckoning call to enjoy this rare moment. Instead of rushing through the speech, I become more animated. For a shy kid, this is a milestone.

That experience is a significant discovery and becomes my gateway into a new world. Public speaking becomes gradually less intimidating and more enjoyable. The fear remains, but each time I feel more confident and capable. Though I don't seek the spotlight, at least I can thrive under it without losing my mind, which is a common experience for people with speaking phobias–which happens to be the majority of people.

I'm ordained as Associate Pastor in a new church development in Moorpark near my home. I get to start part-part-time with hours gradually increasing to part-time as my sons grow and our third son, Nate, arrives. I enjoy relative autonomy over my hours, and I serve alongside a senior pastor who trusts and affirms me.

Weekly children's sermons aren't too taxing except for moments when my lack of English idioms surfaces. Once, during the first service children's sermon on David and Goliath, I tell the kids that David hits him where it counts. Dave, the senior pastor, does not correct me for the second service. So, I stumble blindly into a repeat of my idiom deficiency only to find out later I did something wrong. That becomes a lasting joke between Dave and me. I'm still looking for a way to get him back.

Every time I preach before the congregation, which is once a month, I face the reality that someone has never heard a woman preach or has a problem with it. A fellow female pastor gives me great advice. She says to expect this not to go away and to let success be my answer. She says to focus on the message instead. The message, coming out of the reliability of the source–the Bible–is what lends confidence and authority. So, undeterred by potential critics, I learn how to prepare and preach, and it turns out that the critics are fewer than feared.

Eleven years later I'm intrigued by a new school project, a start-up college preparatory high school–which eventually also includes a middle school–modeled after the philosophy of Westmont College. The mission of the school thrills me, and I apply. In 2000, I'm hired as the first Bible Department Chair and Chaplain of a rigorous educational approach. Chapel consists of mature reflections on what it means to live by a Christian world view, and the classes include philosophical, sociological, cultural, and literary considerations along with biblical instruction.

The first two years I spend my waking hours preoccupied with curriculum writing. I'm like a pilgrim energized by settling into a newly discovered land.

A Pilgrim's Regress

Then I'm slammed with a seismic disrupter: my first breast cancer diagnosis. I stand in front of the first senior class of the school introducing the syllabus for the Christian World View class my colleague Steve and I labored over for one year. This Socratic style class is unique in weaving together several disciplines and preparing students for college–and life. This class is my pride and joy. Andrew is in this class. I wonder what my seventeen-year-old eldest son is feeling and how he will fare as he approaches college applications and my daunting future.

I tell the students I'm not sure I will be teaching them this year. Devoid of a script and plan, I schedule my chemo treatments for Friday and take Monday off. After that radiation comes before school. I'm hoping I can continue to teach. Andrew is a great support to me on the days when classroom management breaks down and unruly class discussions ensue. Some days the floor beckons me to lie down. What I would give for a short nap! A person on the support staff provides me with a mat to put in the teacher conference room. Some people know how to give the most wonderful gifts!

Despite the brutal treatments, I'm able to teach that entire school year, and I miss only eleven days. On Tuesdays and Wednesdays after each of my six chemo cycles, the students admittedly receive a sub-standard quality of education. But I'm encouraged knowing that education is more than the curriculum; education is also about what students see in a teacher's life when it gets tough. This thought sustains me and gives me purpose despite my weakness.

In the first decade of the school there is explosive growth and success. What starts out as a risky venture with 170 students grows to nearly 1000 students in middle and high school and an acceptance rate below fifty percent. The leadership expands the middle school to a new campus next door at the beginning of the recession of 2008, and we establish ourselves as an athletic, academic, and artistic powerhouse.

But growth brings challenges, and challenges bring change. A consultant is hired to take a top-to-bottom look at our philosophy and mission. I continue as chair until my visit to the headmaster's office, when he prefaces our conversation with, "You're not being demoted, but we want to have a more level playing field." Just like that, I'm no longer chair of the department I founded. The first part of his statement leads me to conclude this *is* a demotion, but the second part leaves me puzzled even after I ask him to explain it. I note his use of language, how disclaimers often reveal the truth and vague idioms obfuscate it. This is useful to me when sorting out people's claims. Meanwhile, I'm left reeling from a new disrupter.

The consultant has the name of a famous general. Unlike a general he spends most of his time in listening sessions, but like one he slaps a hundred plus page "comprehensive" report on the table of what I suspect to be a preconceived vision. Why does the word comprehensive rankle me? Like fundamental change, dismantling institutions, or a complete rehaul, is it the dismissal of what is good in the past that bothers me? He proffers a disclaimer that it is not a referendum on the past, but I'm not convinced. The use of the word comprehensive belies the disclaimer. Words have impact.

I understand the new vision and I sympathize with parts of it. Why not ask me if I'm up to the challenge and give me a chance to adapt instead of demoting me? Instead, I feel like the sensitive and protected child I was, the child who is told she's weak and can't handle the truth. I would much rather be told the truth up front than wonder what it really is. I'm left wondering if they really think I'm not competent or what they think of me. Truth is like a hard jolt that ends soon; opaqueness is a softer jab that goes on indeterminately. The demotion leaves me wondering about my worth in the organization.

Other shifts ensue like changing the name from Bible Department to Spiritual Life. The belief is that students with a positive experience of the Bible and Christian formation will buy into the school's vision and mission more. For our department it means the former role of instructor as teacher/pastor shifts to pastor/teacher. Language may be subtle, but a simple shift in word order initiates a shift in world order, at least in our small world. Academic standards, curriculum, grades, and everything else we do are on the table. User-friendliness rises to the top of the list of priorities. Soon every department of the school is touched by the comprehensive plan.

I stay in the department for a few more years. A friend and colleague of mine quietly replaces me as chair. There are no announcements, no direct words, just an opaque move that gradually becomes transparent. I don't begrudge him the position; I respect him and value his friendship. I do begrudge being treated like a child. Sometimes the desire to protect someone from harm ends up causing more harm because the person is left wondering what really happened. This applies to many areas of our lives. We rationalize by saying things like, "She will be hurt if I tell her! I'm not telling him because I don't want him to worry. I want to protect you." The silence often lands differently than intended. We're left with anger and doubt: "Why am I the last to find out? Do they think I'm weak? Do they dislike me? Do they wish me gone?" The truth, though harsher at first, ends up being kinder in the long run. So, because I lack the courage to address the elephant in the room, the elephant eventually squeezes me out of the room.

To change the animal image, like a loyal Labrador, I stay in the department for a few more years until it becomes clear–no, far after it becomes clear–that I'd do better elsewhere. How do you know when to leave a place? For me, it happens in the confluence of factors through discussions and one-on-one interactions. When people try to change my basic educational philosophy, when affirmation dries up, when I'm excluded from policy-setting meetings, or when my skepticism–actually, "snarkiness"–overwhelms my good will, I know it's time. Others make decisions based on a single clue, but I wait for confluence points. Another teacher tells me right after my "not-demotion" she wouldn't stay, but I'm not as decisive. I secretly wish I were, but I want to preserve the good parts of what we've built. I feel like holding on is for the good of the school. I don't want cave to my disrupter. Call it stubbornness, preservation, or old school, I keep holding on like a loyal Labrador.

My turning point comes through a throwaway statement in a meeting that highlights the trajectory of the department and where it's headed. I don't want to head there. I suddenly know it's time to leave. It is not sudden at all; the confluence has just reached a precipice. Perhaps–no, certainly–I am slow to find my voice, and I hold on too long. But once I reach clarity, I act decisively and don't look back.

I apply for a job in the English department, a consideration I've had before. After sixteen years at the school, I'm subjected to an intimidating interview like all candidates. Halfway through the interview, panic sets in as I'm asked to interpret an unfamiliar poem by Gerard Manley Hopkins called "As Kingfishers Catch Fire." With all eyes on me, I look at the page mute. No idea what to do, I send up an inaudible prayer for help. It's the most stress I've ever felt over an examination. But I love that kind of rigor and what it says about the English people! Unsure about the outcome of the interview, I leave the room. To my delight, I'm accepted as instructor of Rhetoric and Style, an expertly crafted course tying together my entire career. A college dream of uniting English, theology, and philosophy comes true. I've come full circle, but there's more to it; there's the beauty and wholeness of the circle that gives my life purpose and meaning, and "Kingfisher" becomes a favorite poem.

Breaking the Spell of the Inside Circle

There's something deeply encouraging about having the sense that you're being prepared for what's ahead. Shortly before my demotion, my friend Pam sends me a timely–and timeless–essay of C.S. Lewis called "The Inner Ring." She has little idea of its future impact. This essay becomes a pillar and foundation for navigating my way around the desire to belong. Lewis's own words–excerpted below–make the case for the allure of fitting in and the harm it creates.

Lewis argues there's an unconscious choice people make to be on the inside that precedes complicity. In the army–and every institution or social group–there are two systems:

> "one is printed in some little red book, and anyone can easily read it up. The other is not printed anywhere. You are never formally and explicitly admitted by anyone. You discover gradually, in almost indefinable ways, that it exists and that you are outside it; and then later, perhaps, that you are inside it.
>
> There are what correspond to passwords, but they too are spontaneous and informal. A particular slang, the use of particular nicknames, an allusive manner of conversation, are the marks. But it is not so constant. It is not easy, even at a given moment, to say who is inside and who is outside. Some people are obviously in, and some are obviously out, but there are always several on the borderline.

There are no formal admissions or expulsions. It has no fixed name. The only certain rule is that the insiders and outsiders call it by different names. From inside it may be called 'You and Tony and me.' When it is very secure and comparatively stable in membership it calls itself 'we.' When it has to be expanded to meet a particular emergency it calls itself 'all the sensible people at this place.' From outside, if you have despaired of getting into it, you call it 'That gang' or 'they' or 'So-and-so and his set' or 'The Caucus' or 'The Inner Ring.'"

Lewis argues that the desire for the inner ring is

"one of the great permanent mainsprings of human action. It is one of the factors which go to make up the world as we know it . . . Unless you take measures to prevent it, this desire is going to be one of the chief motives of your life, from the first day on which you enter your profession until the day when you are too old to care.

And you will be drawn in, if you are drawn in, not by desire for gain or ease, but simply because at that moment, when the cup was so near your lips, you cannot bear to be thrust back again into the cold outer world. It would be so terrible to see the other man's face–that genial, confidential, delightfully sophisticated face–turn suddenly cold and contemptuous, to know that you had been tried for the Inner Ring and rejected. And then, if you are drawn in, next week it will be something a little further from the rules, and next year something further still, but all in the jolliest, friendliest spirit. It may end in a crash, a scandal, and penal servitude; it may end in millions, a peerage and giving the prizes at your old school. But you will be a scoundrel."

The Inner Ring isn't evil in itself but it

"is most skillful in making a man who is not yet a very bad man do very bad things. As long as you are governed by that desire you will never get what you want. You are trying to peel an onion: if you succeed there will be nothing left. Until you conquer the fear of being an outsider, an outsider you will remain.

The quest of the Inner Ring will break your hearts unless you break it. But if you break it, a surprising result will follow . . . you will find yourself all unawares inside the only circle in your profession that really matters. You will be one of the sound craftsmen, and other sound craftsmen will know it. This group of craftsmen will by no means coincide with the Inner Ring or the Important People or the People in the Know. But it will do those things which that profession exists to do and will in the long run be responsible for all the respect which that profession in fact enjoys and which the speeches and advertisements cannot maintain."[5]

Fellowship with the other craftsmen in the English department is a priceless gift. These are people who sharpen and affirm me. The sharpening inspires me to learn and grow; the affirmation heals my wounds. It's the affirmation of a shared philosophy, having each other's backs, and holding the line together that boosts morale. Words of appreciation also boost my professional confidence. I'm finding a place outside the Inner Ring that feels like home.

Lewis concludes that those who break the quest for the Inner Ring find true community; those who don't, can be broken by it. The words "when the cup was so near your lips, you cannot bear to be thrust back again into the cold outer world" chill me. If the officers next to Derek Chauvin had only been wise enough to thrust back the cup, they may have acted decisively to do the right thing. We, of course, observing from a safe distance, are quick to condemn. But what do we do when the cup is near our lips?

The fear of being ostracized bewitches the cup. This is one of the deepest value-distorting human drives. Teachers see it regularly in students giving into the pressure not to "rat." Their focus shifts from the actual wrong to the greater violation of disturbing group cohesion. Students who rat are vilified and cast out, creating fear of reprisal. As a child, I succumb to the same pressure. I'm not aware of what I'm doing at the time, but years later, I blame myself for my stupidity. Shame leads me to push the foolish self under water. But still, she screams for the light of day.

I Am That Child

How do I release my inner child from shame and begin to own her? For years, my unresolved issues bubble up like a forgotten pot left to simmer at the back of the stove. The hurt and lack of resolution with Harry keeps him frozen in time. Childhood tumult combined with my tendency to dismiss difficult emotions contribute to the simmer. Judgmentalism and fear splatter into my relationships. Instead of taking off the lid and turning off the stove, I double down to undo my mistakes and my parents' inadvertent shortcomings. That is my emotional redemption, or so I believe.

5. Lewis, *The Weight of Glory*, 144–45.

Over time, as I learn about childhood development, I gain insight into the centrality of belonging, especially in early adolescence. I watch how middle and high school students claiming to be themselves have a curious way of doing it just like their peers right down to the socks and shoes they wear. They have emotional radars that interpret askance looks as slights and silences as the silent treatment. I hear wrought stories of being without a friend as an incoming freshman, sitting alone in the cafeteria, and how much that first friend still means years later. I also hear about bullying and cruelty. Belonging is, in fact, a human need that spans the generations, only it's more pronounced in childhood. Over time I look back at myself with compassion and sadness for my wounds. Eventually, I stop blaming myself and as I do, I lift the lid and turn off the heat.

A recent pivotal moment of insight stands out to me. I see a rare picture of myself from high school–frequent moves and no cell phones mean fewer photo memories. I'm seventeen dressed in my hippie clothes next to Harry with a vulnerable look on my face. The clothes show my rising voice, but the face hides that voice. I am vulnerable and afraid. As I look at that picture, my throat tightens, tears well up, and something deep and inexplicable stirs from within me. It's as if I'm looking at a stranger, and I feel deep love for that child. I want to affirm her, to tell her it's going to be okay. Then the tears come spilling out and in the confusion of that moment, something crystalizes. It's the feeling that I am still that child, she still lives inside me, even though that child is grown now. Waves of embrace wash over me and I feel whole. It may sound narcissistic to write this, but it's not. I love that girl I despised for so long, that insecure, quiet girl who just wanted to find belonging and security. I was that girl; I am that girl but so much more now. I welcome her into my heart and will no longer cut her off from myself. That experience is a gift to me from my heavenly Father. Therapy is also a gift. Removing the lid helps me understand and own myself.

Owning one part of the past leads to ownership of other parts. When I look back and see God's grace and redemptive power of transforming my failures and disruptive circumstances, I have hope that helps me persevere and embrace the gifts of my disrupters.

Disrupters reveal weakness and failure, but also strength and success. We become wounded healers healing wounds. Failure is not final, redemption has no limits, and gifts derive from the most unlikely people and places.

Part V

Don't Let Your Pain go to Waste

Chapter 11

Embracing is for Non-Huggers Too

THREE SHORT LINES BY Gary Snyder contain a small world that animates the realm of embrace: "Ripples on the surface of water/were silver salmon passing under—different/from the sorts of ripples caused by breezes."[1]

Embracing is a dynamic process with specific actions. First, it's seeing the gifts below the surface that catch us off guard, like salmon ripples. They're easily disguised, but they are rare and true. The second is shifting attention to the salmon ripples. This means focusing on the gifts that remain below the surface. We don't forget the loss, but we frame it in the light of what we still have or new gifts we've discovered. Third is living in a state of receiving and allowing it to change us. Embracing turns a destructive force into a life-giving one.

A caveat is needed here. This step is not essential for healing. Acceptance is sufficient in some cases because some things simply aren't embraceable, like a child's suicide, a drunk driving accident, a betrayal, or a long-term deception. There's simply no way around the fact that some disrupters bestow no gifts. Some situations simply have no silver linings.

There are other disrupters that bestow modest gifts, like a lean Christmas that withholds gifts until the last moment when small packages start to fill some of the empty space on the tree skirt. At first it appears there's not much under the tree, but by Christmas Eve the gifts spill over onto the living room floor. Many are handmade, most are inexpensive, but all are gifts from the heart. A few months later, we might unexpectedly find a forgotten

1. Snyder, "Ripples on the Surface," 1–3.

149

gift stuffed in a closet. When we open it, we feel the delight of unexpected blessings.

Embracing is the Gift of Sight

Embracing a disrupter is an activity of the heart that discovers gifts where it thought there were none. It is a mindset clawed out by pain. Like the verse "Consider it pure joy whenever you face trials of many kinds,"[2] embracing is a refusal to allow our pain to go to waste. It is more enterprising than accepting because it is a search below the surface for hidden and non-material gifts. Such gifts are cherished and remembered long past December. They weren't on the wish list, but the wish list was incomplete without them. Does embracing the disrupter lead to the discovery of gifts or does the discovery of gifts lead to embracing the disrupter? Yes, to both questions. Embracing opens the eyes of the heart to the unforeseen.

Gifts come from unlikely places and people. They come from small children with honest comments and old people with crusty manners. They come from people we write off as "those." They come from broken relationships we give up on and discover are not lost. They come from undesirable places and circumstances we fear, dislike, and avoid. They come from losing control, running out of steam, and giving up on our best efforts. They come when we turn from ourselves, shift our gaze, and look up. Such gifts are unbidden, but they have the power to transform us. They bind and heal, ground and deepen, enliven and inspire. That's why they are among the most precious gifts.

Wounded Healers Heal Wounds

My cancer story is replete with gifts that catch me off guard. Their disguise makes their discovery sweeter, like the times I feel alive in the infusion room. It's strange but true to say that I experience "flow" there. That's because of two special nurses, Tess and Linda. They offer extraordinary care and compassion to their patients. I want to tell them how much it means to me, so I hand each of them an envelope with two written reflections on them from a previous infusion accompanied by my friend Lauren. Lauren is the life of the party, and fun friends are the best company in dreary places

2. Jas 1:2

like infusion centers. When I tell Lauren after the infusion that I wrote something about Linda and Tess, she suggests giving it to them during the next infusion. She stresses the importance of showing appreciation, and I follow her advice. After handing out my envelopes, I sit down in a quiet corner framed by an arboreal view of pink and purple crape myrtle blooms in the parking lot below. Serenity pervades the room.

My first writing is on chemo fears settling in the clinic during my first fearful experience there. The second one is called "Wounded Healers Heal Wounds." It's an attestation that blessing is born of struggle and turmoil. Here is a part of the second writing:

My first time in the infusion room, I notice Linda, one of the oncology nurses. She injects compassion and courage into the space, where patients of all ages sit in cozy recliners with heated blankets connected to lifesaving, yet life-draining, plastic bags of liquid dripping into the superior vena cava. Most sit quietly, some sleep, others talk in hushed tones with companions; some are alone, and many are subdued with drawn faces.

Linda is the lifeblood of the room, pumping sustenance to the nurses, who fill these brave and struggling souls with cheer. She assists the other nurses but confidently asks for help when needed, governed by an understood rule of give and take. Everyone likes and respects Linda. Even a patient once openly skeptical of her ability to change PICC lines–those annoying externally placed ports to transport chemo to the heart–now feels she is the only one who can do the job properly. He drives an hour through L.A. traffic to the suburban office just to have Linda change his PICC line, a rather simple procedure.

I'm intrigued by the cursive tattoo *Blessed* subtly inked on her dark forearm. When I tell her I like it, I'm introduced to a story of her sister–and best friend–whose chronic alcohol abuse creates a family crisis. After many years of supporting and rescuing her, Linda's family tries a new approach: tough love. She tells a grueling story of taking custody of her sister's two children while also mothering her own son as a single mom and oncology nurse. A restraining order against her pleading sister is enforced. It isn't easy to stay strong; old patterns are hard to break, but after two tumultuous years, her sister starts getting the message. She cleans up, proves her parental fitness to a court, and reestablishes a relationship with her children and family. Her sobriety lasts.

What about the tattoo? Celebrating recovery and renewal, the sisters file into a tattoo shop together to ink identical message on their left forearms. The tattoo declares that blessing isn't a prosperity-gospel outcome or a trite #blessed affirmation, but a firm hope born of trials. Their wounds are a part of their story of blessing, which they wear and share. Linda's story connects me to the theme of Henri Nouwen's book *The Wounded Healer*, that wounded healers heal wounds. It's a mystery how a person with scars becomes a healer. The healing takes flight and cross-pollinates to produce beautiful flowers. Linda's healing is the comfort she offers her patients.

Being comforted propels us to eventually embrace our scars. I'm learning to embrace my body–the double mastectomy, single reconstruction, failed DIEP flap surgery, residual numbness, dogged pain, and scars. Ruthless elimination of comparisons to my life before cancer–to normalcy– is an essential step in the process, where "Why me?" becomes "Why not me?" I can't allow curated projections of the charmed life on social media to beguile me; I must embrace my story, my portion. The scars are treasures in earthen vessels, scars that find others in need of healing. Our wounds create passions; passions connect to purpose, and purpose proffers hope.

Comfort is one of those unexpected gifts. My friend Janet has a freak fall in Yosemite that breaks her shoulder three miles from the trailhead. This happens one week into her retirement. That three mile walk out makes me cringe, but she experiences an out-of-body comfort. She is aware of God's presence because, as she attests, of "the overflowing mercies like the doctor and nurse that meet me on the trail and evaluate me. They have tape and make a splint for me. And the man who gives me a sweater off his back so I could have a sling." The nurse at the emergency facility gives the sticks for the splint to Janet's husband, Brad, who makes a cross for her when they return. Janet reports: "I have [the cross] in my bathroom and look at it every time I'm in there, especially in the nights when I have to get up five or six times. I remember that God said, 'I am here, my child.'" For many months she fastidiously nurses the surgical wounds, applying ScarAway, an adhesive to minimize scars. A year later, still concerned about the scars, she realizes that they are a part of her story now, something to reveal and not conceal, something to integrate into her life to comfort others.

At the previous visit to the infusion center, Tess, another devoted nurse, hands out a devotional booklet I asked about earlier. She and Linda read it together on breaks. We joke about how the media push the message that Christians are becoming extinct, but there are many of us "in a campaign of sabotage" as C.S. Lewis states "listening-in to the secret wireless"[3] when we go to church and spreading hope, courage, and cheer wherever God places us. During Tess's hour plus commute each day, she prays for the patients, nurses, and clinic and looks forward to being at work, even Mondays in an infusion center. I'm awed. Her voice and face convey the confidence of a calling where skill, passion, and joy intersect.

After she reads my enveloped writings, Tess approaches me with a hug and words of appreciation, my love language. We talk briefly and deeply as we've done before. A short time later Linda, tears welling up, embraces me and sits down to let me know she is touched. She's trying to take her sister's advice now because it helps her sister feel she is contributing to Linda's life. She talks of being the giver in the relationship, a bit bossy and in control, but that she is working on it. There's a bounce in her step as she leaves.

Why do I feel so alive? The feeling is intense and invigorating; it's almost like I shouldn't be so happy there, but I am. The infusion center with its poisonous drugs is the epicenter of loss. When you're going through cancer, loss looms and overshadows gains like an imminent bankruptcy. You feel bereft, poor, and needy. Pain and fear crowd out pleasure and enjoyment. You have little to offer others as you put your life on hold. Your world narrows down to healing your body. I feel alive because I have something to give again, a contribution to make, something others appreciate. I'm floating on a cloud of appreciation–for the nurses, for a purpose, for joy where I least expect it–like a cherub on a cloud.

Flow and Calling

I'm in a place of "flow" as seen in psychologist Mihaly Csikszentmihalyi's famous investigations of "optimal experience," which reveal what makes an experience genuinely satisfying. During flow people typically feel deep enjoyment, creativity, and a total involvement with life. I'm feeling flow not as a teacher facilitating a discussion of *Lord of the Flies*, not as a colleague playing with evocative poetry at a department meeting, not as a speaker helping teachers wrestle with world view issues, but as a cancer patient in an infusion center, an unlikely place. Flow isn't confined to conventional places; it can't be controlled and manipulated; it just shows up. Flow flexes because it's connected to who you are, not where you are or what you do. I suspect that this is what it means to have a calling. I've had two professional

3. Lewis, *Mere Christianity*, II.2.

callings in my life: pastor and teacher. Is writing a new calling for me? I'm almost afraid to ask.

These brave nurses have a calling. They voluntarily step into the stark realities of life and death every Monday morning offering cheer, dignity, and kindness. They contribute to my welfare with the noble craft of nursing, and I thank them with my writing. It's more than give and take. There's a synergy that forms a kind of choreographed but free-spirited dance. Design and mystery are suspended in perfect balance. Maybe this is what the plastic surgeon discovered after his grief over the death of his daughter took its course, the power of offering himself to others and feeling appreciated. I glimpse the possibilities of life after why.

A calling expresses a unique self, "that being" which lives within us, as Hopkins captures in his evocative poem:

> "Each mortal thing does one thing and the same:
> Deals out that being indoors each one dwells;
> Selves—goes itself; *myself* it speaks and spells,
> Crying *What I do is me: for that I came.*"

The poem is about how things in nature project their essence through what they do. We, too, express ("deal out") the self ("being") that is inside us. "Selves," a noun used as a verb, puts muscle on self-expression. The self that "speaks and spells" knows itself and why it's here. It's here for more than self-expression, but for a beautiful embodiment of justice and grace in limbs and eyes, as the next stanza advances:

> I say móre: the just man justices;
> Keeps grace: thát keeps all his goings graces;
> Acts in God's eye what in God's eye he is —
> Chríst — for Christ plays in ten thousand places,
> Lovely in limbs, and lovely in eyes not his
> To the Father through the features of men's faces.[4]

Our limbs and eyes are Christ's as we walk with grace and justice. This is our calling.

I appreciate people who embody a calling, and I want them to know it. Nurses in infusion centers and offices, clinics, hospitals, or on the field meet us in our vulnerability and treat us with compassion and worth. They work long shifts, keep their heads in emergencies, direct, encourage, and guide their patients. They overlook crankiness and do the tasks most people won't

---

4. Hopkins, "As Kingfishers Catch Fire."

do, all without causing embarrassment or shame. They remain long after our treatment is done, often unaware of their impact on our lives. They celebrate when patients return to say hi like the young man whose transplant worked in the previous year and is now busy keeping up with his children's soccer and school schedules. He stops by the center to greet Linda and Tess. Nurses mourn losses like another oncology nurse who visits her friend with cancer each day after work as his health declines and fails. Nurses deserve to know how vital their work is, how our hearts bond to theirs forever in times of crisis and fear.

Two months after my last chemo, I return to see Linda and Tess. Warm affection greets me at the door. When I remove my cap with a tinge of embarrassment to reveal a cropped buzz, Linda and Tess instruct me, in a "you-go-girl" tone, to stuff the cap in my purse and wear the buzz with pride. Soon, I'm enveloped in a pep talk with them and the rest of the waiting room staff about the sexy look of a buzz. They're pumping me up like a spirited huddle during half-time, and I'm floating on their affirmations, the miracle of flight where wounded healers find wounds to heal.

I leave the clinic, hat stuffed in my purse, confidently braced against the fall chill and my embarrassment. These nurses show me that even in a place no one wants to enter gifts may still be found.

A Tribute to the Caregiver

My greatest unexpected gift comes from Rick. Sure, I expect him to help me because he is my husband of four decades. What catches me off guard is the tenacity of his love. I sometimes fear that secretly he will tire of my complaints and laments, that having a sick wife will be too much for him. After all, this is the second time he's had to step into the caretaker role. It's often an ignored role, and yet without him I don't know how I'd make it through. There's something inexplicable about putting immense pressure on a person and having that person remain in place unmoved. It's a love that resembles God's love, and it helps me fight.

A moment of intimacy with Rick inside a garden wall stands out as a picture of love during cancer treatment. Electric buzzing in my ears, pool-splashing next door, friendly conversing in the green belt beyond the yard, background noises of weed-whackers, freeway traffic, hummingbirds, and breezes fill the aural space around the back yard. My husband and I are engaged in a ritual, a liturgy, a sacred moment behind a garden wall set aside for us.

Errant wisps of hair, gray and brown, stage their unwelcome comeback between chemo treatments. Their intrusion mars my *FOX* look embroidered on the back of the cap Tracey gave me. So, towel draped over my shoulders, I stand with eyes closed while my husband shaves my head clean with his rustic razor. He kisses my forehead.

Inside the garden wall, a quirky intimacy takes shape, decades of "for better or for worse," give and take, love and respect, though honestly, the heavy lifting is more on Rick's side. He is my protector, wall, and safe enclosure, watching, encircling, guarding me. Steadfast and dependable, he does not give or shift, and his love is fresh each morning. I've always loved the way Rick greets me every day. It's more than his being a morning person; he has a living love, bold, resilient, and undying.

Exposed like a gnarled oak in winter, I worry about exhausting him with my needs and complaints, but he is present and listens to droning lists of irritations. It's one thing to say "I do"; it's another thing to stay true. He stays true. Even after a long day of attending to clients as a Clinical Psychologist, he still attends to me. He fills an invisible void. I've heard stories of spouses leaving under these circumstances. This saddens me. How do they cope? How do they find their resilience?

A crisis can reveal complementary traits in a marriage; differences become less annoying, more beneficial. I have spatial awareness; Rick has emotional awareness. He tunes into the feelings of people in the room. On the Enneagram he has a strong "two" component which is a helper. The Enneagram is a well-known tool which points out the strengths and weaknesses of a trait. Type twos are empathetic, sincere, and warm, but they can slip into doing things for others to be needed. In a crisis, however, Rick's type is like finding the right antibiotic for a stubborn infection. Well suited to his work of more than three decades, he is still energized by it. He expends his energy–an overabundance of it–day after day, month after month, year after year to heal his clients. His work yields pine trees instead of thorn bushes, myrtles instead of briers for a vast, nameless–at least to me–network of individuals and families. I can only imagine the healing balm he proffers because he does that for me at my most vulnerable and brittle point.

The caregiver is a sure safety net. Caregivers brace our falls below the sight line. They experience fear, feebleness, and deprivation, but where do they go for support? They're not the ones with cancer. They're not the ones who tumble. I love knowing that our kids ask their dad how it is for him as he keeps our family and friends informed of my setbacks and surgeries, as he ministers to my aching body and bruised spirit. They intuit the special challenges he faces. His friends know it too. They pour into the hospital to stand by him. Rick is like an unflappable switch board operator in the early days of telephone, efficiently plugging in the cables to answer an extensive network of calls. When the white-knuckle days in the hospital pass, he proudly displays the hospital texts he types into a story to remember the wild twists and turns.

If you wonder how to help a person with a life-disrupter, seek out the caregiver. Simply show up and be present. Ask how it's going and be willing to listen without offering advice. Tune into the fatigue, the fear, the special burden of this role. In so doing you will help the patient more than you know.

Shifting to What Remains

Embracing is a gift for non-huggers who wish to improve their hugging skills. It involves first noticing the gifts when they come. Because they often come unexpectedly, they are easy to miss. That's why we need to notice, and when we notice, we need to let others know our appreciation. A second aspect of embracing is shifting from what is lost to what remains. Loss is still there, but it's the background scenery of a photo providing context.

There's a stirring account in Holocaust survivor Dr. Edith Eger's excellent survival story about the moment she first discovers the power of choice and how this power carries her through the trauma and terror of Auschwitz. Hers is a story of extremity, but it's a universal story that pertains to loss in general. Life is a string of losses, both minor and life-shattering, but the challenge is the same. No matter what disrupter we face, we have a choice that affects our happiness.

Edith and her sister, Magda, both teenagers, are new arrivals at Auschwitz as they stand naked for hours with shaved heads awaiting their uniforms. Their mother is already murdered by the infamous Dr. Mengele, and their father, taken away somewhere, is probably dead too. Edith turns to look at her sister, who has somehow managed to stay at her side through the chaos of being processed in the camp. Run through the echoing showers, shorn, and sanitized, they stand dejected under the eyes and taunts of the officers. Edith turns to her sister and observes:

> "She shivers as the sun falls. She holds in her hands her shorn locks, thick strands of her ruined hair. We have been standing for hours, and she grips her hair as though in holding it she can hold on to herself, her humanity.
>
> Magda finally speaks to me. 'How do I look?' she asks. 'Tell me the truth.' The truth? She looks like a mangy dog. A naked stranger. I can't tell her this, of course, but any lie would hurt too much and so I must find an impossible answer, a truth that doesn't wound. I gaze into the fierce blue of her eyes and think that even for her to ask the question, 'How do I look?' is the bravest thing I've ever heard. There aren't mirrors here. She is asking me to help her find and face herself. And so I tell her the one true thing that's mine to say.
>
> 'Your eyes,' I tell my sister, 'they're so beautiful. I never noticed them when they were covered up by all that hair.' It's the first time I see that we have a choice: to pay attention to what we've lost or to pay attention to what we still have.
>
> 'Thank you,' she whispers."[5]

A simple compliment restores her humanity, and that's what they both need to survive. It all starts with the small choice of a sixteen-year-old.

We are defined both by what we still have *and* what we have lost. Paying attention to what we still have is not a matter of ignoring or submerging a loss. That carries its own dangers as Edith finds out after the war when she tries to push the horrors out of her mind. She later realizes that she must face and work on her emotions, a life-long and uneven, but ultimately healing process. Do we pay attention to both?

According to *The Oxford English Dictionary* the word "pay" is not a transaction—as in paying a debt—but it means to render, bestow, or give, and what's bestowed can be attention, a compliment, or allegiance. The idiom conveys a voluntary action of noticing and focusing on something valuable. When we discover what's worth paying attention to, we invest in making that a focused state of mind.

Paying attention to what we still have is not a choice people can make for us; it's ultimately our choice. Others can hold it out as an invitation if offered humbly. They may try to encourage us with statements like, "At least you still have . . . " or "Look at it this way!" like Edith did for Magda, but

---

5. Eger, *The Choice*, 38.

these are less effective, just as change from the outside is less effective than change from within. The choice comes from the center of our motivations, the heart. Change from within sticks.

Choice is like a camera lens shifting its focus from macro to wide angle and back to macro. As it shifts from macro to wide angle, the item is smaller and less imposing. The focus is more expansive, more embracing. It sees the debilitating reality of loss but also a faint hint of what remains. Then the lens zooms to what remains and it magnifies ever so slightly, like a lens apprehending the iridescent wings on a horsefly or the geometric perfection of a common flower. Something within lifts. The lens finds something beautiful and true.

Pain makes it hard for us to shift our perspective from loss to what remains, but even in our pain the gifts come. One night I feel trapped in my body, and rising desire accentuates the loss I'm experiencing. Visions of hiking in Mammoth in the fall intrude into the word game I'm playing to get my mind off my pain, followed by doubts of whether I can enjoy myself before radiation starts. September travel dreams are on hold; my new electric mountain bike gathers dust in the garage; my former Fitbit scores are out of reach, local trails a distant memory, and boring walks along the flat green belt are a trivial substitute. I can usually reign myself in, tell myself to be patient, focus on the gifts I do have, but desire obfuscates a clear view. Is desire the unseen factor in perspective crashes?

I go to sleep with my lament, but to my surprise I arise with a song, an old and familiar but neglected one, greeting me like a surprise gift delivered to the door. I bump into a famous hymn:

> Joyful, joyful, we adore Thee,
> God of glory, Lord of love;
> Hearts unfold like flow'rs before Thee,
> Op'ning to the sun above.
> Melt the clouds of sin and sadness;
> Drive the dark of doubt away;
> Giver of immortal gladness,
> Fill us with the light of day![6]

The frustration of feeling trapped the night before dissolves. How does this happen, this out-of-the-blue remembrance of a song whose dusty memory hides in my mind's attic? It's a gift. David nails it: "Weeping may

---

6. Beethoven, "The Hymn of Joy."

tarry for the night, but joy comes in the morning."[7] Sadness and joy rub shoulders. As Lent prepares the heart for Easter, so privation prepares the soil for bounty. The ancient practice of leaving the soil fallow or idle every seven years so that the weeds and insects are killed off and the soil becomes fertile again applies here. Fallow and fertile describe the same soil.

Sadness and joy describe the same heart, but sometimes they are separated by a yawning chasm, as many experience at the beginning of the pandemic. A visit to Costco with its clogged parking lot, marathon lines, and frantic customers pushing glutted carts reveals the distance between sadness and joy—and fear and peace. Sadness encrusts the heart, jams it shut, seals it off. The immunocompromised, elderly, or vulnerable feel this intensely as do those prone to depression and anxiety. They take precautions and follow the guidelines against the virus, but they are stuck in fear of what's next. Business owners are unsure if they can weather this storm. Milad, a friend of mine, is sealed off from the world behind the massive walls of Bethlehem in the Palestinian Authority. Disease and fear teem inside the walls. Yet, he finds ways to serve food and minister Christ's love by making bags of food to hand out to his neighbors and strangers. Is it even possible to be joyful during times like this?

Open Wide Your Hearts

The heart doesn't automatically unlatch to receive joy and peace. But lament and joy coexist. We need to open wide our hearts to the gifts at the door, to pluck and place them where they can be enjoyed. Author Kate Bowler credibly affirms the coexistence of "events that are wonderful and terrible, the gorgeous and the tragic" when she attests that "these opposites do not cancel each other out." She sees "a middle-aged woman in the waiting room of the cancer clinic, her arms wrapped around the frail frame of her son. She squeezes him tightly, oblivious to the way he looks down at her sheepishly. He laughs after a minute, a hostage to her impervious love. Joy persists somehow" she comments, "and I soak it in. The horror of cancer has made everything seem like it is painted in bright colors." Bowler concludes: "I think the same thoughts again and again: Life is so beautiful. Life is so hard."[8]

---

7. Ps 30:5b

8. Bowler, *Everything Happens*, 123.

Gerard Manley Hopkins's imperatives in an Easter poem invite us further into this posture of receiving joy amidst sadness: "Beauty now for ashes wear,/Perfumes for the garb of woe,/Chaplets for dishevelled hair,/Dances for sad footsteps slow;/Open wide your hearts that they/Let in joy this Easter Day."[9]

These short words "open wide" with their long, pleasant vowels stretched out for notice, evoke a visual image of an Italian woman eagerly flinging open aged green shutters in the morning to see what the day feels like. Smiling, she looks up, wide and open, poised and receptive to the day.

Sometimes I am too tired and focused on my pain, fatigue, or worry to open wide my heart. Many people are figuratively asleep or too preoccupied with their lives to open the shutters with anticipation and hope. We are fearful, distracted, limited by our industry, even cut off from the beauties of nature. These lines of a doleful Wordsworth poem spring to mind: "The world is too much with us; late and soon,/Getting and spending, we lay waste our powers;–/Little we see in Nature that is ours;/We have given our hearts away, a sordid boon!" He exposes the cost of blindness to nature from "getting and spending" and the harm of consumerism that cuts us off from nature, which cannot be bought and sold. Giving our hearts away to "a sordid boon," a vile reward, we lose sight of the intimate interactions in nature, the free play and beauty all around us: "This Sea that bares her bosom to the moon;/The winds that will be howling at all hours,/And are up-gathered now like sleeping flowers;/For this, for everything, we are out of tune;/It moves us not."[10]

We cannot see the intimacy and wild play of the sea baring "her bosom to the moon," the way the moon moves the ocean tides and the stillness of the winds because we are unmoved, asleep, and severed from nature. The quiet moment like up-gathered sleeping flowers, now dewy and opening to the morning light, is thrust out to me by a generous hand saying, "Good morning! Here you go. Enjoy!" All I need is to open wide my heart, notice, and receive. So, I place the still-closed daffodils I bought amid the frantic crowds of the pandemic's start in a white bud vase and grab a half-read book. Solitude and peace surround me.

I often awaken to songs I haven't heard in a long time. What stirs a dormant verse? There's a mystery to it. Some say it's just processes in the

---

9. Hopkins, "Easter Sunday."
10. Wordsworth, "The World Is Too Much With Us."

brain we don't yet understand, but I say it's a gift, a morning kiss from the One who loves me more than anyone.

Huckleberry Hill

Shifting from what's lost to what remains happens in the more mundane parts of life, like thwarted plans. My vacation plans are slammed two years in a row. Minor setbacks in the overall scheme of things, these plans represent more than just a delayed vacation. Rick and I arrange a trip with friends in Sprinter vans through Yellowstone and Glacier National Parks the summer of my recurrence. It's a retirement dream, a milestone celebration of connection with friends and the land where animals are not squeezed out by urban sprawl. Big Sky country's elk, antelope, fox, wolf, bear, eagle, osprey, trout, rivers, smells, and landscapes bring me back to a lost era. I want to linger in the Lamar Valley to spy furtive forest creatures emerge in the long northern dusk, to hike the vanishing glaciers while there is still time, even to boondock in a smartly equipped van. Everything is planned and paid for; the excitement mounts, and then my cancer returns after seventeen years. My life is derailed. One year later, poised to seize the postponed dream, the virus hits. Our dreams are deferred, but our hearts aren't sick because, between these two events, an unexpected gift drops in our lap.

This gift is more than an experience; it is an unearthing. Between my second and third chemo treatments, my friend Tracey invites us to stay in her remote Montana mountain retreat. The effects of chemo have set in, but I decide it's a welcome respite. As our plane shakily approaches the landing in Bozeman's mountain-ringed airport, a wide line of gray storms drops afternoon loads in the west. The partially obscured sun throws a blueish-green blanket on the mountains and meadows below. A downpour of olfactory delight with hints of grass and grain greets us at the terminal. The luggage is delayed by lightning on the runway. We leave the airport to enter Big Sky country–the sky moving, playing, dancing–with weather events flashing, like a Las Vegas marquis.

We head to Tracey's house in Bridger Canyon, which always brings me back to Switzerland's mountains, meadows, streams, and cows. At the top of her driveway, Ross Peak crowns the view triumphantly. This is why they chose the property! Inside the lodge-like great room with a sense of place, furnished with generous timber, wood, and stone, the eye is pulled to a wide view of Sacajawea and Ross Peaks connected by miles of lush pine. The wind roams through the trees pushing a forest fragrance inside, and I am at peace with the prospect of spending a week in this soulful place. I feel connected to the lively solitude of this land.

In the morning we search for huckleberries, the iconic little fruit of the Northwest. We stuff bags into our pockets at the last minute. Not far from the house in the woods, we spot delicate bushes sprinkled with fruit and begin to pick and sample. As we trail away down a bear path with Timber, Tracey's German Shepherd, to watch for us, we stumble on a large patch of deep purple huckleberry bushes laden with fruit. Their sheer amount requires us to sit on the ground to pick them. Like happy children unconcerned about the wet ground, we contentedly immerse ourselves in our task, stuffing our bags and mouths. It's as if time stops and the future doesn't matter. Plump bags full of these wild delights are our reward. As we return to the house, we joke about beating the bears to the berries and leaving some behind for them. The fruit that tastes like blueberries with a tartness of currants and wild forest makes delicious pancakes the next morning.

That next day a visitor arrives on the bear path, a large cinnamon black bear lumbering up with its snout in full operational mode, sucking up thousands of leftover huckleberries, like an industrial vacuum cleaner. Squealing with delight, we jump to the window to watch this fearsome creature from a safe distance. The next day, the bushes are completely stripped of fruit. Feelings of awe mixed with enchantment rouse us.

The gift of huckleberries–and a bear sighting–is more than the experience itself, it's an unearthing, a discovery more than a pursuit. It's a clean, unfiltered, and natural immersion in the moment–the feeling of enchanted freedom–that chases away worry. When you boldly announce, "The future doesn't matter!" you've unearthed a gem. Maybe this is what "unless you become like a child" means. You tap into the wild and carefree default position of a child's heart, which lives closer to the present than the past or future. Like a child, you are pulled by the centripetal force of delight into small moments. The child does not measure out its energy, but it plays until it plops. It revels in a moment of delight. This gift is incorruptible and portable.

Transporting this gift to the present requires intention, not being distracted by the artificial, loud, and urgent that siphon away so much of our time and energy. Distractions from the outside and from within ourselves derail most of us, even seasoned solitude-seekers and creatives like author and poet Mary Oliver: "It is a silver morning like any other. I am at my desk. Then the phone rings, or someone raps at the door. I am deep in the machinery of my wits. Reluctantly I rise, I answer the phone, or I open the door. And the thought which I had in hand, or almost in hand, is gone. Creative work needs solitude. It needs concentration, without interruptions. It needs the whole sky to fly in, and no eye watching until it comes to that certainty which it aspires to but does not necessarily have at once. Privacy, then. A place apart — to pace, to chew pencils, to scribble and erase and scribble again."[11]

Like creativity, enjoying the moment is interrupted by distractions. We often think of distractions as intruders from the outside like demands of the clock that "is fettered to a thousand notions of obligation"—call the dentist, finish the report, buy mustard, remember mom's birthday—but the most perilous distraction comes from within us, from "the intimate interrupter," "the watchful eye we cast upon ourselves"[12] which avoids solitude and concentration. Oliver contends that creativity and art rarely come among crowds and busy places, but in nature or quiet spaces, in swaths of time impervious to interruptions.

Eliminating distractions creates the conditions to access the gift of being in the moment. Moreover, this gift lasts beyond the moment and can be recalled at any time. I take time to remember, sift, and mine the meaning of a past joy. I do more than simply call it to mind; I taste and savor it with my senses and heart–sensitive and attached to it–until its essence emerges, until I know what it means to me. Writing conducts me there. Others find it through prayer and meditation. Whatever the means, I find the purest and most real enchantments with a sober mind and open heart. The apex of "Huckleberry Hill" is the affirmation that the future is unimportant. It's the enchantment of a present moment chasing away future worry, those fleeting experiences of eternity in the now where truth abides. Isn't this a universal craving?

I want to discover more "Huckleberry Hill" times, even during the ennui of the pandemic and staycation. All it takes is memory, feeling, and time. I don't want to regret missed opportunities to receive. What if we feared regret more than not meeting time's demands?

---

11. Oliver, *Upstream*, 23.

12. Oliver, *Upstream*, 30.

Chapter 12

Please, God, Don't Let me Lose
the Lessons of Pain!

PAIN LEADS TO GRATITUDE, gratitude to looking up and around with sharper eyesight. But when the crisis ends it's too easy to look down again to the problems, complaints, and fears of life. As the crisis wanes, I fear losing the lessons of pain. Normalcy threatens that intense appreciation for life and movement toward embrace.

After my chemo treatments, Tess and Linda whoop as another nurse extracts the twelve-inch one millimeter tube from my arm to the heart, the vexing PICC-line that tapped my raw, post-surgical nerves for over two months. PICC-lines are usually easy and benign, but not in this case. It takes five tries over two days on both arms to insert it in the left arm near the surgical failure. Why not in my right arm? Even a relatively easy procedure of inserting a passport under the skin proves difficult. My right superior vena cava is gone with tiny bypass veins forging new paths, like drivers using Waze for the quickest route through traffic. In less than a minute they take out the tube and tell me to return the next day to insert the PICC line on the left side. After three unsuccessful tries it finally works, but it's a constant source of pain and annoyance. Two months later, the nurse removes it within seconds, and the removal marks a turn from immobility to movement, control, normalcy. I am soaring with gratitude, but will it last?

Pain wakes up appreciation, not a feigned "thank you" but a heart-heave, fresh, tasty, and satisfying. It slows me down to notice the things I appreciate in this beautiful life: the support from my husband and kids, the sweet-smelling head of my grandbaby, the welcoming hugs of my preschool granddaughter, even the fact that my family invites me into their challenges and struggles. It's vital to contribute to someone's life when you have cancer because your agency and purpose are stripped down. Being shielded from problems only increases the isolation and ennui. These are just a few of the countless daily-bread gifts. I experience life as received, not produced.

It's entirely possible to pack away the gifts of pain in the closet. The seventeen years between my first cancer and the recent recurrence are times of forgetting for me. Life without treatments, regular appointments, and worry pull me back into the daily grind of plans, control, and petty concerns. I run through my days task-oriented, emotions pushed to the periphery, tending to responsibilities. Sure, there are times of slow-down, but my *life* isn't disrupted. Cancer stops me completely in my tracks, but it leaves something valuable, a place of tears, a deeper dimension of connection to God, people, even myself. I worry that I won't hold onto these benefits.

Swiss Soul Food

Sensory pleasures are the conduits to these benefits, which keep me in the realm of embracing my disrupter. I need to keep my senses alive, to savor this embodied life. A smell, sight, sound, touch, or taste conducts a memory; the memory stirs a feeling and a thought. A soft spring rain in Southern California connects me to joy again. It's between a pour and a drizzle, just enough for the arid soil to say "Ah!" A moist waft of cut grass and sage enters the room, an olfactory delight that awakens the senses. I breathe it in and notice fog ringing the hill above my house. The smell and sight carry a memory of Swiss alpine landscapes, summer heat cooled by the slap of afternoon thunderstorms, steep hillsides decorated with charming chalets and weathered structures for cows with ringing bells, an earthy steam of the sun on rain-splattered paths deluged with amber slugs as big as cigars. The delight stirs the thought of grace and receiving.

Appreciation is a product of the sensory connecting with the transcendent. As a young child living in Germany, we vacation in the chalet of a generous friend in Grindelwald, Switzerland with plunging green valleys below the granite monuments of the Eiger, Moench, and Jungfrau mountains. We stand under the waterfalls of the Lauterbrunnen Valley, enfolded by the whoosh of mist and stream. There I wear my Lederhosen with suspenders over a bare chest. There I fall in love with St. Bernard dogs and

Alpine flora, the redolent meadows bursting into vivid color, the incomparable deep periwinkle of *Enzian* (gentians) and Forget-me-nots. Before *Enzian* are put under protection, my mom offers a prize to the first one to spot one of these delicate funnel-shaped beauties that live at the higher elevations. Wildflower bouquets grace the dinner table. These memories link me to an openhanded God.

This Swiss gift multiplies as I introduce Rick and the boys to Grindelwald on several occasions. The cows, lizards, and amber cigar slugs fascinate the boys. On a trip with my mom and six-year-old son, Nate, he chooses a special travel companion from his vast collection of beanie babies. It's a green snake called Hissy. As we stand under the Lauterbrunnen fall next to the wild stream it creates, the snake suddenly slips out of his hands and into the rushing water. "That's gone!" I hopelessly conclude. Quiet tears of disappointment become a wail from deep in Nate's heart when he realizes his Hissy is gone. How can I deprive him of his beloved companion? I must do something.

With prayer and determination, I hike down the slippery rocks of the stream just steps away from the glacial turbulence of the nearby Weisse Luetschine river tumbling wildly toward twin lakes in the valley below. An hour later, there is still no sign of Hissy. How can I return empty-handed to my hoping son? I'm on the verge of calling off the expedition, when I spot a green mass like moss hidden in the cleft of a stone. I pick my way through tangled bushes over wet rocks and there is Hissy, wrapped around a rock near the precipice of the river, like a capsized kayaker holding on for dear life. I rush back to where Nate is waiting with grandma. His jubilant face and cry of delight as I hold up the soggy snake is worth it all! Hope is restored. Years later, Hissy is packed into a hamper with other stuffed animals, when Reese discovers him, and I tell her the rescue story.

Being human is a rich experience of sensory memory–both good and bad–that grounds us. Do we only remember the good, not the bad? Stuffed in a closet, the bad becomes dusty, crusty, and unredeemed, but when remembered, it breathes and benefits us. Bowler's experience after her grim diagnosis is as if "floating on the love and prayers of all those who hummed around me like worker bees" with everything "like it is painted in bright colors."[1] Is it too bold to claim that pain reveals the bright colors of this life?

---

1. Bowler, *Everything Happens*, 123.

Can You be Happy and Sad at the Same Time?

It's uncomfortable living with the extremes of joy and sorrow, good and bad, friend and foe. Simplistic thinking resolves the tension of opposites by avoiding situations that arouse discomfort. Humans are adept at minimizing pain and maximizing pleasure. It's common to push away one extreme feeling or another, huddle with like-minded people, cast those we disagree with into far-flung corners, or demonize the other, all to decrease the tension of living with painful realities of life. A simple–but profoundly challenging–solution is to feel the pain of knowing opposites. How do you process in your soul the pain that comes from knowing things that are not so great? Look to people who are practiced in this art like Bowler's trained eye that sees "the wonderful and the terrible, the gorgeous and the tragic."[2] This is the eye of appreciation.

Is Ignorance Bliss or Misery?

Perhaps the most profound temptation we face is to prefer ignorance to reality. I remember the moment I discover Santa Claus isn't real, St. Nicholas in my case. Just as Santa calls me to come forward in a family friends' living room, I glimpse a familiar face behind a fake beard. In an instant six years of St. Nicholas hopes and joys collide with the face of Mr. Reinhard, our family friend. Should I continue to walk toward him or announce my revelation? Unwilling to invade my bliss any further, I proceed to sit on his lap. In that moment I implicitly understand that ignorance is truly bliss.

Childhood does and should have a certain amount of bliss. Children do not share the burdens of responsibility and knowing life's complexities. Like a sapling tree that is staked for support, parents protect their children from storms that threaten to break them. Eventually, when the trunk is stable, the stakes are removed. Information is shared on an as-needed and age-appropriate basis. As independence develops and the child's mind becomes more mature, the child stands firmer in the storms of life. So, ignorance has its place for a while.

Ignorance is bliss goes back to a British poem which concludes, "Where ignorance is bliss, 'tis folly to be wise."[3] Adam and Eve illustrate the truth of this idiom when Eve eats the apple from the tree of knowledge after God

2. Bowler, *Everything Happens*, 123.
3. Gray, "Ode on a Distant Prospect" Stanza 10.

specifically asks Adam not to partake. Adam and Eve lose their innocence and special status in Eden and bear the terrible consequences of their disobedience. Through their decision, driven by curiosity, they–and we–lose Paradise.

Since then, *ignorance is bliss* is more of a temptation than a desired state of mind. The temptation to plug our ears is acute in a world overloaded with too much information and dire need. How do we cope with a formidable prognosis, significant loss, or crushing circumstance? Shielding ourselves from the stark realities of life is not the answer. If Jonas Salk, who developed the first vaccine for polio, had been ignorant of the suffering polio caused, there may still be polio. If Mahatma Gandhi had no knowledge of the suffering of his own people, they might not have obtained freedom. We need a game plan to maintain confidence and a semblance of happiness, not to mention to benefit others.

It's not only more real to embrace the juxtapositions of life, but it is also more blessed to do so. When we compartmentalize the wonderful and the terrible, delaying our happiness until the terrible goes away, we pursue a vapid course of action. A commonly promoted parenting myth is, "I'm only as happy as my saddest child." Every parent understands this statement. Our hearts are intricately woven together with our child's heart, and the bond never dissolves, no matter the pain. It is a falsehood, however, to believe the myth that we can only be happy once the terrible is gone. There's a remedy in breathing in both these realities at the same time, of allowing them to take up space in our lives. We can find happiness amid deprivation, sorrow, and pain. We don't have to condemn our disrupters.

It's also like that with the people we know. I think the world of someone until I get to know him or her more and the flaws are revealed. Perhaps someone hurts me deeply and I want to write that person off to ease the pain, but the pain doesn't go away. First thing in the morning it ambushes me and creeps in throughout the day. I feel like I can't cope with the hurt. Then it dawns on me that my heart can feel pain and joy at the same time.

I marvel that the same lungs that breathe in a fragrant rose exhale a heavy sigh of sadness. The same ears that hear a merry fountain perceive a looming portent. The same heart that springs grateful for life's pleasures is also a broken heart. Our hearts and minds are capable of more than we think. When we put them to the test by allowing the juxtapositions room to be, we discover a capacity for joy amid pain where the poor in spirit become the blessed.

Keeping together the wonderful and terrible helps me endure hardship and find joy. Joy resides in the resistance of all or nothing thinking–making people all good or all bad–and living with the tension of good and bad in a person, knowing that this is part of the same person, knowing this is true of me as well. I can affirm, "You are more than the hurt you're causing me." You are loved and valued by God and by me. Once we gain God's eyesight–God sees the evil and the pure–we are better able to cope with the darkness. This joy amid the terrible keeps the terrible from wearing us out.

Embracing the wonderful and the terrible is not only an individual pursuit; it's a community pursuit. Like Alexander in the children's book *Alexander and the Terrible, Horrible, No Good, Very Bad Day*, we discover that some days are like this for other people. We are not alone. Vast networks of people living with opposites offer hope and strength for us on the fraught and free journey of life. We need other people to develop a game plan that resists the temptation to be ignorant of the terrible.

A Community Coalition

I turn to *The Odyssey* for a game plan. Two years after retiring from teaching upon my cancer recurrence, I return to teach a Grammar and Composition class to mostly freshmen. High school English literature is among the best of the world's literature, and I feel blessed to be in a classroom again where I get to discuss great writing with universal application. Homer's classic of Odysseus' return to Ithaka after twenty years of war and hardship provides a valuable lesson on the temptation to believe ignorance is bliss. Lady Kirke, the enchantress, on whose island he has been marooned for a year–admittedly, it wasn't all bad for him there–has just revealed to him the formidable obstacles of the sirens he must face on his journey home. No one would blame Odysseus for preferring *ignorance is bliss* at this point on his treacherous journey. But he does not give in because he wants to see his wife and son, and he has withstood fiercer battles.

Kirke's advice on how to get past the sirens contains a practical lesson for us today. She enjoins Odysseus to "[l]isten with care to this, now, and a god will arm your mind."[4] The verb "arm" indicates that the upcoming temptation is a battle requiring the resolve of a soldier. Kirke does not whitewash the intense consequences of not heeding her advice but warns, "woe to the innocent who hears that sound! He will not see his lady nor

4. Homer, *The Odyssey*, XII. 47.

his children in joy, crowding about him, home from sea; the Seirenes will sing his mind away on their sweet meadow lolling."[5] Ignorance is, in fact, misery.

It is prudent to be aware and foolish to be ignorant. Those who are unaware of the dangers will see death because the sirens will sing away their minds. Homer's diction contrasts the sweetness of the song with the bitterness of its consequences. The phrase "on their sweet meadow lolling" indicates that the temptation does not appear bitter or dangerous, just sweet and inviting, which has parallels to the Adam and Eve narrative. Perhaps *ignorance is bliss* is our great temptation this side of Eden.

Wisdom and knowledge are not, however, enough; Odysseus must have a game plan to make it past the sirens. This is key. He must take action to prevent the knowledge from causing harm. Odysseus is a wise leader here because, rejecting the proposition that *ignorance is bliss*, he shares Kirke's advice with his men to prepare them for what's ahead. To Kirke's flowery description of the temptation Odysseus adds, "Seirenes weaving a haunting song over the sea we are to shun . . . and their green shore all sweet with clover."[6] He understands the hypnotic allure of temptation and the vulnerability of his men, and he takes appropriate and decisive steps to protect them against themselves at this crucial time. Good leaders know when to step in and when to hold back. They know a practical plan inspires confidence to avoid retreat and defeat.

The game plan centers on the limits of willpower, an experience we all have. Research shows that willpower is like a muscle but a weak one which gets tired when you use it too much. Something more is needed. Kirke warns Odysseus to "[s]teer wide" and "plug your oarsmen's ears with beeswax kneaded soft"[7] to completely block their cry. Steering wide is not enough; they are not allowed to hear the siren cry at all. This is a good kind of plugging one's ears. They are plugged not to avoid knowledge but to defeat temptation. It is precisely a lack of awareness of our limits that causes us to put our heads in the sand and pretend all is well.

Odysseus may hear the siren song, but he must be tied to the mast. If he cries to be untied, he will be "lashed to the mast."[8] The verb "lashed" is harsh and cruel, evoking images of slavery. Odysseus will become a slave to

5. Homer, *The Odyssey*, XII. 50–54.

6. Homer, *The Odyssey*, XII.194.

7. Homer, *The Odyssey*, XII. 57–58.

8. Homer, *The Odyssey*, XII. 62.

temptation if he is not lashed tightly to the mast. Odysseus needs his crew to save him from himself when the temptation proves deadly. Willpower, which Odysseus possesses in abundance, is insufficient to get him and his crew home. Because effective leaders and prudent people understand their limits, they maneuver the storms of life with confidence. A good game plan is developed in community with others and is mutually supportive. Without one, we are overcome by fear and temptation, rightly so because the chance of failing is high.

Do you have such a community? If not, take steps to find one. If you do, be honest with them and depend on their help. We all need somebody to lean on when we get knocked down and our heads want to land in the sand. This is where we discover a different kind of strength. This is where we discover a profound appreciation for life.

More Physical and More Spiritual

One of the great surprises in my cancer journey is that the acceptance of the beautiful and terrible strengthens an impulse to enjoy life more. This is the deep secret the Apostle Paul reveals in the statement that God's "power is made perfect in weakness."[9] Cancer makes me more physical and spiritual at the same time. I used to judge people who buy stuff when they have cancer like my miserly germaphobe cousin, Ursula, a doctor's wife in Beverly Hills. Ursula bans germs, luxuries, and controversies from her life. At family gatherings, we are not allowed to cough, sneeze, or bring up God. She entertains us with impressive tricks taught to her ersatz child, Conchita, a groomed poodle with pastel bows and embellished collars. Ursula is an avid bargain-hunter and coupon-clipper. For years, a rumor circulates about her sewing designer labels into bargain basement clothing. (After she dies, I find out it's true.) When leukemia strikes, she abandons a lifetime of fastidious frugality and plunges into a luxury buying spree. I used to mock her spendthrift ways. I understand them now.

Is it a form of denial, giving you something to do instead of thinking about death? Perhaps, but I now think that explanation is too shallow. It is certainly true that many, if not most, people live in denial of death as existentialists and psychologists like Ernest Becker posit, but that's not the whole story. There's something about facing death–not just abstractly–that makes this life so dear. I want to experience the world with all my senses. I

9. 2 Cor 12:9

172

want to absorb the beauty and wonder once again like a child stomping in a puddle in rain boots.

As Christians, why do we think that spirituality diminishes the material, that truly letting go of control means being more other-worldly? Why do we disparage our physical desires even though illness punctuates their pleasure? Are the spiritual effects of cancer really more noble than the corporeal ones?

Throughout my recovery, the stately, mid-century tree that fills the view behind the garden wall, allowing hills to peek through in the distance, is my steadfast companion. This tree fills up my senses every day. People also fill me with delight. Giving family members, friends, cancer survivors, and strangers are the hands, feet, and hearts of this beautiful, embodied life. I admittedly spend too much time on Houzz.com and at garden centers. I savor a fruity red blend in the jacuzzi as the sun sets. Breezes and rushing winds in trees–especially aspen groves–beckon me to a higher place. No Zoom session or online experience comes close to the fullness of the physical.

Cancer also makes me more spiritual, more surrendered, trusting, and at peace. I experience this through time spent in the ER and ICU, and through mounting setbacks and surgeries. God's palpable presence, like a cloud that parts for a moment, an epiphany of sorts, confirms that I am not alone. I realize this is my greatest gift–and need–in this life, and a peacefulness saturates my heart, readying me for what lies ahead. I learn incalculable spiritual lessons. Confined to a bed, my agency and independence stripped away, I grasp more fully that control is an illusion. I live one day at a time because I have no choice. Once I start feeling better, the joy of physicality becomes intense and almost transcendent. In my rush to recovery, however, I fear losing the benefits of pain: the sharpened sense of appreciation, empathy, and connection.

Does Christian spirituality diminish the material? Does it teach that truly letting go of control means being more ethereal? Certainly, there is the reality of being a citizen of heaven, but does this mean I devalue the physical realm? Perhaps by elevating the spiritual over the physical, Christians are adopting a soft form of dualism. Many people today advocate separating the two especially in the public sphere because they fear the spiritual will taint or create bias and prejudice. But this fear demands that people cut off their spirituality from their lives, shutting off the valve to their values and meaning in life. C.S. Lewis argues against ethereal spirituality: "There is no good trying to be more spiritual than God. God never meant man to be a purely spiritual creature. That is why He uses material things like bread and wine to put the new life into us. We may think this rather crude and unspiritual. God does not: He invented eating. He likes matter. He invented it."[10] Contrary to popular appraisals of Christian belief as otherworldly, God affirms the body.

The apostle John and the patristics, the early Christian theologians, promote an embodied life as a core belief, emphasizing the incarnation of Christ against Gnosticism,–"the Word became flesh and dwelt among us"–the human body as a temple of God, and the physical resurrection of believers, among others. That is not to say that the universe is God, but that the transcendent and personal God comes near and cares for us. Why is this important? The gospel, the good news, is that God is with us, Immanuel, and we don't need to attain a higher spiritual plane to experience God because divine love and grace reach us right in our humanity and brokenness. Christianity is not dualism–and it's not for the elite or those with special knowledge–but it is a fully embodied life available to all. We are called "to do justice, and to love kindness, and to walk humbly with [our] God."[11] It's more than ideas and perspectives; we offer heads, hearts, voices, feet, and hands to God and the world.

Embodied spirituality relieves us from the pressure to attain a mindset free from striving, attaining, and suffering, in short, free from being earthen vessels. It celebrates our humanity, a celebration that equips and prepares us for the inevitable struggles that crack our pots. Embodied spirituality is investment in the here and now as a preparation for the future. I have always loved this statement attributed to Martin Luther, "If I knew that tomorrow was the end of the world, I would plant an apple tree today." He invites us to pull out the shovel and get some dirt under our nails today.

Elevating the spiritual over the physical is not only misguided but also perilous. I love watching children play because they speak and spell joy through their faces, limbs, and bodies. At the beach my preschool granddaughters and I make sand-castle cupcakes with saltwater and seaweed frosting. They bite into the gritty cupcake and laugh. The younger one chases seagulls on the soft sand, a perennial human empowerment game. The lounging birds predictably stand up and run as she approaches, but to a toddler this delight evokes a rising squeal. Similarly, my sweet grandmother

---

10. Lewis, *Mere Christianity*, Book II.5.

11. Mic 6:8

who suffered from Alzheimer's was like a child toward the end of her life. We gave her nature and animal picture magazines, which delighted her with every turning page, even if she had seen the pictures dozens of times before. She exulted saying, "Wie drollig!" ("How funny/cute!") because each view was a happy surprise. Why do repetition and familiarity erode wonder as we grow into adulthood?

Many adults think that novelty is needed to experience wonder. They seek out extreme and exotic experiences, which up the ante. There are others who seek metaphysical experiences as a means of recovering wonder, but they end up with a dualism that places the spiritual over the physical realm.

Proud of my Attachments

Some world views support the idea that the spiritual world is better than the physical world. In Buddhism the Four Noble Truths set the goal of life as attaining the end of suffering. The Second Truth identifies one cause of suffering as desire, the desires of pleasure, material goods, and immortality. Desiring these things brings suffering because they cannot be attained.

Gnostic thought, dating to the late first century Greek world, elevates the spiritual over the physical world more decisively than Buddhism. Gnostic thought, as well as Platonic, creeps into the early Christian movement, leading to the view that the afterlife is a disembodied state and other similar body-minimizing beliefs.

In her cancer memoir, Kelly Corrigan tells a story of traveling alone to Nepal at age twenty-nine where she meets a sunny German woman, Sabine, traveling with her three-year-old son, Peter. They fall into a conversation about Buddhism's Third Truth, that suffering ends when you eliminate desires and attachments. Sabine, a Buddhist, clarifies that it's not just material attachments, but attachments "to ideas, to goals, to jobs, to people." Hearing this, Corrigan reflects: "I was proud of my attachments to people . . . I mean, sure, don't attach to marble countertops or the Burberry fall line. But people? I say attach, wrap around, braid yourself into. What's the point of a life without attachments? We *are* our attachments."

Corrigan concludes that Sabine "was lying if she thought she wasn't attached to that boy of hers, who made her eyes flicker every time he leaned into her" and that if attachment turns the wheel of suffering "[t]hen

I choose suffering."[12] Corrigan chooses an embodied life with all its risks and dangers.

Why do people shy away from the embodied life? There's the obvious danger of materialism, a legitimate worry in our consumerist culture, a danger too easily ignored in many communities, including the church. We must guard ourselves against the false promise that consuming will satisfy our wants, much like The Second Truth. Sharing our resources with others is important. There's also the danger of striving to fulfill our desires at a cost to ourselves and others. Reactionary, reflexive, and unconscious spending impulses invite us to slow down and ask ourselves how our spending conforms to our priorities, how it adds value to our lives.

The perils of elevating the spiritual above the physical, however, strike me as more profound. Denying human frailty in favor of an ethereal–perhaps idealized–version of humanity and thwarting legitimate pleasure leads to a more threatening danger. We cut ourselves off from flourishing as human beings. We cannot see, as "The Kingfisher" proposes that Christ plays through our limbs, eyes, and faces; he plays through our uniqueness as individuals–our very features. It's lovely.

Is it possible that we fear expressing our unique selves? Do we cut ourselves off from our best desires and dreams? Lewis suggests this in this noteworthy quote from *The Weight of Glory*: "If we consider the unblushing promises of reward and the staggering nature of the rewards promised in the Gospels, it would seem that Our Lord finds our desires not too strong, but too weak. We are half-hearted creatures, fooling about with drink and sex and ambition when infinite joy is offered to us, like an ignorant child who wants to go on making mud pies in a slum because he cannot imagine what is meant by the offer of a holiday at the sea. We are far too easily pleased."[13]

Perhaps the greatest cost of elevating the spiritual over the physical is imposing a crude, mud-pie imitation of life. What if we felt our desires but put them a good place, not as must-haves? What if we affirmed our humanity as God does? What if we feasted more on this beautiful, wild, matter-and-spirit-entwined life?

12. Corrigan, *The Middle Place*, 125.

13. Lewis, *The Weight of Glory*, 26.

Resisting the Pull

How do I make sure to keep the lessons of pain current? Appreciation is one part of it. Another is resisting the pull of the downstream current again. Comfort and ease are my Lorelei, but the shipwrecks on the rocks are the memorials of those who stop resisting. Learning is about resisting the lure of easy comfort.

Teachers know about the ongoing struggle of learning and growing. That's why classrooms are to me almost sacred spaces, unique and irreplaceable. A discussion starts when a teacher's question, met with silence, is restated and is sometimes met with more silence. If the teacher resists the pressure to fill the void, then the responsibility subtly shifts to the class. Soon a student joins in, followed by another teacher response; then comes a second student comment, a building-on comment from a third, a challenge from a fourth, and a full-fledged discussion is under way. When a classroom discussion hums, the teacher steps back and watches in awe.

There are times, however, when things don't flow, when learning is a struggle, the squirming, sighing, frowning of in-class work, that leads unseasoned teachers to conclude something is wrong, when everything is, in fact, right. If the teacher encourages students through the struggle long enough, a shift becomes visible–repositioning bodies, idiosyncratic pencil-grasping, stabbing pencil sounds, rubbing erasers, and thought-collecting glances out the window as if the sky is a cheat sheet–the hum of productive learning. It's like bobbing in a raft over destabilizing rapids and passing into the wide expanse of a river, deep, swift, and calm.

Lasting learning arrives through struggle and pain. In a crisis, you can't avoid pain, and so it's easier to master its lessons. But, when the crisis passes, the current of comfort pulls you away from productive learning. There's a lot of talk these days about tolerating discomfort to learn new paradigms, and this is important. Like my students, most of us wish learning were familiar, friendly, and relatively easy, but that desire presents a formidable roadblock to growth.

Lasting learning turns out to be counter-intuitive, which means that our usual strategies are counterproductive. In academic learning, re-reading, repetition, "highlighting, underlining, and sustained poring over notes and texts" are the least productive strategies according to the aforementioned book on the science of successful learning. In a section titled "Illusion of Knowing" the authors posit that "rising familiarity with the text and fluency in reading it can create an illusion of mastery."[14] Feeling less effective produces greater learning. This applies to sports, books, and skill development. Through real time studies, they discovered that when people struggle to learn and feel uncertain about obtaining new skills, they, in fact, learn more. Why is this true? There are at least two reasons: frustration and failure pinpoint areas of weakness that need attention, and strategies that are uncomfortable and unfamiliar require greater effort and produce better results.

Our instinct to avoid discomfort and struggle leads to impoverishment, as Leo Tolstoy asserts: "Physical labor seems painful at the beginning; intellectual labor all the more so . . . People have the tendency to stop thinking when it first becomes difficult; and it is at this point, I would add, that thinking becomes fruitful."[15] When questions demanding resolution begin to torment us, we avoid the anxiety they arouse. Tolstoy urges us to push past frustration and embrace discomfort.

The benefits of pushing past frustration expand beyond learning to make us better, more morally developed people skilled at resolving moral questions. If people were forced against their will to confront the moral issues they face, they would not find escapes to resolving moral questions and gravitate toward comfort and ease.

Technology gets in the way of this because it enables us to avoid boredom, struggle, and demanding personal questions. It tends to disconnect us from the past, its metaphors, lessons, and wisdom. Perennial wisdom teaches that human flourishing is a result of delayed gratification borne of struggle. Tolstoy's insight penetrates the surface. Why do people avoid struggle? Perhaps it is because they want to please the animal part of their natures more than the spiritual part.

Saboteurs of Pain's Benefits

Leo Tolstoy's anthropology explains how we impede our own moral development. Humans have two natures: animal and spiritual; the animal part of humanity seeks the path of least resistance, and the spiritual part is the moral conscience or "consciousness," the source of character and true change.

---

14. Brown, *Make it Stick*, 15.

15. Tolstoy, *The Lion and the Honeycomb*, 57.

What stands in the way of becoming a good person? We do, our desire for comfort and the appearance of morality. This is especially true today as people posture and declare their morality in public ways. Tolstoy ascribes this to our need to deceive ourselves. Instead of allowing our conscience to work correctly, we want our actions to appear just. We want to look moral—to ourselves and others. "Life does not accord with our conscience, so we bend our conscience to fit life."[16]

The desire to maximize comfort and avoid anxiety pushes the moral questions away. It's possible to remain months, years, even our whole lives avoiding the resolution of moral questions. We end up not only stunting our own moral development but our purpose as humans. We remain "unable to break through the wall because [we have] unconsciously blunted the blade of thought which alone could penetrate it."[17]

How do we keep our own blades sharp in everyday life to be ready when the crisis hits? What is an effective knife-sharpener for everyday cutlery? We can't rely on the crisis alone to clarify priorities. When we are forced, against our will–as is the case when disrupters hit–to confront the issues we face, it's harder to find escapes and gravitate toward comfort and ease. Pain forces us to check our attitudes of entitlement and offers us the opportunity to purify our character.

Keeping the blade of thought sharp in everyday life requires tolerating discomfort and pain and doing the hard work of resolving moral dilemmas. This is not a quick, superficial exercise like so much of our self-righteous posing today, which is motivated by the desire to see ourselves as moral without doing the work of becoming moral. And this is no small issue if Tolstoy's teleology is right that it is "the resolution of moral questions that constitutes the movement of life."[18] Transformation is our purpose as humans as God seeks to create in us the character of Christ.

Ultimately, I must look at my own heart and ask myself if it is hard. Do I have a heart of stone or a heart of flesh, as Ezekiel 36:25 differentiates? What is a hard heart? In an excellent talk on this subject called "Our Emotions Matter to God," Rankin Wilbourne asserts that it is literally the inability to feel pain. Do I make room for the pain that comes from bending my life to fit my conscience?

---

16. Tolstoy, *The Lion and the Honeycomb*, 57.

17. Tolstoy, *The Lion and the Honeycomb*, 58.

18. Tolstoy, *The Lion and the Honeycomb*, 57.

Pain plows the overwrought soil of the heart, which lies fallow for a season of pruning, weed abatement, and tilling. But then the soil becomes deeper, richer, and more absorbent. It nourishes an abundant harvest.

Feeling pain is an entry point to a life of flourishing. Struggle maintains it. Growth sustains it. Possibilities for a posture adjustment open wide their doors.

Chapter 13

Living Receptively

THE THIRD ACTION OF embracing is to live in a state of receptivity. This doesn't mean being a taker but having a humble posture and allowing the receiving to change us from within. Why is it hard to receive and why is it essential? A culture obsessed with work, control, and accomplishment undervalues the art of receiving. Receiving makes people feel awkward, passive, and lacking control. But undervaluing this art impoverishes us. It may be more blessed to give than to receive, but it's still blessed to receive, and receiving is, in fact, a way of giving. Let's look more deeply at how and why we complicate the humble skill of receiving.

Receiving is for the Strong

An article on why receiving appreciation is especially hard for men zeroes in on Bryce Mathern's last football game of his high school career. "I ran out for a catch and caught the ball for a two-point conversion. In the locker room after the game, the back-up quarterback looked over and said 'Hey, great catch.' I immediately went into a bit of a panic. I said that I fell down after the catch and I should have run the route cleaner. I remember him looking at me for a moment and just saying, 'Great catch.' In that moment, I could not let in the appreciation and lauding. Especially in front of the rest of my football buddies."[1] Discomfort with receiving compliments is a microcosm of our discomfort with receiving in general.

1. Mathern, "Why Receiving Appreciation Can Be So Hard for Men."

It is also hard for women. I compliment a friend on a nice dress, and she tells me she bought it on sale, that it's a tad too tight in the hips, or that it hides her belly bulge well. When my friend tells me my arms look toned, I draw attention to my crepe paper skin. Not wanting to appear like self-absorbed narcissists, we awkwardly deflect compliments: "Uh, thanks, but did you notice my hands shaking and my voice faltering when I got up to speak?" or "I don't like the sound of my voice. Did it sound nasally?" I seldom see a woman accept a compliment with a simple "thank you" without a disclaimer. Why is this?

There are many reasons and ways people resist receiving from others, whether it is a compliment or help in a crisis. Cultural and personality differences play a role. The German culture in which I was raised is stingy with compliments, but they are generous in lending help to friends in need. In every culture, there are people who extend help but don't receive it easily. Some people seal themselves off from others in a crisis. Their privacy is paramount, so they confide in only a small inner circle. Many of their friends feel left out and frustrated that they can't help.

Discomfort with receiving stems from submerged attitudes and beliefs like:

1. I don't want to impose

   The belief that people will like me more if I'm not needy and don't ask too much of them is the driver here. I feel like accepting help from others is inconvenient for them and causes problems.

2. I fear rejection

   Being turned away in the past makes me reluctant to ask again. I believe that I can't rely on others to help me and am used to doing everything myself.

3. I don't want to owe someone

   I dislike the feeling of being dependent on or needing to pay people back, even if they say they don't want anything in return. Receiving help conflicts with my image of being an independent individual. Receiving generates a debt another person can collect at any time.

4. I am undeserving

   I am uncomfortable with being the focus of attention and wonder why people would want to help me. I only allow myself to receive so much and not more.

5.   I like to be in control

Receiving feels awkward, and I'm more comfortable giving. Giving helps me feel like I have something to contribute. Honestly, if I acknowledge I'm needy, then I might even have to admit my problem is not under control and be forced to change.

Do you resonate with any of these beliefs? Why not take a moment to ask yourself why? Some of my inability to receive is connected to not feeling worthy and not wanting to be an imposition or burden on people. Receiving is also convoluted with shame and pride, forming a murky mixture. Skimming the bottom of motivation, I wonder if I feel superior and in charge when I give–and inferior and lacking control when I receive. This self-awareness is not a happy one, but it's helpful for waking the sleeping potential of receiving.

Receiving has the potential of changing us into grace-filled people. On my back after surgeries and treatments, I have no choice but to receive. An exoskeleton of support from family, friends, and acquaintances becomes visible overnight like an intricately woven web. My neighbors Tony and Yvette, both hairdressers with enviable hair and *joie de vivre*, keep making me delicious meals for weeks and months. I am, of course, blessed to be cared for, but I'm also hesitant. Why? Task-oriented and nose-to-the-grindstone for years,–no, for decades–I have an embedded work ethic that stunts my ability to receive for extended periods of time. Receiving creates a debt I want to repay. But once I realize I am blessing Tony and Yvette by receiving their meals, something inside me shifts. I realize I need people, and they need me. Learning to receive is a posture adjustment. It's like a store-front window reflecting my hunched shoulders and bad posture that need correcting. I become aware of ways my posture cramps my style.

The posture of receiving is a lifted hand, and a lifted hand is an open hand. Try lifting your hands and notice how they naturally open. How does it feel to close a lifted hand? It feels wrong, unnecessarily defensive. But this is our posture much of the time. Ultimately, the most important bearing is the one we have toward God. Is it hunched over with clenched fists? Or is it open and available? Is it humble and receptive?

Receiving is an act of grace in an austere world of transactions. It's an Argentine tango dance partner in a sphere of military marches. It's a gift to the giver who feels helpless to change a situation and the giver who wants to make a difference. It is solidarity with those who live on the edge and can do little to change their outcomes. Don't settle for a transaction when the offer of love is extended.

Receiving Is an Interior Designer

Becoming a good receiver has another layer to it. It involves allowing ourselves to change, namely our view of ourselves. Confirmation bias, however, gets in the way of such change. According to the *Encyclopedia of Social Psychology* confirmation bias is "the tendency to process information by looking for, or interpreting, information that is consistent with one's existing beliefs." It works in two ways: it reinforces high and low self-esteem. People naturally prefer feeling good about themselves, so they push away information that tells them they are not as intelligent as they believe, or as good-looking, capable, or whatever bolsters their positive self-esteem. Confirmation bias keeps high-esteem individuals from creating a more realistic view of themselves that leads to more give and take.

This also applies to low self-esteem, and that's where I want to camp out for a moment. Low self-esteem individuals, for instance, might receive plenty of affirmative cues–a smile, a compliment–from people around them, but they don't stick. Why is this? It's not because they miss the cues; it's because the cues contradict their inner bias, which filters the cues with statements like, "That person must not know this skill/subject very well" or "They're probably just being polite and saying nice things because they feel bad for me." We end up remaining stuck in outdated views about ourselves–something we concluded when we were high school freshmen–instead of revamping a sense of self that's based on adult experience. For people with low self-esteem–myself included–compliments can actually trigger *more* self-doubt instead of enhance confidence. Unless we stop to reflect on our own biases, the water will run off the tarp instead of soaking into our soil.

A road trip to Colorado reminds me how important it is to be receptive to gifts from the outside. The trip coincides with another breakout of wildfires in California. A day after the Creek Fire (and others) in which our friends almost lose their home, the smoke wafts into southern Colorado, but the next day a winter storm, bringing snow and rain, causes a sixty-degree plummet in temperature. The Colorado soil opens its mouth and drinks deeply. It is poised and ready to receive. People, however, are not always poised to receive. How can we allow ourselves to drink more deeply because as John Amodeo says, "[t]he parched earth can't let in a life-giving rain if it is covered by plastic tarp." Removing the tarp happens when we become more aware of our confirmation bias.

My self-esteem is often inaccurate, but it tends to be stable and difficult to change. I stubbornly cling to information which *confirms* my perspective–however counter-productive it may be–rather than information which is contradictory. After all, there's something about knowing who I am that's comforting even if it's outdated and inaccurate.

How do I fend off confirmation bias? The first step is to stop and think. Where am I going with this compliment, this offer of assistance? Am I willing to move beyond my discomfort? To act like I'm worthy of help? To receive without having something to offer in return? To not care if I feel weak or indebted? To change my perception of myself?

After some time on my back, I eventually allow myself to believe I am worthy to receive and ask for help, that I'm not weak or indebted to others. I realize that not asking for help makes life even harder because I'm saying no to myself and the giver. Confirmation bias ignores good evidence that carries the potential of an auspicious, more satisfying future.

How do we allow compliments and the gifts of others to get past our tarp-covered soil? Take a deep breath and offer a sincere "thank you" instead of deflecting or minimizing the gift. Savor the moment and push against the unwanted information that piles up to keep you from receiving. Accept and affirm the giver. When we are visibly moved, we move the giver.

Don't Participate in Your Own Sabotage

I don't want to regret missed opportunities to receive. When a free morning is spread out against the sky, why do I hesitate to come and go within its wide expanse? I scan the horizon for distractions, errands, projects, anything to keep me busy, purposeful, and running. Do other people struggle with the gift of free time like I do? Why is it so hard to allow myself the enjoyment of solitude, of being absorbed in a breathing spell? I remind myself I could be monitoring sophomore energy and cell phone use in the classroom, answering parent emails, grading stacks of rewrites, or undergoing cancer treatment. Accustomed to the structure of raising kids, a career, and long months of recovery, I'm conditioned to bolt down desire, like a child running to the ice cream truck, but stopping to look back for permission from mom. Now that I have more time, I hesitate to enjoy it.

Immersion in the moment hits an insidious barrier from within us. Mary Oliver calls it the "intimate interrupter" and "the watchful eye we cast upon ourselves," that blocks such moments. The intimate interrupter, coming not from the outside but from within, is a part of the self that "whistles and pounds upon the door panels and tosses itself, splashing, into the pond of meditation." Before you know it, you've left that timeless space of wrestling down a thought to "find that the imps of an idea have fled back into the mist."[2] The watchful eye criticizes and corrects us, urging us to return to the ordinary world of the clock. It disguises efficiency and performance as productivity.

Oliver instructs that blindfolding the watchful eye happens by refusing the clock: "It is six A.M., and I am working. I am absentminded, reckless, heedless of social obligations, etc. It is as it must be. The tire goes flat, the tooth falls out, there will be a hundred meals without mustard. The poem gets written. I have wrestled with the angel and I am stained with light and I have no shame. Neither do I have guilt. My responsibility is to the ordinary, or the timely. It does not include mustard, or teeth. It does not extend to the lost button, or the beans in the pot. My loyalty is to the inner vision, whenever and howsoever it may arrive."[3]

How do I get good at dissolving guilt and fending off the clock? The fresh aroma of in-the-moment experiences entices me away from the musty smell of the urgent. It's entirely possible to stop smelling this fresh aroma. During the low point in my cancer journey, desire and joy are almost killed, were it not for writing. Writing connects me to my emotions and to others. Often tears flow, deep tears, healing tears. Many people are disconnected from joy in turbulent times. It's hard to smile and be carefree when there is so much dismay. But lying dormant in many crises is the opportunity to discover freshness once again. Simply smelling the aroma keeps us attracted to these moments, like brewing coffee at breakfast or sautéing onions with garlic before dinner. Attraction makes us seek out these moments more.

What are conduits to these receiving moments? I like to use my hands in crafts and gardening. Remember the last time you were in that timeless space where a manual task blocked out the world, like an afternoon nap pushing the background noise to the periphery. Studies show that working with your hands has a calming effect on the brain. In the ICU during Alex's first lung collapse, I immerse myself in the miniature world of

2. Oliver, *Upstream*, 23.

3. Oliver, *Upstream*, 30.

beading during the long hours of recovery. It calms my mind and pushes away worry for a while. Years later, I take a bead-looming class with a friend and five other complete strangers, all of us carried away to a place devoid of small talk, six strangers impervious to the intimate interrupter for a few hours. These moments are like being in a timeless space.

Why is this kind of experience so rare and elusive? Young parents, caregivers, entrepreneurs, those working two jobs, or most people for that matter, avoid this space, pushing it off to a future point. They press the pedal and plow through the day, oblivious to the greedy tyrant of time–stealthy, silent, and steady–robbing their treasure, like a bully with a weapon. The bully is best dethroned by a better, less tyrannical leader, who arrives only by invitation.

I'm inviting gardening back into my life again. I am a periodic gardener depending on the amount of free time I have in different seasons of my life. The gardeners I know are energetic and dynamic people. They never run out of ideas and enthusiasm. Maybe it's the company gardeners keep among the busy pollinators like bees, butterflies, and hummingbirds. Maybe it's the mesmerizing focus of creativity or the connection to God that energizes them. Whatever it is, gardening can be intensely satisfying. Woodsy scents, vivid colors, and dirty hands have a power of persuasion to pull us back to the garden, patio, or arrangement of pots again and again. There's something about tilling soil that tills the soul. The smell of fecund earth connects soil, body, and soul. It reminds us that we are more than transactional beings. We are cultivators and caretakers.

My recent upsurge coincides with the discovery of a YouTube channel called *Garden Answer* hosted by Laura, a young wife and mother of two who hosts the show that reaches over a million followers. She not only gardens, but she also drives a tractor and a forklift; she lays and fixes sprinklers, transplants trees, and much more in her expansive Eastern Oregon garden. I'm drawn to her genuine character.

The first time I watch one of her summer garden tours, I am transposed to an Edenic state of mind. I watch it before bed, and every time I toss and turn throughout the night, gardening images lull me back to sleep. I feel like I've stumbled into a magical world of beauty and productivity, like visiting Pandora in the movie *Avatar*. Her show is a bedtime ritual now. Every night, I look forward to seeing her enthusiasm over the next blend of colors and leaf shapes in her garden and to hear her solutions to gardening failures, which she welcomes as learning experiences. Why am I drawn to her show? It's because it immerses me in a refreshing reservoir.

It's a reservoir of joy that is uniquely human. Each of us taps into it with "just because" kind of activities. We push through distractions, practicalities, and the need to be productive to get there. That's not to say gardening or other "just because" activities are impractical. Sure, gardening has a practical side–for example, harvesting some tomatoes or cutting flowers–but few people garden primarily for the harvest. They do it to take a little time to breathe. They do it for other, more personal reasons, which create a sense of well-being and human flourishing. Think about the activities that make you feel truly alive and happy.

Gardening is a resistance against the mechanistic modern view of humanity as defined by what we can accomplish. It creates character traits undervalued today. We live in a world of instant gratification. These days, it's difficult to convince many young people that a newly emerged bed of tulips is more interesting than a smartphone. Nurturing a seed from a small speck into a mature plant takes time and persistence–two qualities in short supply in our modern lives. Learning to wait is a reality for gardeners.

The balance between producing and waiting at the heart of gardening is an important teacher. Cultivating a garden requires action, doing, and maintenance, but there is just as much, if not more, waiting for results or fruits. I plant something new and envision how it will look in the future. I plant with the future in mind. The look is sparser than I'd like–I want instant results and blooms–but the delay of gratification is good for me. Each day as I walk around to inspect my plants, I see small changes, and that keeps me going, but it's slow. The slowness of growth develops patience. This is one reason gardening is important, especially for younger people.

Waiting gives me a sense of my place as a recipient instead of a producer. So much of our lives has to do with the myth of productivity, that all we do is decide to act and we can control the outcome. Certainly, our actions are key and without them, we have weeds, overgrowth, and disorder, but our actions aren't sufficient. These things used to be self-evident, but moderns have a way of overestimating their efforts, especially moderns who live cut off from nature in bustling cities of concrete. Waiting slows down my clock to tick more in tune with the way things really are. What slows you down, helps you receive, and gives you joy?

Joy is a choice I must make for myself. It doesn't always come on its own. Deciding to garden–or the activity you enjoy–is self-care, and self-care is essential for a good life. Far from being selfish, self-care is a HEPA filter also known as a high-efficiency particulate absorbing or arresting filter to clean out the harmful particulates in the environment. We all know the need to arrest the spread of harmful particulates in our current environment. What about our own social and personal environment? Will we take charge of our lives to not be polluted or stained by the world as James 1:27 exhorts us to do?

Gardening has other beneficial effects. Is it a coincidence that Virginia Woolf experienced an epiphany of what it means to be an artist while walking amid the flower beds in a garden? Neurologist and author Oliver Sacks writes in a short essay titled "Why We Need Gardens" about the impact of visiting gardens on people with neurological illnesses:

> "As a writer, I find gardens essential to the creative process; as a physician, I take my patients to gardens whenever possible. In forty years of medical practice, I have found only two types of non-pharmaceutical 'therapy' to be vitally important for patients with chronic neurological diseases: music and gardens.
>
> A man with Tourette's syndrome, afflicted by severe verbal and gestural tics in the urban environment, grows completely symptom-free while hiking in the desert; an elderly woman with Parkinson's disease, who often finds herself frozen elsewhere, can not only easily initiate movement in the garden but takes to climbing up and down the rocks unaided; several people with advanced dementia and Alzheimer's disease, who can't recall how to perform basic operations of civilization like tying their shoes, suddenly know exactly what to do when handed seedlings and placed before a flower bed.
>
> I cannot say exactly how nature exerts its calming and organizing effects on our brains, but I have seen in my patients the restorative and healing powers of nature and gardens, even for those who are deeply disabled neurologically. In many cases, gardens and nature are more powerful than any medication."[4]

The benefits of gardening–or just visiting gardens–are inexhaustible, but they are a reminder of refreshing reservoirs right in our neighborhood. I hope you take a walk to the reservoir and keep coming back again and again. Spring is a great time to find your own Eden.

4. Sacks, *Everything in its Place.*

No Regrets

Future regret is an effective way to remove the tyrant of time and develop the art of receiving. Oliver's haunting statement reverberates loudly: "The most regretful people on earth are those who felt the call to creative work, who felt their own creative power restive and uprising, and gave to it neither power nor time."[5] Do you feel guilty when you're not working, when the day is spread out like a delicious picnic under the shade of an elm? Is your enjoyment muscle atrophied by a long crisis? Does your intimate interrupter call the shots? Do you fear falling behind and not catching up, losing a competitive edge? Do you look to a future point when you hope things settle down? "Hope deferred makes a heart sick, but a longing fulfilled is a tree of life."[6] What if your greatest fear isn't falling behind the clock but regret, regret over leaving a buried treasure in the ground? Joy is diffident and meek, easily pushed to the shadows by time and obligation. Don't have regrets.

As a survivor of the Great Depression, my dad struggled with enjoying himself. He loved the inexpensive plenty of cafeterias, mess halls, buffets, sales, deals, and discounts. Waste and luxury repelled him. Like many of his generation, he was a saver. He did allow himself one dream: a small retirement home in Santa Barbara. My dad and mom deferred their retirement plans until an indeterminate point in the future past the usual age of retirement. Then he got sick. On the day of his surgery, I walked into the hospital waiting room where my fifty-nine-year-old mother just received the news that it was too late. The pancreatic cancer had spread too far. He left us three weeks later, eight weeks before Andrew was born. You don't know how long you have. "So, teach us to number our days that we may get a heart of wisdom"[7] is a powerful prayer we can offer.

5. Oliver, *Upstream*, 30.
6. Prov 13:12
7. Ps 90:12

Chapter 14

Dreams

I NEVER DREAMED I would receive such a profound gift, and I almost didn't. It came in a very unorthodox, some might argue foolish, manner. Regardless of the manner, I'm deeply grateful for the gift.

Thirty-seven years of silence and Harry surfaces. Yes, on Facebook. It starts casually. "What are you up to? How have you been? I moved from Minnesota to Colorado." We exchange news about our lives; it's harmless banter that goes on for a while. Then he gets serious and delivers a bombshell statement. He tells me that through his relationship struggles, it is clear to him that I'm the love of his life. Warning signals sound. Is he hitting on me? Guided by the protective arms of prudence, I halt the discussion and cut off further contact with him. Disaster averted.

Later that day while I'm alone, my emotions flood me, overwhelming my reason like a toddler's temper tantrum. I can neither explain nor control the flood. I cry inconsolably for more than two hours, which is a long time for someone not easily given to tears. Devoid of words and explanations, I feel like that same hurt teenage girl many years ago. My mind flounders as it tries to sort through the murky waters and make sense of what I'm feeling.

Thirty-seven years of silence with intermittent noise that grates in the background of my life in John-Cage discordance are suddenly penetrated by this haunting statement. Over the years the background noise wafts in and out like a weak radio signal. We pick up the annoying channel from time to time, like the time the sound system plays mariachi music through the speakers during our wedding ceremony, and we all look around to see where it is coming from. It doesn't affect the service itself and makes us laugh later as it becomes a part of our wedding story. This noise, however, is jarring and disruptive, and we don't want it to be a part of our marriage story.

Early in the process I tell Rick about my contact with Harry. He is visibly upset, and we have many difficult conversations about what just happened. But as quickly as Harry comes, he fades away again into cyberspace offering us a reprieve from the emotional turmoil. During this time, I feel like I am being tested. I often say that everyone has his price, but I don't really think it applies to me in any significant way. I've not been tempted in the way of unfaithfulness or other ways that dissuade me from my values. But now my hubris is my nemesis. Humbled by the realization that I'm not above temptation puts me in a big boat with others who struggle to stay true. Will the boat with people who know their vulnerabilities ultimately be my rescue boat? I pray it will.

An internal struggle ensues that threatens to turn my boat upsidedown. Will I stick to my values, or will my emotions overwhelm my reason? It would be a lie to say it's easy and straightforward, that I simply decide to do the right thing, and everything falls right into place. Over the next few weeks, my spiritual training kicks in. The Apostle Paul's words come into focus: "for while bodily training is of some value, godliness is of value in every way, as it holds promise for the present life and also for the life to come."[1] The spiritual training of life-time rituals, practices, and commitments boosts stamina to meet moments of crisis. I make the decision to trust that God is good and that his principles are for my good. Eventually, practiced trust overrules my unruly emotions. Rick and I weather the storm and our relationship becomes stronger.

Weeks pass with no more messages. Relief. Then suddenly another message arrives: "I'm riding my motorcycle to California and would like to see you." This time he communicates from a new account with no followers. He tells me about his personal life of brokenness and redemption, addiction, and that his third marriage has just ended. That's when it becomes clear that he's trying to hit on me, and I resolve never to fall for his manipulative ways again! I tell him I am open to seeing him, but only with Rick present, though I don't think I can ask Rick to meet this ridiculous request. No one in his right mind would advise such a thing.

---

1. 1 Tim 4:8

An Unorthodox Healing

I refuse the idea of seeing Harry and hope the situation just goes away, but the idea of meeting him stalks me. My therapist's comment that Harry is frozen in time in my mind and heart has a ring of truth to it. I never had an anger session with my girlfriends to rail against how he treated me and that I didn't deserve it. I never experienced closure. Like Penelope, I never got to put a pall on the casket and bury the relationship in peace. Harry still appears in my mind as a twenty-something young man and the old feelings are trapped in my childhood self. Frozen like the long Narnian winter of the wicked witch, my heart needs a springtime thaw. Deep in my heart I know what I need. I need to see him.

I'm fully aware of the unreasonable request I'm placing on Rick and how unconventional–no, foolish–it is for a wife to ask this of her husband. Even so, I'm undeterred. Shame notwithstanding, I tell him I want to see him and ask if he would come with me. To my surprise, he agrees.

We make plans to meet him on a Saturday afternoon at Shutters Restaurant in Santa Monica. The restaurant has an outdoor patio going down to the boardwalk from the street above. As we walk to the restaurant, Rick asks me what happens if he turns out to be attractive. I realize this is a big risk for Rick, for both of us. A feeling of nervous anticipation takes hold of me worse than the anxiety before my ordination exam before the Presbytery. I seldom drink wine during the day, but that afternoon I chug down Chardonnay to settle jitters as we wait. It's like being on a blind date only with the opposite desired outcome because I don't want him to be attractive.

Will he look like a dapper retired gentleman in a crisp white shirt, linen jacket, and expensive shoes? No, he's on a motorcycle, so he'll probably have a cool Peter Fonda look of bad-ass leather with hair askew and a helmet in hand. Rick asks me, "What if he looks like Cary Grant or George Clooney?" and I respond, "What if he does?" In my mind's eye, he still looks like a taller version of George Harrison in his early twenties, and I am unable to think of him as an older man. The moment arrives, but the wine doesn't calm my anxious heart.

The first thing I notice as he descends the stairs to the patio is his legs, white and pasty, bereft of hair, that relaxation of the flesh visible beneath Saturday shorts men wear to putter around the garage. He is older and less remarkable. Appreciation for Rick's fit and firm body wells up inside me. As soon as I see those legs, I'm entwined in the most unusual experience I've ever had. Seeing those legs unfreezes decades of time and catches me up to the present. It's like time-lapse photography condensing thirty-seven years into one short moment. The therapist is right about Harry being frozen in time like a bug in amber. Previously trapped and rigid, my emotions escape to see the light of day, and they are baptized by the fresh water of truth. Reality washes over my obsolete perceptions. All of this happens within the span of the next ninety minutes.

He sits down and we begin to talk; first it's chit chat, then he starts telling us the outlines of his life, his problems with addiction, divorces, and his career as a family counselor. His manner of talking hasn't changed. He speaks without inquiry, bringing back that familiar tone and personality that left me wanting more. The pain of the past resurrects as does the bitter resolve to never be at the mercy of a man's withholding again.

But then comes a statement that catches me off-guard and anoints my head with oil. He asks for my forgiveness for *damaging* me. He doesn't say "hurt" but "damage." Words have power and precise words have targeted power. His words pour over my wounds a healing oil. They validate the pain of that teenage child damaged by a man six years her senior. I feel a wound closing up almost instantaneously. I've never experienced anything like it before, and it's more than I expect or imagine.

I learn of why Harry never contacted me. He doesn't excuse it but explains it. His dad gave him a strict warning to not hurt me again, telling Harry if he contacted me, he would not speak to him again. His dad knew of the harm but was unaware of how good intentions actually create more harm in the long run. When we seek to protect someone from harm, we often end up not sparing them at all.

We talk of other things. I mention I am looking into buying a motor-cycle and he suggests a Vespa, a scooter for lightweight riders. I tell him I'm getting a Harley, but that goes over his head. He still doesn't take me seriously; he thinks of me as small and insignificant. At that moment I'm flooded with appreciation for a husband who takes me seriously, listens to me, and wants to know what I think and feel. It would have been so easy to follow a familiar script with the stunted voice of a child as the main player, but I am blessed not only to have a new script, but also a new role. I realize what a gift it is to have a husband who encourages and challenges me. Rick and I conclude our time together with the impression that he is somewhat self-absorbed. He doesn't ask about my mom, and there are few questions of my life or our family. Some things don't change, but other things do, and I am grateful to for the things that do change.

As we get up to leave, we go to the parking lot where his motorcycle is parked. Rick incredulously tells me to get on the back for a picture. I look at him with disbelief! "Why are you asking me to do this," I motion. This is how we used to ride up the winding roads to the commune. He once dropped the bike with me on the back on an oil slick. As I sling my leg over the bike and sit down, my healing is complete. I don't understand how it happens, but from that point on, Harry disappears from my mind and heart. I can hardly remember his face after that experience. It's like something is deleted and something is added. The hurt, the sting, the unresolved feelings simply drop away and never come back again. A deeper connection to Rick is added. Almost a decade later, that miracle still holds. I wish I knew how it happened, but all I know is the past catches up to the present to hand me a priceless gift of reality. Truth truly sets us free.

Rick later tells me he was nervous as well. What if Harry was a dashing older man? What if he still had power over his wife? That Rick was willing to take this risk for me defies logic, but the logic of love is sometimes irrational. It's that logic that heals me.

Two Disparate Themes Join Together

I can see more clearly now why truth and integrity are important to me. For a long time, my life has two disparate themes, not a single narrative, but a tension between two themes that vie for attention: belonging and freedom, fitting in and finding my voice, cohesion and truth. These two themes often oppose each other and make for a disjointed narrative. My mom notices the freedom theme as a toddler at a family camp in the mountains. We are walking and suddenly I sit down refusing to walk anymore. My dad has to carry me. My mom takes in the information to adjust her parenting of that autonomous self she sees in me. She values that stubborn light that refuses to be extinguished. I, too, view my autonomy as a force now, the force of my voice crying to be heard.

The other theme is wanting to belong, which works in the opposite direction to make me compliant. My mom tells me that during my years in Germany adults like me and want to be with me because I'm proper and obedient. I want a group and a voice, but I let the group define me. Later on I let a relationship define me and my voice grows even quieter. Then, when that relationship ends, I banish the compliant self and exchange it for the freer one. I want nothing to do with the bruised reed that broke. I feel ashamed of my weakness.

As an adult my insecurities become less dominant, but they are still there. I can't accept my childhood self, but I can prove to myself that it's no longer calling the shots. I stretch myself to do uncomfortable things. I go to seminary when only twenty percent of ministerial students and an even lower percentage of ordained pastors are women. I become an Associate Pastor at a start-up church. My passion for the gospel, Bible study, and Christian formation guides me through the challenge of being a woman in a man's world. Later I join a start-up school where I have the privilege of founding a department and leading a staff of mostly men.

My middle adult years are a time of internal bridge construction to join the childhood and adult parts of myself. The quests for individuation and intimacy come together into a whole as I make peace with my shamed self. God's forgiveness builds the bridge to forgiving myself, but I must establish it for myself. Integrity is the joining of different parts into a whole so that they work together to make something strong. A bridge that can handle the weight of traffic and shifts in the soil is said to have integrity. It stands up under duress. My bridge is starting to stand up as well, able to hold up under strong pressure and weight.

The weight of cancer has shifted my perspective in many ways. I see my life as smaller and more focused than I used to see it. I suppose facing death has that effect. It makes me realize what really matters and what remains once I'm gone. I often doubt the impact of my life and wonder if I've accomplished much. But I've learned that being loved and loving has a big impact. I may be remembered by a few people for a while, but ultimately, I will be forgotten. That's how life is and it's okay. I am not forgotten by God who has prepared a place for his people in his kingdom. There I will find my rest and joy far beyond what I can ask or imagine.

Another gift comes from a conversation Andrew has with my mom after a health scare she survives. He asks her to be more expansive in showing love to her kids. The outworking of that conversation amazes me as she opens her heart to me by hugging and listening to me more. At first, I'm skeptical but it sticks. She is genuinely trying to reveal her heart and to change, a remarkable thing for someone inching toward ninety-six years of age. Will I allow her to change? I must look at my own heart to examine my willingness to forgive.

Two additional shifts are a growing acceptance of discomfort and a willingness to speak my voice even if it feels vulnerable and scary. I face a recalcitrant reluctance to do the latter, like a boat stuck in ice at the Arctic Circle. I need an icebreaker ship to clear a passage through the frozen waters. A disrupter is such a ship providing access to other ships previously denied access. But old habits are hard to break. It's hard to expose family secrets, be vulnerable, and put myself out there for others to see my vulnerable, unvarnished self. My inner train conductor's voice may be muffled, but I can still hear his desperate cries under the muzzle demanding obedience. He injects shame to stifle my story. "You will hurt your family! You should not expose yourself!" he cries. It feels almost too uncomfortable to disobey his voice until I remember the gifts of cancer, chief among which is its clearing away the ice that keeps me from new waters. I want to embrace this gift.

I feel the way a person raised in poverty with little expectation to escape the slum might feel. Opportunities to move out are met with doubt and fear. A lack of role models coupled with a lack of belief in oneself to succeed create a reluctance to take positive action. "Take the opportunity! Determine your future!" are glib cheers. I must go against deep and familiar patterns of thought and behavior. It starts with silencing the voices of doubt and shame and seeing them for what they are: false motives. I must come to the point of believing my story *is* worth telling even if it I run the risk of criticism, that it is mine to share in hopes that it might connect with others' stories. This is how I find my footing and purpose in hardship.

In a recent interview of a podcast called The School of Purpose, University of Connecticut sociologist Brad Wright interviews me about my cancer journey. We spend surprisingly little time on the details of the physical journey and most on the lessons derived. Many of the lessons boil down to purpose. Cancer has given me a renewed sense of purpose, which keeps me going. He asks me about my plans for the future, and I reply that I no longer talk in terms of plans but dreams.

Is it logical to act on dreams in the face of an uncertain future? Yes! After Brittany's second transplant, she and her husband buy a house and a puppy, plant a garden, and she enrolls in a second master program. She hopes to adopt a baby. Rick and I also take the opportunity to buy our dream house, and I plant a garden. Is it responsible to make future investments? Planting is investing in the moment for more than a moment. Planting gives purpose. I see myself as a gardener of my family, students, and friends. I prepare the soil, sow the seeds, and nurture the seedlings. The harvest is up to God.

I dream that my life will be like a vineyard with an abundant harvest. A few years ago, I took a picture of a truckload of purple grapes in a California vineyard. The array of colors from burgundy to boysenberry combined with dust, smudge marks, and dew multiplied into an explosion of color as exciting as the juice under its skin and the wine it would create, like Homer's description of Alkinoos's garden of "the vine's fruit empurpled in the royal vineyard there."[2] I have always loved fruit and what it symbolizes. I've written poems about it and packed it on a farm in college. Fruit is what I dream about: for my family, friends, students, parishioners, and lamenting souls; fruit that keeps on bearing and ripening to bursting fullness.

While I wander like a pilgrim toward this dream, I want to taste and see the moment for more than a moment, to savor this life without making an idol of it. And when the dark disrupter hits, I will know I've lived with purpose.

I shall keep the servant's whisper at the victory parade near, "Memento mori" because I need his whisper.

2. Homer, *The Odyssey*, VII.129.

Bibliography

Beecher Stowe, Harriet. *Uncle Tom's Cabin*. New York: Aladdin, 2002.

Bowler, Kate. *Everything Happens for a Reason and Other Lies I've Loved*. New York: Random House, 2018.

Bowler, Kate. "Living a Chronic Life in a Fix-it-now World." *Washington Post*, June 17, 2019, Opinion.

Brooks, David. *The Second Mountain*. New York: Random House, 2019.

Brown, Peter, et al. *Make it Stick*. Cambridge, MA: Harvard University Press, 2014.

Corrigan, Kelly. *The Middle Place*. New York: Hachette Books, 2009.

Eger, Edith. *The Choice*. New York: Scribner, 2017.

Entz, Yolanda. *Yola: Forgive and Remember Nazi Rule*. Maitland, FL: Xulon Press, 2009.

Feiler, Bruce. *Life is in the Transitions*. New York: Penguin, 2020.

Gray, Thomas. "Ode on a Distant Prospect of Eton College." Stanza 10.

Homer. *The Odyssey*. translated by Robert Fitzgerald. New York: Farrer, Strauss, and Giroux, 1998.

Johnston, Abigail. "Strength." *No Half Measures*, April 19, 2021, https://nohalfmeasures. blog/2021/04/19/strength/

Keller, Timothy. *Reason for God*. New York: Dutton, 2008.

Lamott, Anne. *Bird by Bird*. New York: Anchor Books, 1994.

Lewis, C.S. *The Abolition of Man*. New York: HarperCollins, 1974.

Lewis, C.S. *Mere Christianity*. San Francisco, CA: HarperCollins, 1952.

Lewis, C.S. *The Weight of Glory*. New York: HarperCollins, 1980.

Mathern, Bryce. "Why Receiving Appreciation Can Be So Hard For Men," 30 June 2014, https://goodmenproject.com/featured-content/hlg-why-do-men-have-such-a-hard-time-receiving-appreciation/

McCullough, David. *The Pioneers*. New York: Simon & Shuster, 2019.

Midkiff, Sarah. "Chris Cuomo Had A Major Existential Crisis–But He's All Good Now." *Yahoo News*, April 14, 2020. https://www.yahoo.com/lifestyle/chris-cuomo-had-major-existential-211430642.html?fr=yhssrp_catchall

Morrison, Latasha. *Be the Bridge*. Colorado Springs, CO: WaterBrook, 2019.

Murekatete, Jacqueline. "Facing Today: A Facing History Blog," 30 April 2019, https:// facingtoday.facinghistory.org/interview-with-rwandan-genocide-survivor-jacqueline-murekatete

Oliver, Mary. *Upstream*. New York: Penguin Books, 2016.

Ramsey, K. J. *This Too Shall Last*. Grand Rapids: Zondervan Reflective, 2020.

Rivera, Joe. "Jalen Rose's Passionate Plea After the Death of George Floyd." *Sporting News,* May 29, 2020, https://www.sportingnews.com/us/nba/news/jalen-rose-george-floyd-death/1ves33v5h2z6b1whfrhmyhyhl8

Sachs, Oliver. *Everything in its Place.* New York: Knopf, 2019.

Tolstoy, Leo. *The Lion and the Honeycomb:* "Why Do Men Stupefy Themselves?" London: Collins, 1987.

Van Der Kolk, Bessel. *The Body Keeps the Score.* London: Penguin, 2015.

Wilkerson, Isabel. National Endowment for the Humanities, 2015 https://www.neh.gov/about/awards/national-humanities-medals/isabel-wilkerson

Wilson, Reid. *Stopping the Noise in Your Head.* Health Communications, Inc., 2016.

Wright, N. T. *Surprised by Hope.* New York: HarperCollins, 2008.